A Handbook of
Commercial Correspondence

A Ashley

Oxford University Press

Oxford University Press
Great Clarendon Street
Oxford OX2 6DP

Oxford New York
Auckland Bangkok Buenos Aires Cape Town
Chennai Dar es Salaam Delhi Hong Kong
Istanbul Karachi Kolkata Kuala Lumpur
Madrid Melbourne Mexico City Mumbai
Nairobi São Paulo Shanghai Singapore
Taipei Tokyo Toronto

with an associated company in Berlin

Oxford and *Oxford English* are trade marks of
Oxford University Press.

ISBN 0 195 457206 4
© Oxford University Press 1992

First published 1984
Second edition 1992
Twelfth impression 2002

Printed in Hong Kong

Note
The companies, organizations and people
mentioned in the specimen letters and
documents in this book are entirely fictitious,
and any similarity with actual companies,
organizations or people is coincidental.

Acknowledgements
The Publishers and Author are grateful to the
following for permission to reproduce the
documents on the pages quoted: Barclays
Bank International Ltd (pp. 152, 155); British
Airways (p. 191); Overseas Containers Ltd.
(p. 209); Lloyd's of London (p. 230); the
London Chamber of Commerce and Industry
(p. 210).

Contents

Introduction

Correspondence is essential in establishing and confirming transactions in commerce. Typed or produced on a word processor it reflects you or your business. Therefore *what* is written and *how* it is expressed is as much a part of a business education as accountancy and economics.

A Handbook of Commercial Correspondence has been planned to give students and business people a working knowledge of commercial writing and practice in modern contexts. It covers all aspects of transactions from addressing and laying out a letter to orders and procedures involving representative agencies, banking, insurance, shipping and delivery, complaints, non-payment of accounts, and so on. Later units deal with telegrams, telexes, faxes, and electronic mail, miscellaneous correspondence, memorandums and reports, and personnel appointments.

After the first two units, which deal with the presentation and style of commercial letters, each unit follows a regular pattern:

1 An introduction to the transaction or transactions with which the unit is concerned and an explanation of the terminology used in them and the functions of the organizations likely to be involved in them.
2 An analysis of the objectives to be achieved when writing relevant letters and lists of alternative phrases, sentences or paragraphs which can be substituted in different cases.
3 Specimen letters and specimen transactions, together with questions and comments on the language, style, and roles of the correspondents.
4 A brief review of the units and a summary of the vocabulary.

The book is intended for business people, secretaries, teachers, and business studies students.

Business people and secretaries

As a handbook this should prove invaluable in outlining letters, using alternative expressions, and adding to your knowledge of commerce.

British and overseas business people will gain from the simple, direct language used and see how it is possible to be polite without seeming timid, direct yet not rude, concise rather than abrupt, and firm but not inflexible.

The letters and documents used reflect authentic transactions so that overseas business people, in particular, will get the sense of commercial practice in the UK and a detailed understanding of the terminology and the sometimes confusing roles of different commercial organizations, e.g. merchant banks and commercial banks, Lloyd's and insurance companies, The Baltic Exchange and The Shipping Conference.

Teachers

The information on commercial practice and the specimen letters and transactions in this book have been carefully built up to suit the needs of business students, whether English-speaking or learners of English, as well as giving the teacher, who might not be familiar with commerce, a good grounding in the subject.

The opening units quickly introduce terms which are repeated throughout, and each transaction is planned so that teachers and students are fully aware of the roles of the correspondents and the organizations they are dealing with. Where there is continuity in a transaction, following through from order to completion, students should be encouraged to refer back to previous correspondence.

The short questions following the specimen letters will reinforce understanding of the language and nature of the transaction. Role plays based on the transaction can be acted out by groups in negotiations between buyers and sellers and communications between the various organizations involved in the transactions, such as banks and agencies.

The brief review and vocabulary summary at the end of each unit can be used later in the course as revision material. Careful use of the Index will focus attention on those areas of commercial practice or terminology with which students are having difficulty.

Students

This book allows you to work by yourself, taking you through the different stages of business transactions. By studying the information and correspondence as you progress through each unit you should be able to understand the roles of the correspondents and the agencies they are dealing with. There is no need to worry about the commercial terms as they are constantly repeated and you will soon become used to them. Nevertheless, there are detailed explanations of them, and if you have any problems you can use the Index to refresh your memory.

Each unit contains two kinds of material to read. The first explains the style and content of a particular kind of business letter, and gives you information about the organizations involved, e.g. banks, insurance and shipping companies. The second kind of material is the letters themselves. Study both kinds carefully, and also the various documents illustrated in the book, and you will get a clear picture of commerce, commercial terminology, and the functions of the various organizations.

Where there is a reference to previous correspondence, e.g. 'This letter follows on from the correspondence at 3.3.4 and 4.3.5', go back and remind yourself what happened before this part of the transaction. You should also complete the short questions at the end of letters to make sure you understand them.

The reviews at the end of each unit are not only summaries, but references to be used later in the book if you need to remind yourself of a topic.

Finally, do not try to take short cuts by skipping any units. Even if you think you are familiar with the subject, read it again as revision.

Structure and presentation

1

Layout 1 (sender's address, dates, inside address, order of addresses, style and punctuation of addresses, 'for the attention of', salutations, the body of the letter, complimentary closes, signatures); layout 2 (letterheads, references, per pro, company position, enclosures); layout 3 ('private and confidential', subject titles, copies); addressing envelopes.

1.1
Layout 1

The letter shown on the next page is from a private individual in Denmark to a company in the UK. It shows some of the features of a simple business letter.

1.1.1
Sender's address

In correspondence that does not have a printed letterhead, the sender's address is written on the top right-hand side of the page.

In the UK, in contrast to the practice in some countries, it is not usual to write the sender's name before the sender's address.

1.1.2
Date

The date is written below the sender's address, sometimes separated from it by a space. In the case of correspondence with a printed letterhead, it is also usually written on the right-hand side of the page (see 1.2).

The month in the date should not be written in figures as they can be confusing; for example, 11.1.93 means 11th January 1993 in the UK but 1st November 1993 in the USA. Nor should you abbreviate the month, e.g. Nov. for November, as it simply looks untidy. It takes a moment to write a date in full, but it can take a lot longer to find a misfiled letter which was put in the wrong file because the date was confusing.

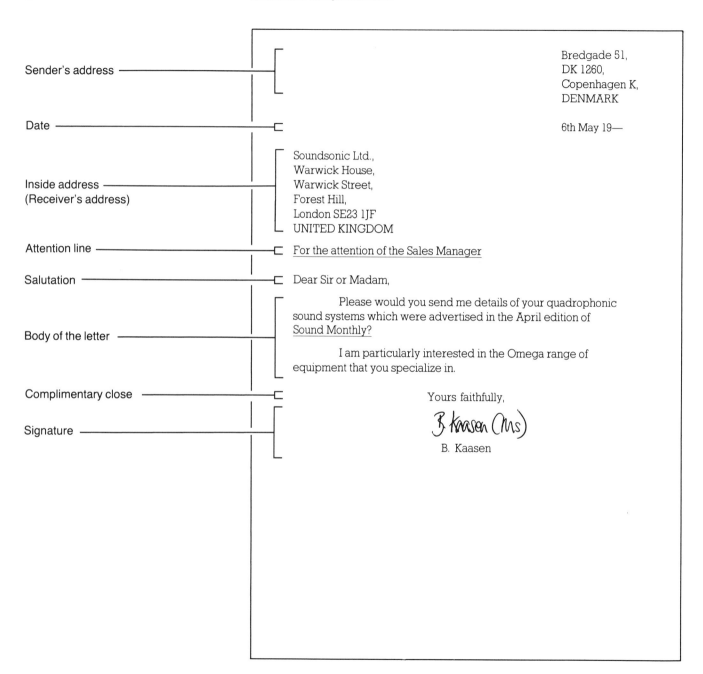

Sender's address

Bredgade 51,
DK 1260,
Copenhagen K,
DENMARK

Date

6th May 19—

Inside address
(Receiver's address)

Soundsonic Ltd.,
Warwick House,
Warwick Street,
Forest Hill,
London SE23 1JF
UNITED KINGDOM

Attention line

For the attention of the Sales Manager

Salutation

Dear Sir or Madam,

Body of the letter

Please would you send me details of your quadrophonic sound systems which were advertised in the April edition of Sound Monthly?

I am particularly interested in the Omega range of equipment that you specialize in.

Complimentary close

Yours faithfully,

Signature

B. Kaasen (Mrs)

B. Kaasen

Many firms leave out the abbreviation 'th' after the date, e.g. 24 October instead of 24th October. Other firms transpose the date and the month, e.g. October 24 instead of 24 October. These are matters of preference, but whichever you choose you should be consistent throughout your correspondence.

1.1.3
Inside (or receiver's) address

This is written below the sender's address and on the opposite side of the page.

1 *Surname known*
If you know the surname of the person you are writing to, you write this on the first line of the address, preceded by a courtesy title and either the person's initial(s) or his/her first given name, e.g. *Mr J.E. Smith* or *Mr John Smith*, not *Mr Smith*.

Courtesy titles used in addresses are as follows:

Mr (with or without a full stop; pronounced /'mɪstə/; the unabbreviated form *mister* should not be used) is the usual courtesy title for a man.

Mrs (with or without a full stop; pronounced /'mɪsɪz/; no unabbreviated form) is used for a married woman.

Miss (pronounced /mɪs/; not an abbreviation) is used for an unmarried woman.

Ms (with or without a full stop; pronounced /mɪz/ or /məz/; no unabbreviated form) is used for both married and unmarried women. Many women now prefer to be addressed by this title, and it is a useful form of address when you are not sure whether the woman you are writing to is married or not.

Messrs (with or without a full stop; pronounced /'mesəz/; abbreviation for *Messieurs*, which is never used) is used occasionally for two or more men (*Messrs P. Jones and B.L. Parker*) but more commonly forms part of the name of a firm (*Messrs Collier & Clerke & Co.*).

Special titles which should be included in addresses are many. They include academic or medical titles: *Doctor* (*Dr.*), *Professor* (*Prof.*); military titles: *Captain* (*Capt.*), *Major* (*Maj.*), *Colonel* (*Col.*), *General* (*Gen.*); aristocratic title: *Sir* (which means that he is a Knight; not to be confused with the salutation *Dear Sir* and always followed by a given name – *Sir John Brown*, not *Sir J. Brown* or *Sir Brown*), *Dame, Lord, Baroness*, etc.

Esq (with or without full stop; abbreviation for *Esquire* and pronounced /es'kwaɪə/) is seldom used now. If used, it can only be used instead of *Mr* and is placed after the name. Don't use *Esq* and *Mr* at the same time: *Bruce Hill Esq*, not *Mr Bruce Hill Esq*.

All these courtesy titles and special titles, except *Esq*, are also used in salutations. (See 1.1.7)

2 *Title known*
If you do not know the name of the person you are writing to, you may know or be able to assume his/her title or position in the company, (e.g. *The Sales Manager, The Finance Director*), in which case you can use it in the address. (See the letter at 3.3.3.)

3 *Department known*
Alternatively you can address your letter to a particular department of the company (e.g. *The Sales Department, The Accounts Department*). (See the letter of 3.3.2.)

4 *Company only*
Finally, if you know nothing about the company and do not want to make any assumptions about the person or department your letter should go to, you can simply address it to the company itself (e.g. *Soundsonic Ltd., Messrs Collier & Clerke & Co.*).

1.1.4
Order of inside addresses

After the name of the person and/or company receiving the letter, the order and style of addresses in the UK, as recommended and used in this book, is as follows:

Name of house or building
Number of building and name of street,
    road, avenue, etc.
Name of town or city and postcode
Name of country

Industrial House
34–41 Craig Road
Bolton BL4 8TF
UNITED KINGDOM

Some European addresses may place the numbers of the building after the name of the street. It is also common to substitute the name of the country with an initial before the district code number. Look at the two examples below:

Facoltà di Medicina
Via Gentile 182
I–70100 Bari

Lehrstul für Bodenkunde
Amalienstrasse
D–8000 München 40

(You are advised to follow the above order and style, even though variations are possible: for example, the name of the county, e.g. Lancashire, may, if known, be written on the line below the name of the town or city; the postcode may be written on a separate line; the name of the town, as well as the country, may be in capital letters.)

See also 1.4 *Addressing envelopes.*

1.1.5
Style and punctuation of addresses

Both the addresses may be 'blocked' (i.e. each line is vertically aligned with the one above) as in the letter at 1.1, or 'indented', as below:

Bredgade 51,
  DK 1260,
    Copenhagen K,
    DENMARK

There are no rules stating that one style or the other must be used, though blocking, at least in addresses (see 1.1.8 for blocking and indenting the body of a letter), is more common. In any case you must be consistent, i.e. do not block the sender's address and then indent the inside address.

If punctuation is used, each line of the address is followed by a comma, except the last line, as in the letter at 1.1. But the majority of firms now use open punctuation, i.e. without any commas, as in the letter at 1.2.

1.1.6
'For the attention of'

An alternative to including the recipient's name or position in the address is to use an 'attention line' as in the letter at 1.1. and as here:

International Industries Ltd
1–5 Greenfield Road
Liverpool L22 0PL

For the attention of the
Production Manager

Dear Sir,

1.1.7
Salutations

Dear Sir opens a letter written to a man whose name you do not know.

Dear Sirs is used to address a company.

Dear Madam is used to address a woman, whether single or married, whose name you do not know.

Dear Sir or Madam is used to address a person of whom you know neither the name nor the sex. Notice that Ms Kaasen in the letter at 1.1 uses this form; she does not assume that the Sales Manager of Soundsonic must be a man. See also 2.6.1. *Titles, names and addresses.*

When you do know the name of the person you are writing to, the salutation takes the form of *Dear* followed by a courtesy title and the person's surname. Initials or first names are not generally used in salutations: *Dear Mr Smith*, not *Dear Mr J. Smith* or *Dear Mr John Smith.*

The comma after the salutation is optional (*Dear Sir*, or *Dear Sir*).

Note that in the USA a letter to a company usually opens with *Gentlemen*, followed by a colon, not with *Dear Sirs.*

1.1.8
The body of the letter

This may be indented, as in the letter at 1.1, or blocked, as in the letter at 1.2. It is a matter of choice. Whichever style you use, you must be consistent and use that style all through the letter.

It is usual to leave a line space between paragraphs in the body of the letter; if the blocked style is used, this is essential.

1.1.9
Complimentary closes

If the letter begins *Dear Sir, Dear Sirs, Dear Madam* or *Dear Sir or Madam*, it will close with *Yours faithfully.*

If the letter begins with a personal name – *Dear Mr James, Dear Mrs Robinson, Dear Ms Jasmin* – it will close with *Yours sincerely.*

Avoid closing with old-fashioned phrases such as *We remain yours faithfully, Respectfully yours*, etc.

The comma after the complimentary close is optional (*Yours faithfully*, or *Yours faithfully*).

Note that Americans tend to close even formal letters with *Yours truly* or *Truly yours*, which is unusual in the UK in commercial correspondence. But a letter to a friend or acquaintance may end with *Yours truly* or the casual *Best wishes.*

The position of the complimentary close – on the left, right or in the centre of the page – is a matter of choice. It depends on the style of the letter (blocked letters tend to put the close on the left, indented letters tend to put them in the centre) and on your firm's preference.

1. 1. 10
Signatures

Always type your name after your handwritten signature and your position in the firm after your typed signature. This is known as the signature block. Even though you may think your signature is easy to read, letters such as 'a', 'e', 'o', 'r', and 'v' can easily be confused.

It is, to some extent, a matter of choice whether you sign with your initial(s) (*D. Jenkins*) or your given name (*David Jenkins*), and whether you include a courtesy title (*Mr, Mrs, Miss, Ms*) in your signature block. But if you give neither your given name nor your title, your correspondent will not be able to identify your sex and may give you the wrong title when he/she replies. It is safer, therefore, to sign with your given name, and safest of all to include your title.

Including titles in signatures is, in fact, more common among women than among men, partly because many women like to make it clear either that they are married (*Mrs*) or unmarried (*Miss*) or that their marital status is not relevant (*Ms*), and partly because there is still a tendency to believe that important positions in a company can only be held by men. It would do no

harm for men to start including their titles in their signatures.

In the letter at 1. 1, Ms Kaasen gives her title in her handwritten signature. It is also possible to include the title in the typewritten signature, usually in brackets, as in these two examples:

Yours faithfully,

(Miss) T. Shurgold

Yours sincerely,

J. Howatt (Mr)

SOUNDSONIC Ltd.

Warwick House, Warwick Street, Forest Hill, London SE23 1JF

Chairman John Franks O.B.E.   Directors S.B. Allen M.Sc., N. Ignot, R. Lichens B.A.

Telephone (081) 566 1861   Fax: (081) 566 1385   Telex: 819713

Your ref: 6 May 19—
Our ref: DS/MR

Date: 11th May 19—

Ms B. Kaasen
Bredgade 51
DK 1260
Copenhagen K
DENMARK

Dear Ms Kaasen,

Thank you very much for your enquiry which we received today.

I am enclosing our catalogue and price-list for the equipment you said you were interested in. I would like to draw your attention to pages 31–35 in the catalogue where you will find full details of the Omega range.

We would welcome any further enquiries you have, and look forward to hearing from you.

Yours sincerely,

Mary Raynor (Ms)

p.p. D. Sampson
Sales manager

Enc.

1.2
Layout 2

Here is the firm's reply to the letter from the prospective customer in Denmark. It shows some further features of a normal business letter, and uses the kind of layout (blocked, open punctuation, etc.) which this book regards as standard.

—— Letterhead

—— References

—— Per pro
—— Company position

—— Enclosure

1.2.1
Letterheads

The printed letterhead of a company gives a great deal of information about it.

1 *Type of company*
The abbreviation *Ltd.* after the company's name tells you that the company has *limited liability*, which means that the individuals who own the company, or part of it, i.e. the shareholders, are only responsible for their holding (the capital they have contributed) and no more than that if the company goes bankrupt. It is a warning to people giving the company credit that in bankruptcy they can only get what the company owns, not the personal possessions of its shareholders. The abbreviation *PLC* (*Public Limited Company*) is used to show that the company's shares can be bought by the public; *Ltd.* continues to be used for private limited companies whose shares are not available. In the USA the term *Incorporated* (*Inc.*) is used.

SOUNDSONIC Ltd.
SP Wholesalers PLC
Hartley-Mason Inc.

The abbreviation *& Co.* tells you that the company is a *partnership* between two or more people. If it is a family concern, the word *Son, Sons, Bros* (*Brothers*) or, very occasionally, *Daughter(s)* may be added. Partnerships may have limited liability or unlimited liability.

F. Lynch & Co. Ltd.
R. Hughes & Son Ltd.

If neither *Ltd.* nor *& Co.* appear after the company's name, then it may be a *sole trader*, a single person doing business in his own name and on his own account.

If the company is a *joint stock company*, the names of the directors will appear on the letterhead.

2 *Board of Directors*
The name of the Chairman (or, in the USA, the President), who runs the concern, may be given, as well as the names of the Directors, who decide the overall policy of the firm. The Managing Director (in the USA, Chief Executive), who takes an active role in the day-to-day running of the company, may be mentioned if he is different from the Chairman.

3 *Addresses*
In addition to the address of the office from which the letter is being sent, the letterhead may also give the address of the head office or registered office if different and the address of any *branches* or other offices the company owns (see the letter at 3.3.3).

Telephone, telex, fax numbers, and a cable (telegram) address may also be given.

4 *Registered number*
This usually appears in small print, sometimes with the country or city in which the company was registered.

The VAT number (Value Added Tax) may also be given. See the letter at 3.3.2.

1.2.2
References

References are quoted to indicate what the letter refers to (*Your Ref.*) and the correspondence to refer to when replying (*Our Ref.*).

References may either appear in figures, e.g. 661/17 in which case 661 may refer to the chronological number of the letter and 17 to the number of the department, or, as in the letter at 1.2, in letters, DS/MR, in which case DS stands for Donald Sampson, the writer, and MR for his secretary, Mary Raynor.

Note that the 'Your Ref.' given in the letter at 1.2 is a date, as B. Kaasen had not mentioned any reference in the original letter.

See also 1.3.2 *Subject titles*.

Yours faithfully,

(Mrs) Rosemary Phipps

p.p. J. Mane
Managing Director

1.2.3
Per pro

The term *per pro* (p.p.) is sometimes used in signatures and means *for and on behalf of*. Secretaries sometimes use *p.p.* when signing letters on behalf of their bosses.

Yours faithfully,

(Ms) T. Lovette

(Ms.) T. Lovette
Chief Accountant

1.2.4
Company position

When signing on behalf of your company, it is useful to indicate your position in the firm in the signature.

Enc.
Bill of lading (5 copies)
Insurance certificate (1 copy)
Certificate of origin (1 copy)
Bill of exchange (1 copy)

1.2.5
Enclosures

If there are any enclosures, e.g. leaflets, prospectuses, etc., with the letter, these may be mentioned in the body of the letter. But many firms in any case write *Enc.* or *Encl.* at the bottom of the letter, and if there are a number of documents, these are listed.

1.3
Layout 3

The final letter in this section shows some further features of a business letter.

SOUNDSONIC Ltd.

Warwick House, Warwick Street, Forest Hill, London SE23 1JF

Chairman John Franks O.B.E.   Directors S.B. Allen M.Sc., N. Ignot, R. Lichens B.A.

Telephone (081) 566 1861   Fax (081) 566 1385   Telex: 819713

Your ref:

Our ref: DS/MR

Date: 21 July 19—

Ms B. Kaasen
Bredgade 51
DK 1260
Copenhagen K
DENMARK

Private and confidential → Private and confidential

Dear Ms Kaasen,

Subject title → Non-payment of invoice 322/17

I am sorry to see that, despite several reminders, you have not yet paid the above-mentioned invoice. Unless, therefore, the account is cleared within 14 days of the above date, I shall have no alternative but to place the matter in the hands of our solicitors.

Yours sincerely,

Mary Raynor (Ms)

p.p. D. Sampson
Sales manager

Copies → c.c. Messrs. Poole & Jackson Ltd., Solicitors

1.3.1
'Private and confidential'

This phrase may be written at the head of a letter, and more importantly on the envelope, in cases where the letter is intended only for the eyes of the named recipient.

There are many variations of the phrase – 'Confidential', 'Strictly Confidential' – but little difference in meaning between them.

1.3.2
Subject titles

Some firms open their letters with a subject title. This provides a further reference, saves introducing the subject in the first paragraph, immediately draws attention to the topic of the letter, and allows the writer to refer to it throughout the letter.

It is not necessary to begin the subject title with *Re*: e.g. *Re: Application for post of typist.*

1.3.3
Copies

c.c. (= carbon copies) is written, usually at the end of the letter, when copies are sent to people other than the named recipient.

Sometimes you will not want the named recipient to know that other people have received copies. In this case, *b.c.c.* (= blind carbon copies) is written on the copies themselves, though not, of course, on the top copy.

1.4
Addressing envelopes

Envelope addresses are written in a similar way to inside addresses (see 1.1.3, 1.1.4, 1.1.5) but, for letters in or going to the UK, the postcode is usually written on a line by itself at the end of the address, and the name of both the town and the country are written in capital letters.

```
Mr G. Penter
49 Memorial Road
ORPINGTON
Kent
BR6 9UA
```

```
Messrs W. Brownlow & Co.
600 Grand Street
LONDON
W1N 9UZ
UNITED KINGDOM
```

1.5
Points to remember

1 The layout and presentation of your letter are important as they give the reader the first impression of the firm's efficiency.
2 There are two styles of letter, blocked and indented. Both are acceptable, but the blocked style will probably save time.
3 Write both addresses in as much detail as possible and in the correct order.
4 Make sure you use the recipient's correct title in the address and salutation. If in doubt as to whether a woman is single or married, use *Ms.*
5 Do not abbreviate dates.
6 Choose the correct salutation and complimentary close. When you begin with *Dear Sir* or *Dear Sirs* or *Dear Madam* or *Dear Sir or Madam*, end with *Yours faithfully*. But if you use a personal name in the salutation, then close with *Yours sincerely*.
7 Make sure your references are correct.
8 Make sure your signature tells your reader what he/she needs to know about you.

1.6
Words to remember

letterhead
sender's address
inside (receiver's) address
postcode

telex number
registered number
VAT number
cable/telegram address
fax/telefax

salutation
courtesy title
Dear Sir/Sirs/Madam/Sir or Madam
Dear Mr . . ./Mrs . . ./Miss . . ./Ms . . .
USA: Gentlemen:

complimentary close
Yours faithfully/sincerely
USA: Yours truly
signature

blocked style
indented style
open punctuation

attention line
for the attention of
private and confidential
references
Your Ref:
Our Ref:
subject title
p.p. (per pro)
Enc./Encl. (enclosure)
c.c. (carbon copy)
b.c.c. (blind carbon copy)

Ltd. (limited liability)
PLC (public limited company
USA: Inc. (incorporated)
& Co. (and company)
sole trader
joint stock company

Board of directors
Chairman, *USA:* President
Managing Director, *USA:* Chief
  Executive (CEO)
Sales Manager
Finance Director
Chief Accountant

Content and style

2

Length; order and sequence; planning your letter; style and language; clarity; accuracy.

This unit gives you some general ideas on how to write business letters: how much information to give, how to plan your letter, what sort of style to use, how to make your letters as clear, informative and accurate as possible. They are, however, only general ideas, your real appreciation of what to do and what not to do in commercial correspondence will only come as you read through and study the following units.

2.1
Length

Students often ask how long their letter should be. The answer is, as long as necessary, and this will depend on the subject of the letter; it may be a simple subject, e.g. thanking a customer for a cheque, or quite complicated, e.g. explaining how a group insurance policy works. It is a question of how much information you put in the letter: you may give too little (even for a brief subject), in which case your letter will be too short, or too much (even for a complicated subject), in which case it will be too long. Your style and the kind of language you use can also affect the length (see 2.4). The right length includes the right amount of information.

The three letters that follow are written by different people in reply to the same enquiry from a Mr Arrand about the company's product.

2. 1. 1
Too long

There are a number of things wrong with a letter of this sort. Though it tries to advertise the products and the company itself, it is too wordy. There is no need to explain that stores or shops are stocking for Christmas; the customer is aware of this. Rather than draw attention to certain items the customer might be interested in, the letter only explains what the customer can already see, that there is a wide selection of watches in the catalogue covering the full range of market prices. In addition, the writer goes on unnecessarily to explain which countries the firm sells to, the history of the company, and its rather unimpressive motto.

Dear Mr Arrand,

Thank you very much for your enquiry of 5 November which we received today. We often receive enquiries from large stores and always welcome them, particularly at this time of the year when we know that you will be stocking for Christmas.

We have enclosed our winter catalogue and are sure you will be extremely impressed by the wide range of watches that we stock. You will see that they range from the traditional to the latest in quartz movements and include ranges for men, women, and children, with prices that should suit all your customers, from models costing only a few pounds to those in the upper-market bracket priced at several hundred pounds. But whether you buy a cheaper or more expensive model we guarantee all merchandise for two years with a full service.

Enclosed you will also find our price-list giving full details on c.i.f. prices to London and explaining our discounts which we think you will find very generous and which we hope you will take full advantage of.

We are always available to offer you further information about our products and can promise you personal attention whenever you require it. This service is given to all our customers throughout the world, and as you probably know, we deal with countries from the Far East to Europe and Latin America, and this fact alone bears out our reputation which has been established for more than a hundred years and has made our motto a household world – Time for Everyone.

Once again may we thank you for your enquiry and say that we look forward to hearing from you in the near future?

Yours sincerely,

2. 1. 2
Too short

There are a number of points missing from this letter, quite apart from the fact that, since the writer knew the name of his correspondent he should have begun the letter *Dear Mr Arrand* and ended *Yours sincerely*.

1 There is no reference to the date or reference number of the enquiry.
2 Catalogues should be sent with a reply to an enquiry; it is annoying for a customer to have to wait for further information to be sent.

Dear Sir,

Thank you for your enquiry. We have a wide selection of watches which we are sure you will like. We will be sending a catalogue soon.

Yours faithfully,

3 Even if a catalogue is sent, the customer's attention should be drawn to particular items that would interest him in his line of business. He might be concerned with the upper or lower end of the market. He might want moderately priced items, or expensive ones. There may be a completely new line that should be pointed out to him.

4 A price-list should also be included if prices are not listed in the catalogue, and any special discounts that are available should be quoted as well as delivery dates if possible.

2.1.3
The right length

Here is a letter that is more suitable. See 2.3 for the points listed.

2.1.4
A warning

Your letter should be neither too long nor too short. It is better to include too much information than too little. Your reader cannot read your mind. If you leave out vital information, he won't know what he wants to know, unless he writes back again and he may not bother to do that. If you include extra information, at least he'll have what he wants, even though he may be irritated by having to read the unnecessary parts. Provided, of course, that you include the vital information as well as the extras: the worst letter of all is the one that gives every piece of information about a product – except the price.

Dear Mr Arrand,

Thank you for your enquiry of 5 November.

We have enclosed our winter catalogue and price-list giving details of c.i.f. London prices, discounts and delivery dates.

Though you will see we offer a wide selection of watches, may we draw your attention to pp. 23–28, and pp. 31–36 in our catalogue which we think might suit the market you are dealing with? And on page 25 you will notice our latest designs in pendant watches which are becoming fashionable for both men and women.

As you are probably aware, all our products are fully guaranteed and backed by our world-wide reputation.

If there is any further information you require, please contact us. Meanwhile, we look forward to hearing from you soon.

Yours sincerely,

1

2 Content and style

2.2
Order and sequence

As well as containing the right amount of information, your letter should also make all the necessary points in a logical sequence, with each idea or piece of information linking up with the previous one in a pattern that can be followed. Do not jump around making a statement, switching to other subjects, then referring back to the point you made a few sentences or paragraphs before.

2.2.1
Unclear sequence

Consider this badly-written letter. There is no clear sequence to the letter, which makes it difficult to understand.

Dear Sir,

We are interested in your security systems. We would like to know more about the prices and discounts you offer.

A business associate of ours, DMS (Wholesalers) Ltd., mentioned your name to us and showed us a catalogue. They were impressed with the security system you installed for them, so we are writing to you about it. Do you give guarantees with the installations?

In your catalogue we saw the Secure 15 which looks as though it might suit our purposes. DMS had the Secure 18 installed, but as we mentioned, they are wholesalers, while we are a chain of stores. We would like something that can prevent robbery and shoplifting, so the Secure 15 might suit us.

How long would it take to install a system that would serve all departments? Could you send an inspector or adviser to see us at some time?

If you can offer competitive prices and guarantees we would put your system in all our outlets, but initially we would only install the system in our main branch.

We would like to make a decision on this soon, so we would appreciate an early reply.

Yours faithfully,

Dear Mr Jarry,

We are a chain of retail stores and are looking for an efficient security system. You were recommended to us by our associates DMS (Wholesalers) Ltd. for whom you recently installed an alarm system, the <u>Secure 18</u>.

We need an installation which would give us comprehensive protection against robbery and shoplifting throughout all departments and the <u>Secure 15</u> featured in your catalogue appears to suit us. However if one of your representatives could come along and see us, he would probably be able to give us more advice and details of the available systems.

Initially we will test your system in our main branch, and if successful, then extend it throughout our other branches, but of course a competitive quotation and full guarantees for maintenance and service would be necessary.

Please reply as soon as possible as we would like to make a decision within the next few months. Thank you.

Yours sincerely,

2.2.2
Clear sequence

Here is a better version of the same letter, in which the ideas and information are in logical order.

2.3
Planning your letter

The way to get the right amount of information in your letter, and to get it in the right order, is by planning your letter in advance. Ask yourself: what do you want your letter to achieve and what response do you want? Note down everything you want to include in it before you start writing; then read your notes again to see (a) that you have included all the necessary information, (b) that you haven't included any unnecessary information, and (c) that you have put the information in the right order.

Here, for example, is the plan for the letter at 2.1.3.

1st para
  acknowledge enquiry

2nd para
  enclose catalogue, price-list

3rd para
  draw attention to watches suitable for Arrand, and latest designs

4th para
  mention guarantees and reputation

5th para
  encourage further contact

2.3.1
First paragraph

The first sentence or paragraph of a letter is an important one since it sets the tone of the letter and gives your reader his first impression of you and your company. Generally speaking, in the first paragraph you will thank your correspondent for his letter (if replying to an enquiry), introduce yourself and your company if necessary, state the subject of the letter, and set out the purpose of the letter. Here are two examples:

Thank you for your enquiry dated 8 July in which you asked us about our range of cosmetics. As you have probably seen in our advertisements in fashion magazines, we appeal to a wide age-group from the teenage market through to more mature women, with our products being retailed in leading stores throughout the world.

Thank you for your letter of 19 August which I received today. We can certainly supply you with the industrial floor coverings you asked about, and enclosed you will find a catalogue illustrating our wide range of products which are used in factories and offices throughout the world.

2.3.2
Middle paragraphs

This is the main part of your letter and will concern the points that need to be made, answers you wish to give, or questions you want to ask. As this can vary widely with the type of letter that you are writing, it will be dealt with in the relevant units. It is in the middle paragraphs of a letter that planning is most important, to make sure that your most important, to make sure that your

points are made clearly, fully and in a logical sequence.

2.3.3
Final paragraph

When closing the letter, you should thank the person for writing, if your letter is a reply and if you have not done so at the beginning. Encourage further enquiries or correspondence, and mention that you look forward to hearing from your correspondent soon. You may also wish to restate, very briefly, one or two of the most important of the points you have made in the main part of your letter. Here are some examples:

Once again thank you for writing to us, and please contact us if you would like any further information. To go briefly over the points I have made – all prices are quoted c.i.f. Yokahama; delivery would be six weeks from receipt of order; and payment should be made by bank draft. I look forward to hearing from you soon.

I hope I have covered all the questions you asked, but please contact me if there are any other details you require. May I just point out that the summer season will soon be with us, so please place an order as soon as possible so that it can be met in good time for when the season starts. I hope to hear from you in the near future.

We are sure that you have made the right choice in choosing this particular line as it is proving to be a leading seller. If there is any advice or further information you want we shall be happy to supply it, and look forward to hearing from you.

Dear Sir,

I beg to acknowledge receipt of your letter of the 15th inst. in connection with our not clearing our account which was outstanding as at the end of June.

Please accept our profuse apologies. We were unable to settle this matter due to the sudden demise of Mr Noel, our accountant, and as a result were unaware of those accounts which were to be cleared. We now, however, have managed to trace all our commitments and take pleasure in enclosing our remittance for £620 which we trust will settle our indebtedness.

We hope that this unforeseen incident did not in any way inconvenience you, nor lead you to believe that our not clearing our balance on the due date was an intention on our part to delay payment.

We remain, yours, etc. . . . .

Dear Mr Aldine,

I am replying to your letter of 15 July asking us to clear our June balance.

I apologize for not settling the account sooner, but due to the unfortunate death of Mr Noel, our accountant, we were not able to settle any of our outstanding balances.

Please find enclosed our cheque for £620, and accept our apologies for any inconvenience.

Yours sincerely,

Dear Mr Rohn,

I have already written to you concerning your outstanding debt of £591. This should have been cleared three months ago. You don't seem to want to co-operate in paying us, and therefore we will sue you if your debt is not cleared within the next ten days.

Yours, etc.

2.4
Style and language

2.4.1
Simplicity

Commercial correspondence often suffers from an old-fashioned, pompous style of English which complicates the message and gives the reader the feeling that he is reading a language he does not understand. In this letter, all the writer is trying to do is explain why he delayed paying his account, but, because of the style, the letter is too long, and is difficult to write and read.

Here is a simpler version of the letter. Mr Aldine will be satisfied with it because it tells him, in a simple and clear style, what he wants to know. First, his customer remembers his name. Second, he has apologized. Third, Mr Aldine knows his was not the only account that has not been paid, and knows why. Finally, he has his cheque.

2.4.2
Courtesy

Your style should not, however, be so simple that it becomes discourteous. Here is an example of a letter that is so short and simple that it sounds rude.

In this version of the same letter, notice the stylistic devices that are used to make it more polite: complex sentences, joined by conjunctions, rather than short sentences; passive rather than active; full forms rather than abbreviated forms.

2.4.3
Idioms and colloquial language

It is important to try to get the right 'tone' in your letter. This means that, generally speaking, you should aim for a neutral tone, avoiding pompous language on the one hand (as in the first letter at 2.4.1) and informal or colloquial language on the other hand.

A letter may be given the wrong tone by the use of inappropriate *vocabulary, idioms, phrasal verbs*, and *short forms*, among other things. Here are a few examples of each, together with a preferred alternative:

you've probably guessed
   you probably know
you'll get your money back
   the loan will be repaid
to go into property
   to invest in property
a couple of hundred quid
   two hundred pounds
prices are at rock bottom
   prices are very low
prices have gone through the roof
   prices have increased rapidly

These are perhaps extreme examples, but the general point is that you should be very wary of using idiomatic or colloquial language in your letters. Apart from the danger of being misunderstood if your correspondent is a non-native speaker of English, you may also give an impression of over-familiarity.

Dear Mr Rohn,

I refer to the previous letter sent on 10 October in which you were asked to clear the balance of £591 which has been outstanding since July. As you have not replied to the letter you leave little choice for me but to place the matter in the hands of solicitors. However, I am reluctant to do this and am offering you a further ten days to settle the account.

Yours sincerely,

2.5
Clarity

Your correspondent must be able to understand what you have written. Confusion in correspondence often arises through a lack of thought and care, and there are a number of ways in which it can happen.

2.5.1
Abbreviations

Abbreviations can be useful because they are quick to write and easy to read. But both parties need to know what the abbreviations stand for.

The abbreviations *c.i.f.* and *f.o.b.*, for example, are recognized internationally as meaning *cost, insurance*, and *freight* and *free on board*. But can you be sure that your correspondent would know that *o.n.o.* means *or nearest offer*?

Some international organizations, e.g. NATO, are known in all countries by the same set of initials, but many are not, e.g. EEC (European Economic Community) and UNO (United Nations Organization). National organizations, e.g. CBI (Confederation of British Industry) and TUC (Trades Union

Congress), are even less likely to be known by their initials in other countries. Note, for telephone purposes, that with a few exceptions (NATO is one of them) these abbreviations are not usually pronounced as a word, but as separate letters: /ti: ju: si:/ not /tʌk/.

If you are not absolutely certain that an abbreviation will be easily recognized, do not use it.

2.5.2
Figures

We saw, at 1.1.2, that the use of figures instead of words for dates can create problems.

Numerical expressions can also cause confusion. For example, the decimal point in British and US usage is a full point rather than a comma as used in most continental European countries, so that an English or American person would write 4.255 where a French person would write 4,255 (which to an English person would mean four thousand two hundred and fifty-five).

If there is a possibility of confusion, therefore, write out the expression in both figures and words, e.g. £10,575.90 (ten thousand five hundred and seventy-five pounds, ninety pence).

(Conversely, be wary of the words *billion* and *trillion* which mean different things in the UK and USA. For a full treatment of numerical expressions, see Appendix 4 in the *Oxford Advanced Learner's Dictionary*.)

2.5.3
Prepositions

Special care should be taken when using prepositions. There is a big

difference between *The price has been increased* to £15.00, *The price has been increased* by £15.00, and *The price has been increased* from £15.00.

2.6
Accuracy

Careless mistakes in a letter can create a bad impression on your reader. Spelling, punctuation, and grammar should all be checked carefully, but there are some other ways in which inaccuracy may spoil your letter.

2.6.1
Titles, names, and addresses

Make quite sure that you use the correct title in the address and salutation, that you spell your correspondent's name correctly (nothing creates a worse impression than a mis-spelled name), and that you write his/her address accurately.

Do not make assumptions about your correspondent's sex if you do not know it. If you are writing, for example, to a Chief Buyer who you do not know, do not assume that he/she must be one sex or the other: use *Dear Sir or Madam* rather than *Dear Sir* or *Dear Madam*. If you know the person's name but not his/her sex (either because he/she only signs with an initial, or because his/her given name is new to you), then use *Mr/Mrs . . .*, e.g. *Dear Mr/Mrs Barron*.

2.6.2
References

When replying to a letter, make sure you quote all references accurately. Your correspondent will not be pleased if it is not immediately clear which letter you are replying to.

2.6.3
Prices, measurements, etc.

Special care must be taken when quoting prices or giving specifications such as measurements, weights, etc. A wrongly-quoted price in a letter can cause complications.

2.6.4
Enclosures

Always check that you have actually enclosed the documents you have mentioned in your letter. And check that you have enclosed the right documents: if, for example, you say in the body of the letter, that you are enclosing 'our leaflet PB/14', do not then enclose leaflet PB/15. Or, when sending a covering letter with an order, make sure you have quoted the order number accurately in your letter.

2.7
Points to remember

1 Include just the right amount of information in your letter. (But better to include too much than too little.)
2 Plan your letter before you start writing, to make sure it says everything you want to say and says it in a logical sequence.
3 Use a simple but polite style of language. Beware of idioms.
4 Your letter should be clear and unambiguous. Take care with abbreviations and figures.

5 Accuracy is important. Pay special attention to titles, names and addresses, references, prices and specifications, enclosures.

2.8
Words to remember

length
order and sequence
style and language
clarity
simplicity
courtesy
accuracy

idioms
colloquial language
abbreviations
a statement
a sentence
a paragraph

to open a letter
to introduce oneself
to acknowledge an enquiry
to draw attention to something
to point out something
to make a point
to restate a point
to enclose a catalogue
to encourage further contact
to close a letter

Enquiries

3

Methods of enquiry; asking for catalogues, price-lists, prospectuses; asking for details; asking for samples, patterns, demonstrations; suggesting terms, methods of payment, discounts; asking for goods on approval or on sale or return; asking for an estimate or tender.

3.1
Methods of enquiry

J. SINCLARE LTD.,
41 Lewis Place,
Coulsdon, Surrey.
1 October 19—

Your Ref: Box 3124

Please could you send me details of the refrigerators advertised in yesterday's 'Evening Post'?

An enquiry can be made by telephone, telegram (cable), telex, fax, or postcard. If you use a postcard, it is not necessary to begin with a salutation (*Dear Sir*, etc.) nor end with a complimentary close (*Yours faithfully*, etc.) Your address, the date, and reference is sufficient.

If you need to give more information about yourself or ask the supplier for more information, you will need to write a letter. The contents of this will depend on three things: how well you know your supplier; whether your supplier is at home or abroad; and the type of goods you are enquiring about – there is a difference between asking IBM about the cost of installing a complex computer and asking a publisher how much a book would cost.

3.2
Writing letters of enquiry

3.2.1
Opening

Tell your supplier what sort of firm you are.

We are a co-operative wholesale society based in Zurich.

Our company is a subsidiary of Universal Business Machines and we specialize in . . .

We are one of the main producers of industrial chemicals in Germany, and we are interested in . . .

How did you hear about the firm you are writing to? It might be useful to point out that you know a firm's associates, or that they were recommended to you by a consulate or Trade Association.

We were given your name by the Hoteliers' Association in Paris.

You were recommended to us by Mr John King, of Lasworn & Davies, Merchant Bankers.

We were advised by Spett. Marco Gennovisa of Milan that you were interested in supplying . . .

The British Embassy in Madrid told us that you were looking for an agent in Spain to represent you.

It is possible to use other references:

We were impressed by the selection of gardening tools that were displayed on your stand at this year's Gardening Exhibition held in Hamburg.

Our associates in the packaging industry speak highly of your Zeta packing machines and we would like to
have more information about them. Could you send us . . .

3.2.2
Asking for catalogues, price-lists, prospectuses

It is not necessary to give a lot of information about yourself when asking for catalogues, brochures, booklets, etc. This can be done by postcard, but remember to supply your address, unless it is already printed, phone number, telex, and fax number if you have one. It would also be helpful if you could briefly point out any particular items you are interested in.

Could you please send your current catalogue and price-list for exhibition stands? We are particularly interested in 'furniture display' stands.

Would you let us have your summer brochure for holidays to Greece and the Greek Islands, and supply details of any low fares and tariffs for the month of September?

I would appreciate your sending me an up-to-date price-list for your building materials.

I am planning to come and study in London next autumn and I would like a prospectus for your college giving me information about fees and special courses in computing.

We have heard about your latest equipment in laser surgery and would like more details. Please send us any information you can supply, marking the letter 'For the Attention of Professor Kazuhiro', Tokyo General Hospital, Kinuta-Setagayaku, Tokyo, Japan.

3.2.3
Asking for details

When asking for goods or services you must be specific and state exactly what you want. If replying to an advertisement you should mention the journal or newspaper, the date, and quote any box number or department number given, e.g. Box No. 341; Dept. 4/12B. And if referring to, or ordering from a catalogue, brochure, leaflet, or prospectus, always quote the reference, e.g. Cat. No. A149; Holiday No. J/M/3; Item No. 351; Course BL 362.

I am replying to your advertisement in the June edition of 'Tailor and Cutter'. I would like to know more about the 'steam pressers' which you offered at cost price.

I am interested in holiday No. J/M/3, the South Yugoslavian tour.

I will be attending the auction to be held in Turner House on 16 February this year, and am particularly interested in the job lot listed as Item No. 351.

Could you please give me more information about course BL 362 which appears in the language learning section of your summer prospectus?

I would appreciate more details about the 'University Communications System' which you are advertising on Grampian Television.

3.2.4
Asking for samples, patterns, demonstrations

You might want to see what a material or item looks like before placing an order. Most suppliers are willing to provide samples or patterns so that you can make a selection. However, few would send a complex piece of machinery for you to look at. In that case you would be invited to visit a showroom, or the supplier would offer to send a representative. Nevertheless, if it is practical, ask to see an example of the article you want to buy.

When replying, could you please enclose a pattern card?

We would also appreciate it if you could send some samples of the material so that we can examine the texture and quality.

Before selling toys we prefer to test them for safety. Could you therefore send us at least two examples of these children's cars in the 'Sprite' range?

I would like to discuss the problem of maintenance before deciding which model to install in my factory. I would be grateful if you could arrange for one of your representatives to call on me within the next two weeks.

3.2.5
Suggesting terms, methods of payment, discounts

Firms sometimes state prices and conditions in their advertisements or literature and may not like prospective customers making additional demands. However, even if conditions are quoted, it is possible to mention that you usually expect certain concessions. Although it is true that once a supplier has quoted a price and stated terms, he may be unwilling to change them, by suggesting your terms you indicate that certain conditions may persuade you to place an order.

We usually deal on a 30% trade discount basis with an additional quantity discount for orders over 1,000 units.

As a rule our suppliers allow us to settle by monthly statement and we can offer the usual references if necessary.

We would also like to point out that we usually settle our accounts on a documents against acceptance basis with payment by 30-day bill of exchange.

Could you let us know if you allow cash or trade discounts?

We intend to place a substantial order, and would therefore like to know what quantity discounts you allow.

3. 2. 6
Asking for goods on approval or on sale or return

Sometimes wholesalers and retailers want to see how a line will sell before placing a firm order with the supplier. They may be able to do this by getting goods *on approval* or on a *sale or return* basis. In either case the supplier would have to know the customer well, or would want trade references. He will also place a time limit on when the goods must be returned or paid for.

Your leaflet advertising your latest publications of History magazines interested us, and we would like to stock a selection of these. However, we would only consider placing an order provided it was on the usual basis of sale or return. If this is acceptable we will send you our official order.

In the catalogue we received last week from you, we saw that you are introducing a new line in artificial furs. While we appreciate that increasing pressure from wildlife protection societies is reducing the demand for real skins, we are not sure how our customers at this end of the market will react. But we would like to try a selection of designs. Would it therefore be possible for you to supply us with a range on an approval basis to see if we can encourage a demand for synthetic furs? Three months would probably be enough to establish a market if there is one.

3. 2. 7
Asking for an estimate or tender

Estimates are quotations to complete a job of work, for example, putting a new roof on a factory or installing machinery. Tenders are similar quotations, but in a written form and often used when the job is much larger, e.g. building a complete factory. Very often, when this sort of work is for a government, or is a large undertaking, an advertisement is placed in the newspapers.

Advert: *The Irish Tourist Organization invites tenders from building contractors to erect seating for 10,000 people for the Dublin Summer Festival. Tenders should be in by 1st March 19— and will be studied on price and suitability of construction plans.*

Advert: *The Zena Chemical Company invites tenders from private contractors for the disposal of chemical waste. Strict government regulations will be in force so only those licensed to deal with toxic substances should apply. Further details from . . .*

A company may write *circular letters* to several companies inviting offers to complete a construction job or to effect repairs or decorating.

We are a large chain of theatres and are looking for estimates from upholsterers to re-cover the seats in our two main theatres in Manchester.

We are writing to a number of building contractors to invite estimates for the conversion of Northborough airfield into a sports and leisure centre. The work will include erecting buildings, providing facilities, e.g. ski slopes, parachute jumps, etc., and should be completed by next December. If you can provide a competitive estimate please contact us at . . .

As you might have read in the newspaper our firm has taken over International Motors PLC and we are in the process of automating their Hamburg factory. At present we are writing to several engineering designers who may be interested in converting the plant to a fully automated production unit. Enclosed you will find specifications, but we would welcome your surveyors to come and inspect the site with a view to supplying an estimate for the reconstruction.

3.2.8
Closing

Usually a simple 'thank you' is sufficient to close an enquiry. However, you could mention that a prompt reply would be appreciated, or as the examples show, that certain terms or guarantees would be necessary.

Thank you for your attention. We hope to hear from you in the near future.

We would be grateful for an early reply.

Finally, we would like to point out that delivery before Christmas is essential and hope that you can offer us that guarantee.

If the concessions we have asked for could be met, we would place a substantial order.

Prompt delivery would be necessary as we have a fast turnover. We would therefore need your assurance that you could meet all delivery dates.

You can also indicate further business, or other lines you would be interested in if you think they could be supplied. If a supplier thinks that you may become a regular customer, rather than someone who has placed the odd order, he would be more inclined to quote competitive terms and offer concessions.

If the product is satisfactory, we will place further orders with you in the future.

If the prices quoted are competitive, and the quality up to standard, we will order on a regular basis.

Provided you can offer favourable quotations, and guarantee delivery within four weeks from receipt of order, we will place regular orders with you.

3.3.
Specimen letters

3.3.1
Short enquiries

A *Request for a catalogue and price-list*

> Dear Sir,
>
> Please would you send me your Spring catalogue and price-list quoting c.i.f. prices, Le Havre? Thank you.
>
> Yours faithfully,

B *Request for a prospectus*

> Dear Sir,
>
> I would like some information about your Proficiency courses in English beginning this July.
>
> Please send me a prospectus, details of your fees, and information about accommodation in London for the period July–December. If possible I would like to stay with an English family. Thank you.
>
> Yours faithfully,

C *Request for general information*
Note that the reference to trade prices in this letter tells the manufacturer that he is dealing with a retailer or wholesaler, not a private individual.

> Dear Sir,
>
> Could you please send me details of your tubeless tyres which are being advertised in garages around the country?
>
> I would appreciate a prompt reply quoting trade prices.
>
> Yours faithfully,

Disc SA

251 rue des Raimonières F–86000 Poitiers Cédex
Tél: (33) 99681031 Télécopie: (33) 102163

Réf: PG/AL   12 May 19—

The Sales Dept.
R.G. Electronics AG
Havmart 601
D–5000 Köln 1

Dear Sirs,

We are a large record store in the centre of Poitiers and would like
to know more about the tapes and cassettes you advertised in this
month's edition of 'Hi Fi News'.

Could you tell us if the cassettes are leading brand names, or made by
small independent companies, and whether they would be suitable for
recording classical music or only dictations and messages? It would
also be helpful if you could send us some samples and if they are of the
standard we require, we will place a substantial order. We would also
like to know if you are offering any trade discounts. Thank you.

Yours faithfully,

P. Gérard

P. Gérard

3.3.2
Reply to an advertisement

In this letter the customer is replying to
an advertisement for cassettes which he
saw in a trade journal. The advertiser
gave little information, so the writer will
have to ask for details.

Questions

1 Why does M. Gérard say they are a
   'large' record store?
2 Is he interested in high-quality
   cassettes or low-quality cassettes?
3 What two things does he require
   before he places an order?
4 How did he hear about the advert?
5 If the letter began *Dear Mr . . .* what
   would the complimentary close be?
6 Is M. Gérard asking about any
   special concessions?
7 Which words in the letter correspond
   to the following: *publication*;
   product's name; *vocal instructions*;
   examples; *large*?

3.3.3
Enquiry from a buying agent

Firms often have agents in other countries who either sell or buy products for them (see Unit 10 *Agents and agencies*). In this letter the agent is acting on behalf of her principals in Canada.

Sanders & Lowe Ltd.

Import and Export, (London Office), Planter House, Princes Street, London   EC1 7DQ

Birmingham Office: 28 Bradshaw Street, Birmingham B5 1TQ
Manchester Office: 343 Oxford Street, Manchester M27 2LR
Liverpool Office: 54 Bakers Road, Liverpool L3 9HW
Stockport Office: 5 Island Road, Stockport SM3 12K

Directors: L.W. Lowe, D.R. Sanders

Telephone: 071 543 1615
Fax: 071 543 1925
Telex: 928537

Reg. No. England 155134
VAT No. 013 7001 21

Your ref: ———   Our ref: 180/MB   Date: 7 June 19—

The Sales Manager
Glaston Potteries Ltd.
Clayfield
Burnley BB10 1RQ

Dear Sir or Madam,

We are writing to you on behalf of our principals in Canada who are interested in importing chinaware from England.

Could you send us your latest catalogue and price-list, quoting your most competitive prices?

Our principals are a large chain store in North America and will probably place substantial orders if the quality and prices of your products are suitable.

We look forward to hearing from you soon.

Yours faithfully,

L.W. Lowe (Mrs)

F. Lynch & Co. Ltd.

(Head Office), Nesson House, Newell Street, Birmingham B3 3EL

Telephone No.: 021 236 6571   Fax: 021 236 8592   Telex: 341641

Satex S.p.A
Via di Pietra Papa
00146 Roma
ITALY

Your ref:

Our ref: Inq. C351

6 February 19—

Dear Sirs,

We were impressed by the selection of sweaters that were displayed
on your stand at the 'Menswear Exhibition' that was held in Hamburg
last month.

We are a large chain of retailers and are looking for a manufacturer
who could supply us with a wide range of sweaters for the teenage
market.

As we usually place very large orders, we would expect a quantity
discount in addition to a 20% trade discount off net list prices, and our
terms of payment are normally 30-day bill of exchange, documents
against acceptance.

If these conditions interest you, and you can meet orders of over 500
garments at one time, please send us your current catalogue and price-
list. We hope to hear from you soon.

Yours faithfully,

L. Crane

L. Crane
Chief Buyer

3.3.4
Enquiry from a retailer to a foreign manufacturer

This letter is from a Birmingham chain of
retail shops to an Italian manufacturer.
Here the retailer explains how he got to
know about the manufacturer, and
suggests that a quantity discount and
acceptance of his method of payment
would persuade him to place an order.
He is stating his terms in his enquiry
because he feels that as a bulk buyer
he can stipulate conditions. But you will
see from the reply (4.3.5) that although
the Italian manufacturer wants the order,
he does not like the terms, and
suggests conditions that are more
suitable to him.

Questions
1 How did Lynch & Co. get to know
   about Satex?
2 What market are Lynch & Co.
   interested in?
3 How many sweaters are they likely to
   order?
4 What discounts are they asking for?
5 How will payment be made?
6 What expression does Mr Crane use
   to show Lynch is a large firm?
7 Should any references be quoted in
   reply to this letter?
8 Which words in the letter correspond
   to the following: *shown*; *group of
   shops*; *selection*; *less*; *present*?

3.3.5

Request for goods on approval

Mr Hughes, the customer, has dealt with Homemakers before and the enquiry has a casual tone about it. He has enclosed a provisional order because he is confident that Mr Cliff, the supplier, will agree to offering the kits on approval so that Mr Hughes can test the demand for them. In this case references are not necessary; if they were, Mr Hughes could offer another supplier or his bank as a referee. The reply to this letter is at 4.3.6.

Questions

1 Why does Mr Hughes want the goods on approval?
2 Does he expect Mr Cliff to agree? How do you know?
3 When does he want the kits?

R. Hughes & Son Ltd.

21 Mead Road, Swansea, Glamorgan 3ST 1DR

Telephone: Swansea 58441   VAT No. 215 2261 30
Telex: 881821

Mr R. Cliff,   17th November 19—
Homemakers Ltd.,
54–59 Riverside,
Cardiff CF1 1JW

Dear Mr Cliff,

Thank you for your last delivery. You will be pleased to hear that the dressing tables are selling well.

A number of my customers have been asking about your bookcase and coffee table assembly kits which are listed in your Summer catalogue under KT 31, and we would like to test the demand for them. Would it be possible for me to have, say, half a dozen units of each kit, on approval, before placing a firm order?

I have enclosed an order, No. B1463, in anticipation of you agreeing, and as there is no particular hurry for the units, you could send them along with your next delivery.

Yours sincerely,

R. Hughes

R. Hughes

Encl. Order B1463

SUPERBUYS Ltd.

Superbuy House, Wolverton Road, London SW16 7DN

Telephone: 081 327 1651	Reg. No.: 94116 London
Telex: 303113	VAT No. 516 841030
Fax: 081 327 1935	

The Manager   Date: 10th January 19—
Wembley Shopfitters Ltd.
Wycombe Road
Wembley
Middlesex HA9 6DA

Dear Sir,

We are opening a new branch of 'Superbuys' in Wembley High Street
in March and would like to know if you could send someone along to
give us an estimate for refitting.

From our designer's plan enclosed, you can see that the premises were
once used as a warehouse and would need extensive alterations which
would include putting in counters, shelves, windows, rewiring, and
reflooring.

The work would have to be completed before the end of February and
you would be required to sign a contract to that effect. If the job
interests you, please contact Mr Keith Bellon our Managing Director on
081 327 1651 ext. 119 to arrange an appointment.

Yours faithfully,

Jean Landman

Jean Landman
Secretary to K. Bellon

Encl. Wembley Plan AC/1342

3.3.6
Request for an estimate

A supermarket is asking a firm of
shopfitters for an estimate to put in
counters, shelves, windows, etc. The
reply to this letter is at 4.3.7.

Questions

1 Why is an estimate needed? Why is it
  not possible to give a firm quotation?
2 What has to be done before the
  estimate can be given?
3 Can Wembley Shopfitters take as
  long as they want to complete the
  job?
4 Do Superbuys expect a letter in
  reply?
5 How should Mr Bellon be contacted?
6 Has anything been included with the
  letter?
7 How were the premises originally
  used?

3.4
Points to remember

1 Enquiries can take the form of telephoned, telexed, or faxed requests for information. Only use these forms if you can make your enquiry very brief. For fuller enquiries, write a letter.
2 Give details of your own firm as well as asking for information from your prospective supplier.
3 Be specific and state exactly what you want. Quote box numbers, catalogue references, etc. to help your supplier to identify what you want.
4 Ask for samples if you are uncertain about a product.
5 You can suggest terms and discounts, but be prepared for your supplier to make a counter-offer.
6 You can be direct in your letter, yet still polite. Notice how the use of the passive can soften a request: *I want a prompt reply* is impolite; *A prompt reply would be appreciated* is better. Notice also how short sentences can create an abrupt effect, while a complex sentence can modify: *We are large wholesalers. We are interested in your range of shirts* is not as good as *We are large wholesalers and are interested in your range of shirts*.
7 Close with a simple 'thank you' or 'I look forward to hearing from you', unless you want to indicate the possibility of substantial orders or further business.

3.5
Words to remember

to make an enquiry about a product
to enquire about a product

a company
a supplier
a customer
a wholesaler
a retailer
a bulk buyer
an agent
a principal
an associate
a representative
a subsidiary
a co-operative society
a Trade Association

a catalogue
a brochure
a booklet
a prospectus
a price-list
a leaflet
a showroom
a demonstration
a circular letter
a trade journal

samples
patterns

to offer concessions
to quote a price
to suggest/state terms
cash discount
trade discount
quantity discount
monthly/quarterly statement
documents against acceptance
bill of exchange

to place an order
goods on approval
goods on sale or return

to stock a product
to hold/carry (a) stock of a product

to invite/seek a tender or estimate
to provide/supply a tender or estimate

a reference
to ask for trade references
to provide/supply trade references

Replies and quotations

4

Confirming that you can help; 'selling' your product; suggesting alternatives; referring the customer elsewhere; catalogues, price-lists, prospectuses, samples; demonstrations, representatives, showroom visits; quotations; prices; transport and insurance costs; discounts; methods of payment; quoting delivery; fixed terms and negotiable terms; giving an estimate.

4.1
Replying to letters of enquiry

4.1.1
Opening

Mention your prospective customer's name. If the customer signs the letter *Mr B. Green*, then begin *Dear Mr Green*, not *Dear Sir*, which indicates that you have not bothered to remember the enquirer's name.

Thank the writer for his/her enquiry. Mention the date of his/her letter and quote any other references that appear.

Thank you for your enquiry of June 6th 1984 in which you asked about . . .

I would like to thank you for your enquiry of May 10 and am pleased to tell you that we would be able to supply you with the . . .

We were pleased to hear from your letter of 10 December that you were impressed with our selection of . . .

Thank you for your letter, NJ 1691, which we received this morning.

4.1.2
Confirming that you can help

Let the writer know as soon as possible if you have the product or can provide the service he/she is enquiring about. It is irritating to read a long letter only to find that the firm cannot help.

We have a wide selection of sweaters that will appeal to all ages, and in particular the teenage market which you specified.

Our factory would have no problem in turning out the 6,000 units you asked for in your enquiry.

We can supply from stock and will have no trouble in meeting your delivery date.

I am pleased to say that we will be able to deliver the transport facilities you require.

We can offer door-to-door delivery services.

4.1.3
'Selling' your product

Encourage or persuade your prospective customer to do business with you. A simple answer that you have the goods in stock is not enough. Your customer might have made ten other enquiries, so remember it is not only in sales letters that you have to persuade. Mention one or two selling points of your product, including any guarantees you offer.

We think you have made an excellent choice in selecting this line, and once you have seen the samples we are sure you will agree that this is unique both in texture and colour.

Once you have seen the Delta 800 in operation we know you will be impressed by its trouble-free performance.

We can assure you that the Omega 2000 is one of the most outstanding machines on the market today, and our confidence in it is supported by our five-year guarantee.

4.1.4
Suggesting alternatives

If you do not have what the enquirer has asked for, but have an alternative, offer it to him. But do not criticize the product he originally asked for.

... and while this engine has all the qualities of the model you asked for, the 'Powerdrive' has the added advantage of having fewer moving parts, so less can go wrong. It also saves on oil as it ...

The model has now been improved, its steel casing having been replaced by plastic which is lighter, more durable, and stronger.

Of course leather is an excellent material to work with in the upholstering of furniture, but escalating costs have persuaded customers to look for something more competitive in price. Fortunately, Tareton Plastics have produced an amazing substitute, 'Letherine', which has the same texture, strength and quality of leather, but is less than a quarter of the cost. The samples enclosed will convince you ...

4.1.5
Referring the customer elsewhere

It is possible, of course, that you may not be able to handle the order or answer the enquiry. Your correspondent may be asking about a product you do not make or a service you do not give. If this is so, tell him and if possible refer him elsewhere.

I regret to say that we no longer produce the type of stapler you refer to, since we find there is no longer sufficient demand for it. I am sorry we cannot be of help to you.

The book you mention is not published by us, but by Greenhill Education Ltd. If you would care to write to them, their address is . . .

We no longer manufacture pure cotton shirts as their retail prices tend only to attract the upper end of the market. All our garments are now poly-cotton, which is stronger, needs little ironing, and allows variations in patterns. However, if you are still set on pure cotton garments, we advise you to contact Louis Fashions Ltd. at . . .

Even if the product is yours, you may still have to refer the enquirer elsewhere.

I confirm that the product you require is one of ours, but since we are only able to deal with wholesalers, not retailers, may I refer you to R. L. Depré SA, rue Montpellier 28, Paris . . .?

Our agents in Italy are Intal S.p.A, Via Alberto Poerio 79, Rome, and they carry a full stock of our goods.

4. 1. 6
Catalogues, price-lists, prospectuses, samples

Make sure that you enclose current catalogues and price-lists if you are sending them. And if prices are subject to change, then let your customer know. It is bad policy to suddenly send a letter telling him that prices have been increased by 10% after you have quoted a firm price. And if you are sending samples, let your customer know they will follow the letter immediately by separate post.

Please find enclosed our current catalogue and price-list quoting c.i.f. prices Kobe. The units you referred to in your letter are featured on pp. 31–34 under catalogue numbers Y32–Y37.

When ordering could you please quote these numbers? The samples you asked for will follow by separate post.

We have enclosed our booklet on the Omega 2000 and are sure you will agree that it is one of the finest machines of its kind. It can be adapted to your specifications and details of this are on page 12 under the heading 'Structural Changes'.

We have sent you our summer catalogue which unfortunately is only printed in English. However, we have enclosed a German translation for the relevant pages (41–45) and hope this will prove helpful.

. . . and we have enclosed our price-list, but should point out that prices are subject to change as the market for raw materials is very unstable at present.

4. 1. 7
Demonstrations, representatives, showroom visits

Certain products, e.g. heavy equipment, machinery, installations, may need demonstrating. In these cases the company might send a representative, or adviser if equipment is to be installed. They could, however, suggest that the customer visits their agent in his own country, or a stockist with a showroom.

We have enclosed all the details about the Laren welder, but feel that a demonstration will give you more of an idea of its capabilities. We would therefore like to invite you to our centre in Birmingham where the equipment is set up so that you can see the machine in action.

As the enclosed illustrated booklet cannot really show the efficiency of the Farnon word processor, can we send our representative to you with a model of the machine, and he can give you a demonstration? If you are interested in a visit, please fill in the enclosed pre-paid card and return it to us.

The enclosed catalogue will give you an idea of the type of sound equipment we produce, but may we suggest that you visit our agent's showrooms in Rotterdam where you can see a wide range of units? The address is . . .

We will be able to install the equipment within three months, but would like to send Mr T. Griffith, our chief engineer, to look over your plant and prepare a report on the installations, taking into account your particular requirements.

4.1.8
Closing

Always thank the customer for writing to you. If you have not done so in the beginning of the letter, you can do so at the end. You should also encourage further enquiries.

Once again we would like to thank you for writing to us and would welcome any further points you would like us to answer.

Please write to us again if you have any questions, or call us at the above telephone number.

I am sorry we do not have the model you asked for, but I can promise you that the alternative I have suggested will certainly meet your expectations, and remember we offer a full guarantee for three years.

We hope to hear from you again, soon, and can assure you that your order will be dealt with promptly.

4.2
Quotations

In your reply to an enquiry, you may want to give your prospective customer a quotation. Below is a guide to the subjects you should cover in your quotation.

4.2.1
Prices

When a manufacturer, wholesaler or retailer quotes a price, he may or may not include other costs and charges such as transport, insurance, and taxes (e.g. in the UK, Value Added Tax or VAT). Prices which include these extra costs are known as *gross prices*; those which exclude them are known as *net prices*.

The net price of this article is £10.00, to which must be added VAT at 17½%, making a gross price of £11.75.

We can quote you a gross price, inclusive of delivery charges, of £37.50 per 100 items. These goods are exempt from VAT.

A firm's quotation is not necessarily legally binding, i.e. they do not always have to sell you the goods at the price they quoted in their reply to an enquiry. However, when prices tend to fluctuate, the supplier will add a provision to their quotation stating that their prices are subject to change. If the company makes a firm offer, it means they will hold the goods for a certain time until you order, e.g. firm 14 days. Again, this is not legally binding, but suppliers generally keep to their offer to protect their reputation.

The prices quoted above are provisional, since we may be compelled by increased costs of raw materials to increase our prices to customers. I will inform you immediately if this happens.

We can offer you a price of £6.29 per item, firm 21 days, after which the price will be subject to an increase of 5%.

Whenever possible you should quote prices in your customer's currency, allowing for exchange fluctuations.

The price of this model of cassette-player is 2,800 Belgian francs at today's rate of exchange.

We can quote you a price of 150,000 Italian lire per 100 units, though I regret that, because of fluctuating exchange rates, we can only hold this price for four weeks from today's date.

4.2.2
Transport and insurance costs

The International Chamber of Commerce use a set of terms for delivery in overseas contracts – these are called *Incoterms*. Their use is optional, but deals are much clearer if contracts are subject to *Incoterms 1990*.

GROUP C – *Main carriage paid*

CFR (Cost and Freight) named port of destination e.g. the port the goods are going to.

Delivery has occurred when the goods are on the ship at the port of shipment. The seller pays all the costs to this point and freight charges to the named port of destination. S/he provides the buyer with all the transport documentation showing

freight paid to that point. The goods and transit risks become the buyer's when the goods have gone over the ship's rail at the port of shipment.

CIF (Cost, Insurance & Freight) named port of destination

Delivery occurs as in **CFR** (above) and the risks are the same, but the exporter pays cargo insurance.

CFR and **CIF** can only be used for sea and inland waterways.

CPT (Carriage Paid To) named place of destination

Delivery happens when goods are given to the carrier (if more than one, the first carrier, or a freight forwarder). The seller pays the costs of delivery to the named place and the buyer's risks start from there.

CIP (Carriage and Insurance Paid) named place of destination

Delivery occurs as in **CPT** with the buyer's risks being the same. The only change is the exporter pays the cost of cargo insurance.

GROUP D – *Arrival*

DAF (Delivered at Frontier) named place

Delivery happens when the buyer gets the goods at a named place on the frontier, cleared for export, but not cleared for import. The buyer assumes all risks from here. The exporter pays all the costs to this point, but does not pay for unloading or import clearing charges.

DES (Delivered Ex Ship) named port of destination

Delivery happens when buyer gets goods at named port. He then assumes all risks, but the exporter pays all costs to that point, but not unloading or import clearance.

DEQ (Delivered Ex Quay – Duty Paid) named port of destination

Delivery happens when the buyers gets the goods on his/her quay (dock) and assumes all risks from that point. The seller pays all charges to that point including import and customs clearance costs.

DES and **DEQ** can only be used for sea and inland waterways.

DDU (Delivered Duty Unpaid) named place of destination

Delivery takes place when buyer gets the goods at the named place in the importing country and takes all the risks thereafter. The seller pays all costs to this point, but not duties and taxes.

DDP (Delivered Duty Paid) named place of destination

Delivery happens as in **DDU**, with the buyer taking the same risks. The seller pays all costs to this point including taxes and duties.

GROUP E – *Departure*

Ex-Works (EXW) e.g. from the factory or warehouse

Seller packs and prepares goods for despatch with delivery taking place at his/her factory or warehouse. The buyer now takes all transit risks.

GROUP F – *Main carriage unpaid*

FCA (Free Carrier) named place e.g. where the carrier – the plane or ship etc., pick up the goods

Delivery occurs when the seller gives the goods to the carrier (airline, shipping company, or freight forwarder) who is named by the buyer. The seller will pay all the costs up to this point, including export formalities and licences. From this point the buyer takes the risks for the goods and transit.
This term is used for any type or combination of types of transport.

FAS (Free Alongside Ship) with port of shipment named e.g. where the goods are leaving from

Delivery occurs alongside the ship named by the buyer at the named port of shipment. The buyer has the expense of loading. The seller pays costs up to and including delivery alongside the ship, including all documentation. The goods and transit risks are the buyer's when the goods are delivered within the period stated in the contract of sale. This term is only used for sea and inland waterways e.g. canals.

FOB (Free on Board) named port of shipment e.g. where the goods are leaving from.

Delivery takes place when goods are on board the named ship at the buyer's named port. The seller pays all costs of loading. The buyer's risks for the goods and transit begin once the goods have been put over the ship's rail.
The term is only used for sea and inland waterways.

4.2.3
Discounts

Manufacturers and wholesalers sometimes allow discounts to be deducted from the net or gross price. They may allow a *trade discount* to sellers in similar trades; or a *quantity discount* for orders over a certain amount; or a *cash discount* if payment is made within a certain time, e.g. seven days, or a loyalty discount when firms have a long association.

We allow a 3% discount for payment within one month.

The net price of this model is £7.50, less 10% discount for quantities up to 100 and 15% discount for quantities over 100.

We do not normally give discounts to private customers but because of your long association with our company we will allow you 20% off the retail price.

The prices quoted are c. & f. Yokohama, but are subject to a 20% trade discount off net price, and we will allow a further 20% trade discount off net prices for orders of more than 2,000 units.

4.2.4
Methods of payment

When quoting terms, you may require, or at least suggest, any of several methods of payment (letter of credit, bill of exchange, etc.) For a full treatment of this subject, see 6.3.1/2 and 9.5/7.

If you would send us your personal cheque for the amount quoted, we will then send the article by registered mail.

Payment for initial orders should be made by sight draft, payable at Den Norske Creditbank, Kirkegaten 21, Oslo 1, cash against documents.

4.2.5
Quoting delivery

If the enquiry specifies a delivery date, confirm that it can be met, or if not, suggest an alternative date. Do not make a promise that you cannot keep; it will give you a bad reputation, and if a delivery time is a condition of ordering, the customer could sue you if you break the contract, or reject the goods.

. . . and we are pleased to say that we can deliver by December 1st for the Christmas rush.

As there are regular sailings from Liverpool to New York, we are sure that the consignment will reach you well within the time you specified.

We have the materials in stock and will ship them immediately we receive your order.

As there is a heavy demand at this time of year for heaters, you will have to allow at least six weeks for delivery.

We could not deliver within two weeks of receipt of order, as we would need time to prepare the materials. However, if you could let us have a month, we could guarantee delivery within that period.

4.2.6
Fixed terms and negotiable terms

It is possible to quote terms in two ways: by stating your price and discounts without leaving room for negotiation, or suggesting that the customer could write again and discuss them. In the two examples below, the companies make firm quotes, indicating that methods of payment and discounts are fixed.

All list prices are quoted f.o.b. Southampton and are subject to a 25% trade discount with payment by letter of credit.

The prices quoted are ex-works, but we can arrange freight and insurance if required, and unless otherwise stated, payment is to be made by 30-day bill of exchange, documents against acceptance.

In the next two examples, the use of the adverbs *normally* and *usually* soften the tone of the statements to indicate that although the firm prefers certain terms, these can at least be discussed. In the final example the supplier even asks 'if this arrangement is satisfactory'.

We usually offer an 18% trade discount on f.o.b. prices, and would prefer payment by irrevocable letter of credit.

Normally we allow a 23% trade discount off net prices with payment on a documents against payment basis. Please let us know if this arrangement is satisfactory.

4.2.7
Giving an estimate

Companies which are asked to estimate for a particular job of work may include the estimate in tabulated form in a letter (see 4.3.7). More often, however, they will send their official estimate form with a covering letter.

As you know, our representative has visited your factory to discuss the extension which you wish to add to it, and I now have pleasure in enclosing our official estimate.

The enclosed estimate covers labour and parts and carries a six-month guarantee on all work completed.

4.3
Specimen letters

4.3.1
Short replies

1 *Catalogue and price-list:*
reply to 3.3.1A

Dear Mr Raval,

Thank you for your enquiry of 31 January. We are enclosing our Spring catalogue and current price-list quoting c.i.f. prices Le Havre.

We would like to draw your attention to the trade and quantity discounts we are offering in our Special Purchases section pp. 19–26 which may be of particular interest to you.

Please contact us if we can be of any further help to you.

Yours sincerely,

2 *College prospectus:*
reply to 3.3.1B

Dear Miss Iwanammi,

Please find enclosed our prospectus covering courses from July to December. Details of fees and accommodation in London for that period are covered in the booklet 'Living in London' which accompanies the prospectus.

At present we still have places available for students taking the Proficiency course beginning in July, but would ask you to book as soon as possible so that we can reserve a place for you in the class and arrange accommodation with an English family.

We are sure you will enjoy your stay here and look forward to seeing you.

Yours sincerely,

3 *General information:*
reply to 3.3.1C

Dear Mr Wymer,

Thank you very much for your enquiry. You will find enclosed a catalogue giving detailed information about our tubeless tyres and including the impressive results we have achieved in rigorous factory and track tests. Please note the items on safety and fuel economy which have proved the main selling points of this product.

With regard to trade discounts, we are allowing 25% off list prices to bona fide retailers and wholesalers, with quantity discounts for orders over £3,000.

We will be pleased to supply any further information you require.

Yours sincerely,

R. G. Electronics AG

Havmart 601
D-5000 Köln 1
Tel: (221) 32 42 98
Fax: (221) 83 61 25
Telex: 6153291

Your Ref: PG/AL

P. Gérard   14th May 19—
Disc S.A.
251 rue des Raimonières
F-86000 Poitiers Cédex

Dear Mr Gérard,

Thank you for your enquiry of 12 May in which you asked about the tapes we advertised in this month's edition of 'Hi Fi News'.

The cassettes are ferrous based and high quality Cr O_2 which as you know means they would be suitable for any type of recording. They are 'Kolby' products which is a brand name you will certainly recognize, and the reason their prices are so competitive is that they are part of a bankrupt stock that was offered to us.

Because of their low price and the small profit margin we are working on, we will not be offering any trade discounts on this consignment. But we sell a wide range of cassettes and have enclosed a price-list giving you details of trade, quantity, and cash discounts on our other products.

We have sent, by separate post, samples of the advertised cassettes and other brands we stock, and would urge you to place an order as soon as possible as there has been a huge response to our advertisement. Thank you for your interest.

Yours sincerely,

R. Gerlach

R. Gerlach
Sales Director

Encl. price-list

4.3.2
Catalogues and samples

In the letter at 3.3.2 M. Gérard wrote to R. G. Electronics AG to enquire about tapes and cassettes; he implied that his store was a large one, that he was only interested in high quality products, and that he might place a substantial order. This is the reply.

Questions

1 How does Herr Gerlach refer to M. Gérard's enquiry?
2 Why are the cassettes being sold cheaply?
3 Does Herr Gerlach offer any discounts?
4 Can Disc S.A. order whenever they want to?
5 Are these the only cassettes that R. G. Electronics sell?
6 What other material has been sent to Disc S.A.?

4.3.3
'Selling' the product

This is a reply to the buying agent who wrote at 3.3.3 on behalf of her principals in Canada. As the agent made no reference to any particular line of chinaware she was interested in, nor mentioned terms, this letter is in the nature of a sales letter.

Questions

1 How does Mr Merton draw attention to his firm's many products?
2 How does he imply that his firm has an international reputation?
3 What discount does he offer?
4 How does he encourage further enquiries?
5 Do Glaston offer any concessions?
6 How do Glaston quote their prices?
7 Which words in the letter correspond to the following: *putting in*; *range*; *select*; *allowance*; *when we receive your indent*?

GLASTON POTTERIES Ltd.

Clayfield, Burnley BB10 1RQ

Tel: 0315 46125	Registered No. 716481
Telex: 8801773	VAT Registered No. 133 5341 08
Fax: 0315 63182	Your ref: 180/MB

Mrs L. Lowe   10 June 19—
Sanders & Lowe Ltd.
Planter House
Princes Street
London EC1 7DQ

Dear Mrs Lowe,

It was a pleasure to receive your letter today, and we are enclosing the catalogue and price-list you asked for.

You will see that we can offer a wide selection of dinner and tea services ranging from the rugged 'Greystone' earthenware breakfast sets, to the delicate 'Ming' bone china dinner service.

You can choose from more than fifty designs which include the elegance of Wedgwood, the delicate pattern of Willow, and the richness of Brownstone glaze.

We would be pleased to add your clients to our list of customers throughout the world and could promise them an excellent product with a first-class service. We would be glad to accept orders for any number of pieces, and can mix sets if required.

You will see that our prices are quoted c.i.f. to Eastern Canadian seaboard ports and we are offering a special 10% discount off all net prices, with delivery within three weeks from receipt of order.

If there is any further information you require, please contact us, and once again thank you for your letter.

Yours sincerely,

J. Merton

J. Merton (Mr)
Sales Manager

Enc.

D & S Charcot S.A.R.L.

place du 20 août 79 B–4000 Liège

Tel: (32) 49–240886
Télécopie: (32) 49–16592

The Chief Buyer   11 March 19—
Caravela
Rua das Ameixoeiras 1291
P-1700 Lisboa

Dear Mr Monteiro,

Thank you for your enquiry, but I regret to say that we have run out of our stock of K153 and K157 units and do not expect another delivery until later this month.

At present we are testing a consignment recently imported from Taiwan, but these do not have a Belgian Standards Institute stamp of approval and we would like to test them thoroughly before putting them on the market. Nevertheless, if we find they are satisfactory, or we get a delivery of K153s/7s from our manufacturers we will contact you at once.

Yours sincerely,

D Charcot

D. Charcot
Manager

4.3.4
Offer of an alternative

The wholesaler is out of stock of the adapters that his customer has asked for, so he is offering a substitute. However, he has not yet tested the new product and knows nothing about its performance or safety.

Questions

1 What is M. Charcot's problem?
2 How does he show his customer that he is concerned about safety?
3 Why is safety particularly important in this case?
4 Does M. Charcot rely on his customer to write to him again?
5 Can M. Charcot still get the units he asked for?
6 Which organization establishes safety regulations in Belgium?

4.3.5

Quotation of terms

This is a reply to the general enquiry at 3.3.4. in which Mr Crane of F. Lynch & Co. asked for certain concessions. Notice how, in the reply, Mr Causio of Satex does not turn down the requests but suggests a counter-offer.

Questions

1 How does Mr Causio confirm that he can supply the sweaters?
2 Does Mr Causio agree to all Mr Crane's requests concerning discounts?
3 How does Mr Causio suggest that the method of payment could be changed in the future?
4 What enclosures have been made?
5 What sort of payment does Mr Causio ask for?
6 How does Mr Causio suggest his firm deals internationally?
7 What expression does he use to say his firm has different clothes in different styles?
8 Which words in the letter correspond to the following: *bulk discount*; *bill paid on presentation*; *clothes*; *reconsider*; *discount*?

Satex S.p.A.

Via di Pietra Papa, 00146 Roma

Telefono: Roma 769910
Telefax: (06) 681 5473
Telex: 285136

Mr L. Crane, Chief Buyer   Vs. rif.: Inq   C351
F. Lynch & Co. Ltd.   Ns. rif.: D/1439
Nesson House
Newell Street   21 February 19—
Birmingham B3 3EL
UNITED KINGDOM

Dear Mr Crane,

We are pleased to receive your enquiry, and to hear that you liked our range of sweaters.

There would certainly be no trouble in supplying you from our wide selection of garments which we make for all age groups.

We can offer you the quantity discount you asked for which would be 5% off net prices for orders over £2,000, but the usual allowance for a trade discount in Italy is 15%, and we always deal on payment by sight draft, cash against documents. However, we would be prepared to review this once we have established a firm trading association with you.

Enclosed you will find our summer catalogue and price-list quoting prices c.i.f. London.

We are sure you will find a ready sale for our products in England as have other retailers throughout Europe and America, and we do hope we can reach an agreement on the terms quoted.

Thank you for your interest; we look forward to hearing from you soon.

Yours sincerely,

D. Causio

D. Causio

Encl.

HOMEMAKERS Ltd.

54–59 Riverside, Cardiff CF1 1JW

Telephone: (0222) 49721   Registered No. C135162
Telex: 38217

24 November 19—

R. Hughes & Son Ltd.
21 Mead Road
Swansea
Glamorgan 3ST 1DR

Dear Mr Hughes,

It was nice to hear from you again, and to learn that our products are
selling well in Swansea and that your customers have become
interested in our new do-it-yourself range.

You can certainly have the assembly kits you asked for (Cat. No. KT31)
and there will be no need to wait until you receive another delivery;
I will tell my driver to drop them off on his next delivery to Swansea
which will be on Monday.

The provisional order, No. B1463, which you enclosed will be sufficient,
but would you return any part of the consignment you have not sold
within two months?

I look forward to your next order, and hope to see you when I come to
Swansea in December.

Yours sincerely,

R. Cliff

4.3.6
Goods on approval

As we saw in 3.3.5, these two firms
know one another quite well, so Mr Cliff
does not find it necessary to ask for
references or a guarantor before
allowing Mr Hughes the goods on
approval. A provisional order is enough
to confirm that Mr Hughes has asked for
the goods, and the driver will get him to
sign a delivery note, once he has
brought the consignment, as further
proof that Mr Hughes has received
them.

4.3.7
An estimate

This illustrates an estimate sent in tabulated form in the body of a letter. It is a reply to the letter at 3.3.6.

Wembley Shopfitters Ltd.

Wycombe Road, Wembley, Middlesex HA9 6DA

Telephone: 081 903 2323   Reg: London 481629   VAT: 314 6519 28

Mr K. Bellon   24 January 19—
Superbuys Ltd.
Superbuy House
Wolverton Road
London SW16 7DN

Dear Mr Bellon,

<u>Estimate for refitting 'Superbuys'</u>
<u>Wembley High Street Branch</u>

Our foreman visited the above premises on Thursday and reported back to our costing department who have now worked out the following estimate for fixtures and fittings which includes materials and labour.

	£
Fitting 200m of 'Contact' Shelving in main shop and store room.	420.00
Erecting 15 steel stands plus shelves 23m × 6m @ £52.00 each.	780.00
Laying 3,320 sq.m. 'Durafloor' flooring @ £9.00 per sq.m.	29,880.00
Fitting 3 window frames plus glass 13m × 10m @ £79.00 each.	237.00
Rewiring; fixing power points, boxes, etc. 36 'Everglow' light fittings @ £12.00 each.	432.00
Total	31,749.00
plus VAT @ 17.5%	5,556.00
	37,305.00

cont.

– 2 –

We are sure you will agree that this is a very competitive estimate especially when you consider that the materials we use are of the best quality and backed by a one-year guarantee against normal wear and tear. We can also promise that the job will be completed before the end of February provided that no unforeseeable circumstances arise.

If you have any further questions, please contact Mr T. Mills on 081 903 2323 ext. 21, who, as senior supervisor, will be able to give you any advice or information you require. We look forward to hearing from you soon.

Yours sincerely,

P. Lane

P. Lane
Director

Questions

1 Where is the brief subject matter of this letter?
2 Which department estimates this amount for the job?
3 Why does Mr Lane consider this a competitive offer?
4 What provision is mentioned if the job is to be completed in February?
5 What does the sign @ mean?
6 Is the figure £31,749 a net or gross total?
7 What is the position of Mr Mills?
8 What does the expression *normal wear and tear* mean, and why is it mentioned?
9 Which words in the letter correspond to the following: *place of work*; *calculated*; *assessment*; *supported*; *problems not anticipated*?

4.4
Points to remember

1 The reply to an enquiry does not only tell your customer whether you can provide the goods or services he has asked about, but also indicates what sort of firm you are; whether you are aware, conscientious, and efficient.

2 Avoid opening with expressions like 'We are in receipt of your enquiry' or 'With reference to your enquiry' or 'In reply to your enquiry'. These openings tend to sound rather cold.

3 Avoid phrases like 'We are taking the liberty of sending you . . .' or 'We hasten to reply to your esteemed enquiry of the 10th inst.;' you will sound like a firm that should have gone out of business a century ago.

4 If you use expressions like 'It was with the utmost pleasure that we received . . .' or 'We deeply regret that we cannot supply you with . . .', you will appear at best desperate or, worse, insincere. A straightforward 'Thank you for . . .' or 'I would like to thank you for . . .' or 'I am sorry that . . .' is enough.

5 Make sure that you do not leave out information, and have supplied the printed matter that you think will help your customer.

6 Assure your customer that you have faith in your product, which means that you have to 'sell' it.

7 A reply to an initial enquiry is the first impression your customer will have of you, and that will be how he judges you. So a direct approach, telling the customer what the product is, why he should buy it, how much it will cost, and what concessions you are offering, will create an impression of an efficient company that can handle his order smoothly.

8 After you have written your reply, check it to make sure that you have answered all the customer's questions, and included all the points you wanted to make. Ask yourself if the letter flows, or seems short and sharp; if it sounds helpful, or just informs the customer. The best test of all, of course, is to ask yourself if you would order something from a firm that has sent you the letter you have written.

4.5
Words to remember

a representative
an adviser
a stockist
a guarantor

retail price
wholesale price
net price
gross price
prices inclusive of delivery charges
to quote a firm price
to hold a price for 21 days (firm 21 days)

VAT (Value Added Tax)
goods exempt from VAT

to quote terms
fixed terms
negotiable terms
quantity discount
cash discount
letter of credit
bill of exchange
sight draft
cash against documents
documents against payment
documents against acceptance

ex-works/ex-factory
f.o.r.   (free on rail)

FAS   (free alongside ship)
FOB   (free on board)
CFR   (cost and freight)
CIF   (cost, insurance, and freight)
DES   (delivered ex ship)
DEQ   (delivered ex quay - duty paid)
carriage paid
carriage forward

to handle an order
to supply from stock
to quote a delivery date
to meet a delivery date
to deliver a consignment
a delivery note

Orders

5

Placing an order (covering letters, confirming payment, discounts, delivery dates, methods of delivery, packing); acknowledging an order; advice of despatch; delays in delivery; refusing an order (out of stock, bad reputation, unfavourable terms, size of order).

5.1
Placing an order

Orders are usually written on a company's official order form (see 5.4.2 for an example) which has a date and a reference number that should be quoted in any correspondence which refers to the order. Even if the order is telephoned, it must be confirmed in writing, and an order form should always be accompanied by either a compliment slip or a covering letter. A covering letter is preferable as it allows you the opportunity to make any necessary points and confirm the terms that have been agreed.

The guide below is for an outline of a covering letter. You may not want to make all the points listed, but look through the guide to see what could be mentioned.

5.1.1
Opening

Explain there is an order accompanying the letter.

Please find enclosed our Order No. B4521 for 25 'Clearsound' transistor receivers.

The enclosed order (No. R154) is for 50 reams of A4 bank paper.

Thank you for your reply of 14 May regarding the cassettes we wrote to you about. Enclosed you will find our official order (No. B561) for . . .

Your letter of 12 October convinced me to place at least a trial order for the 'Letherine' material you spoke about. Therefore, please find enclosed . . .

5. 1. 2
Payment

Confirm the terms of payment.

As agreed you will draw on us at 30 days, documents against acceptance, with the documents being sent to our bank at . . .

We would like to confirm that payment is to be made by irrevocable letter of credit which we have already applied to the bank for.

Once we have received your advice, we will send a banker's draft to . . .

. . . and we agreed that payments would be made against quarterly statements . . .

5. 1. 3
Discounts

Confirm the agreed discounts.

We would like to thank you for the 30% trade discount and 10% quantity discount you allowed us.

Finally, we would like to say that the 25% trade discount is quite satisfactory.

. . . and we will certainly take advantage of the cash discounts you offered for prompt settlement.

Although the rather low trade discount of 15% disappointed us, we will place an order and hope that this allowance can be reviewed at some time in the near future.

5. 1. 4
Delivery

Confirm the delivery dates.

It is essential that the goods are delivered before the beginning of

November in time for the Christmas rush.

Delivery before February is a firm condition of this order, and we reserve the right to refuse goods delivered after that time.

Please confirm that you can complete the work before the end of March, as the opening of the supermarket is planned for the beginning of April.

5. 1. 5
Methods of delivery

Many firms use *forwarding agents* (see 11.3.5) who are specialists in packing and handling the documentation for shipping goods. Nevertheless, you should still advise the firm as to how you want the goods packed and sent to ensure prompt and safe delivery, so that if the consignment does arrive late, or in a damaged state, your letter is evidence of the instructions you gave.

. . . and please remember that only air freight will ensure prompt delivery.

Please send the goods by Red Star express as we need them urgently.

We advise delivery by road to avoid constant handling of this fragile consignment.

Could you please ship by scheduled freighter to avoid any unnecessary delays?

5. 1. 6
Packing

Advise your supplier how you want the goods packed. Note, in the first example, that crates are often marked with a sign – a diamond, a target, a square, a lion, etc. – that can be recognized by the supplier and customer.

Each piece of crockery is to be individually wrapped in thick paper, packed in straw, and shipped in wooden crates marked ◇ and numbered 1 to 6.

The carpets should be wrapped in thick grease-proof paper which is reinforced at both ends to avoid wear by friction.

The machines must be well greased with all movable parts secured before being loaded into crates, which must be marked.

5.1.7
Closing

We hope that this will be the first of many orders we will be placing with you.

We will submit further orders, if this one is completed to our satisfaction.

If the goods sell as well as we hope, we shall send further orders in the near future.

I look forward to receiving your advice/ shipment/acknowledgement/ confirmation.

5.2
Acknowledging an order

As soon as an order is received by a supplier, it should be acknowledged. This letter can be quite short, as the letter at 5.4.3.

Thank you for your order No. 338B which we received today. We are now dealing with it and you may expect delivery within the next three weeks.

Your order, No. 6712/1 is now being processed and should be ready for despatch by next week.

We are pleased to say that we have already made up your order, No. 9901/ 1/5 for 50 canteens of 'Silverline' cutlery, and are now making arrangements for shipment to Rotterdam.

5.3
Advice of despatch

When the supplier has made up the order and arranged shipment, the customer is informed of this in an advice. This may be done on a special form (see 5.4.7) or in a letter.

Your order, No. D/154/T, has now been placed on board the SS Mitsu Maru sailing from Kobe on 16 May and arriving Tilbury, London, on 11 June. The shipping documents have already been sent to your bank in London for collection.

We are pleased to advise you that the watches you ordered – No. 88151/24 – were put on flight BA 165 leaving Zurich 11.00, 9 August arriving Manchester 13.00. Please find enclosed air waybill DC 15161/3 and copies of invoice A113/3.

Please be advised that your order, No. YI/151/C, has now been put on the Glasgow–London express and can be collected at Euston station. Enclosed is consignment note No. 1167153 which should be presented on collection. You should contact us immediately if any problems arise. Thank you for your order, and we hope we can be of service in the future.

5.4
Specimen letters
and forms

5.4.1
Placing an order: covering letter

This letter follows on from the correspondence at 3.3.4 and 4.3.5. F. Lynch & Co. have decided to place an order with Satex S.p.A. and are sending a covering letter with the form.

Questions

1 In the letter at 3.3.4 Lynch & Co. said they were likely to order over 500 sweaters, but their actual order is only for 150. What might be the reason for this?
2 How will Lynch & Co. pay?
3 How soon do they want the sweaters?
4 If the sweaters they have ordered are out of stock, would they accept substitutes?

F. Lynch & Co. Ltd.

(Head Office), Nesson House, Newell Street, Birmingham B3 3EL

Telephone: 021 236 6571   Fax: 021 236 8592   Telex: 341641

Satex S.p.A
Via di Pietra Papa
00146 Roma
ITALY

Your ref: D/1439
Our ref: Order DR4316

9 March 19—

Attn. Mr D. Causio

Dear Mr Causio,

Please find enclosed our order, No. DR4316, for men's and boys' sweaters in assorted sizes, colours, and designs.

We have decided to accept the 15% trade discount you offered and terms of payment viz. documents against payment, but would like these terms reviewed in the near future.

Would you please send the shipping documents and your sight draft to Northminster Bank (City Branch), Deal Street, Birmingham B3 1SQ.

If you do not have any of the listed items in stock, please do not send substitutes in their place.

We would appreciate delivery within the next six weeks, and look forward to your acknowledgement.

Yours sincerely,

Lionel Crane

Lionel Crane
Chief Buyer

Enc. order form No. DR4316

ORDER   No. **DR 4316**

F. Lynch & Co. Ltd.

(Head Office), Nesson House, Newell Street, Birmingham B3 3EL

Telephone: 021 236 6571   Fax: 021 236 8592   Telex: 341641

Satex S.p.A
Via di Pietra Papa
00146 Roma

ITALY   Authorized *L. Crane* ....

Quantity	Item description	Cat. No.	Price c.i.f. London
50	V Neck: 30 Red/20 Blue	R 432	£13.80 each
30	Roll Neck: 15 Black/15 Blue	N 154	£ 9.40 "
30	Crew Neck: 15 Green/15 Beige	N 154	£16.00 "
40	Crew Neck: pattern	R 541	£12.60 "
	Note: Subject to 5% quantity discount		

Comments: 15% Trade Disc. Pymt. D/P Del. 6 weeks   **Date:** 9 March 19—

5.4.2
Order form

This is Lynch & Co.'s official order form.

Questions

1 When should the order be delivered?
2 How will Lynch & Co. pay?
3 Who is L. Crane?
4 What sort of discounts have been agreed?
5 If the order was faxed to Satex, which number would be used?
6 Which reference identifies the sweaters?
7 Besides the price, what other costs are covered to London?
8 If Lynch & Co. need further correspondence with Satex on this order, what reference would they use?

5.4.3
Acknowledgement of order

Satex S.p.A. will now prepare Mr Crane's order, but in the meantime let him know that the order has been received.

Satex S.p.A.

Via di Pietra Papa, 00146 Roma

Telefono: Roma 769910
Telefax: (06) 681 5473
Telex: 285136

Mr L. Crane, Chief Buyer   Vs. rif.: Order DR4316
F. Lynch & Co. Ltd.   Ns. rif.: D/1140
Nesson House
Newell Street   13 March 19—
Birmingham B3 3EL
UNITED KINGDOM

Dear Mr Crane,

Thank you for your order (No. DR4316) which we are now making up. We have all the items in stock and will be advising you in the near future.

Yours sincerely,

D. Causio

D. Causio

Satex S.p.A.

Via di Pietra Papa, 00146 Roma

Telefono: Roma 769910
Telefax: (06) 681 5473
Telex: 285136

Mr L. Crane, Chief Buyer   Vs. rif.: Order DE4316
F. Lynch & Co. Ltd.   Ns. rif.: D/1141
Nesson House
Newell Street   29 March 19—
Birmingham B3 3EL
UNITED KINGDOM

Dear Mr Crane,

We would like to advise you that your order has been shipped on the
SS Marconissa and should reach you within the next ten days.
Meanwhile our bank has forwarded the relevant documents and sight
draft for £1,662.60 to the Northminster Bank (City Branch) Birmingham

We are sure you will be pleased with the consignment and look
forward to your next order.

Yours sincerely,

D. Causio

D. Causio

5.4.4
Advice of despatch

This letter confirms that Satex S.p.A. have sent the order. When he receives this letter, Mr Crane will go to the Northminster Bank, where he will be asked to accept a sight draft, i.e. pay a bill of exchange immediately. After he has paid this, he will be handed the shipping documents (bill of lading, insurance certificate, and commercial invoice) so that he can collect the goods. Remember, this was a c.i.f. transaction where the supplier paid cost, insurance, and freight, and on a documents against acceptance basis, i.e. once the bill of exchange has been accepted, the documents would be handed over.

5.4.5
Placing an order

This letter and the next one follow on from the correspondence at 3.3.3 and 4.3.3. There are three parties involved: the manufacturers, Glaston Potteries; the buying agents, Sanders and Lowe; and their principals in Canada, MacKenzie Bros. Here, Mrs Lowe is writing on behalf of her principals and forwarding their order. Notice the instructions she gives and notice that she has already phoned the manufacturer to agree terms of payment which were not mentioned in the manufacturer's letter at 4.3.3.

Questions

1 Sanders & Lowe have completed their job, which was to find a supplier. So who must Glaston Potteries write to now?
2 What advice has been given on packing?
3 What method of payment has been arranged?
4 Will substitutes be acceptable if Glaston Potteries are out of stock of any items?
5 Why should there be no problem for Glaston Potteries to deliver within four weeks?
6 Which words used in the letter correspond to the following: *cups, saucers, plates, etc.*; *boxes*; *breakables*; *made*; *different*; *stated*; *relevant*; *completed*?

Sanders & Lowe Ltd.

Import and Export, (London Office), Planter House, Princes Street, London   EC1 7DQ

Birmingham Office: 28 Bradshaw Street, Birmingham B5 1TQ
Manchester Office: 343 Oxford Street, Manchester M27 2LR
Liverpool Office: 54 Bakers Road, Liverpool L3 9HW
Stockport Office: 5 Island Road, Stockport SM3 12K

Telephone: 071 543 1615
Fax: 071 543 1925
Telex: 928537

Reg. No. England 155134
VAT No. 013 7001 21

Directors: L.W. Lowe, D.R. Sanders

Your ref: ——   Our ref: 185/MB   Date: 2 July 19—

Mr J. Merton
Sales Manager
Glaston Potteries Ltd.
Clayfield
Burnley BB10 1RQ

Dear Mr Merton,

Please find enclosed an order (R1432) from our principals, MacKenzie Bros. Ltd., 1–5 Whale Drive, Dawson, Ontario, Canada.

They have asked us to instruct you that the 60 sets of crockery ordered should be packed in six crates, ten sets per crate, with each piece individually wrapped, and the crates marked clearly with their name, the words 'fragile', 'crockery', and numbered 1–6.

They have agreed to pay by letter of credit, which we discussed on the phone last week, and they would like delivery before the end of this month, which should be easily effected as there are regular sailings from Liverpool.

If the colours they have chosen are not in stock, they will accept an alternative provided the designs are those stipulated on the order.

Please send any further correspondence relating to shipment or payment direct to MacKenzie Bros. and let us have a copy of the commercial invoice when it is made up.

Yours sincerely,

L. Lowe

L.W. Lowe (Mrs)

Enc. Order R1432

GLASTON POTTERIES Ltd.

Clayfield, Burnley BB10 1RQ

Tel: 0315 46125
Telex: 8801773
Fax: 0315 63182

Registered No. 716481
VAT Registered No. 133 5341 08

MacKenzie Bros. Ltd.   14 July 19—
1–5 Whale Drive
Dawson
Ontario
CANADA

Dear Sirs,

Order R1432

The above order has now been completed and sent to Liverpool Docks
where it is awaiting loading onto the SS Manitoba which sails for Dawson,
Canada on the 16 July and arrives on 30 July.

Once we have the necessary documents we will hand them to Burnley City
Bank, your bank's agents here, and they will forward them to the Canadian
Union Trust Bank.

We have taken special care to see that the goods have been packed as per
your instructions, the six crates being marked with your name, and
numbered 1–6. Each crate measures 6ft × 4ft × 3ft and weighs 5 cwt.

We managed to get all items from stock with the exception of Cat. No. G16
which we only had in red. But we included it in the consignment as it had
the Willow pattern you asked for.

If there is any further information you require, please contact us. Thank you
very much for your order, and we look forward to hearing from you again
soon.

Yours faithfully,

J Merton

J. Merton (Mr)
Sales Manager

5.4.6
Advice of despatch

Glaston Potteries have made up the
MacKenzie order and now advise them.
MacKenzie Bros. will already have
opened a letter of credit (see 9.7) at their
bank, The Canadian Union Trust Bank,
in favour of their suppliers, Glaston
Potteries. The Canadian bank will now
wait until they have confirmation of
shipment from *their* agents in England,
Burnley City Bank, and will then transfer
the money so that Glaston Potteries can
be paid.

Questions

1 How will the consignment be sent?
2 What will happen to the documents
  once Glaston Potteries receive them?
3 How have the goods been packed
  and the crates marked?
4 What did Glaston do about the item
  they could not supply?
5 When will the consignment arrive in
  Canada?
6 Which words in the letter correspond
  to the following: *made up*; *send*; *in
  accordance with*; *apart from*; *due
  in*?

5.4.7
Advice note

At 5.4.6, Glaston Potteries advised MacKenzie Bros. of despatch in a letter. Here D & S Charcot use a form.

D & S Charcot S.A.R.L.   Advice note

place du 20 août 79 B-4000 Liège

Tel: (32) 49–240886
Télécopie: (32) 49–16592

The Chief Buyer
Caravela
Rua das Ameixoeiras 1291
P–1700 Lisboa
Your order No. D163/9

The following consignment has been sent to you by rail today. Please confirm receipt and quote consignment note No. 8817561 915.

Quantity	Goods (Description)
4 doz	ERC adaptors 13 amp
68	Dimmer switches 250 watt
100	1-metre fluorescent fitting with defuser
4 doz	Jacar 4-metre extension leads 3kW (3,000 watt)
6 doz	13 amp point fittings

Comments: Paid on Pro Forma inv. B3171.   **Date:** 5 September 19—

5.5.
Delays in delivery

If goods are held up either before or after they are sent, you must keep your customer informed. Let him know what has happened, how it happened, and what you are doing to correct the situation.

I was surprised and sorry to hear that your consignment (Order No. B145) had not reached you. On enquiry I found that it had been delayed by a local dispute on the cargo vessel SS Hamburg on which it had been loaded. I am now trying to get the goods transferred to the SS Samoa which should sail for Yokohama before the end of next week. However, I shall keep you informed.

I am writing to tell you that there will be a three-week delay in delivery. This is due to a fire at our Greenford works which destroyed most of the machinery.

Nevertheless, your order has been transferred to our Slough factory and is being processed there. I apologize for the delay which was due to circumstances beyond our control.

We regret to inform you that there will be a hold up in getting your consignment to you. This is due to the cut in supplies from Gara where civil war suddenly broke out last week. We have contacted a possible supplier in Lagos and he will let us know if he can help us. If you wish to cancel your order, you may, but I think you will find most manufacturers are experiencing the same difficulties at present.

5.6
Refusing an order

There are a number of reasons for a firm refusing an order, and some of the most common are given below. Whatever your reason, you must be polite: the words *reject* and *refuse* have a negative tone to them, therefore it is better to use *decline* or *turn down* instead.

5.6.1
Out of stock

You may be out of stock of the product ordered, or indeed you may no longer make it. Note that, in either case, you have an opportunity to sell an alternative product (see 4.1.4), but remember not to criticize the product you can no longer supply.

We are sorry to say that we are completely out of stock of this item and it will be at least six weeks before we get our next delivery, but please contact us then.

We no longer manufacture this product as demand over the past few years has declined.

Thank you for your order for heavy-duty industrial overalls. Unfortunately we have run out of the strengthened denim style you asked for. As you have particularly requested only this material, we will not offer a substitute, but hope we will get delivery of a new consignment within the next two months. We hope you will contact us then.

We received your order for ACN dynamos today, but regret that due to a strike at the ACN factory we are unable to fulfil the order, and we realize that other models will not suit your requirements. Hopefully the dispute will be settled soon so that we will be able to supply you. You can rely on us to keep you informed of the developments.

5.6.2
Bad reputation

The customer may have a bad reputation for settling their accounts or, in the case of a retailer of, say, electrical or mechanical products, may have offered a poor after-sales service which could in turn affect your reputation. In these cases, it is better to indicate terms on which you would be prepared to accept his order, or, as in the last three examples, find a diplomatic way of saying 'no'.

We would only be prepared to supply on a cash basis.

We only supply on payment against pro-forma invoice.

As there is heavy demand we have very few of these products in stock, and are serving on a rota basis. It seems unlikely that we could deliver within the next four months.

As our plant is closing for the summer vacation we would not be able to process your order for the date you have given. Therefore, regretfully we have to decline it.

I am sorry to say that we must turn down your order as we have full order books at present and cannot give a definite date for delivery.

5.6.3
Unfavourable terms

The supplier may not like the terms the customer has asked for, either for delivery:

Delivery could not possibly be promised within the time given in your letter.

Two months must be allowed for delivery, as we ourselves have to get raw materials and rely on our own suppliers.

Or discount:

It would be uneconomical for us to offer our products at the discounts you suggest as we work on a fast turnover and low profit margins.

The usual trade discount is 15% in this country, which is 5% lower than the figure mentioned in your letter.

The discount you asked for is far more than we offer any of our customers.

Or payment:

We only accept payment by letter of credit.

We never offer quarterly terms on initial orders, even to customers who can

provide references. However, we might consider this sort of credit once we have established a trading relationship.

Our company relies on quick sales, low profits, and a fast turnover, and therefore we cannot offer long-term credit facilities.

5.6.4
Size of order

The quantity required might be too large:

We are a small firm and could not possibly handle an order for 20,000 units.

Our factory does not have facilities to turn out 30,000 units a week.

The quantity required might be too small:

We only supply orders for ball pens by the gross, but suggest you try a stationery wholesaler rather than manufacturer.

The shirts we manufacture are sold in one colour and by the dozen. We never sell individual garments.

Our factory only sells material by 30-metre rolls which cannot be cut up.

Panton Manufacturing Ltd.

Panton Works, Hounslow, Middlesex, TW6 2BQ

Tel: 081 353 0125
Telex: 21511
Fax: 081 353 6783

Registered No. England 266135

Mr H. Majid,   8th October 19—
Majid Enterprises,
Grant Road,
Bombay,
INDIA

Dear Mr Majid,

I am writing to you concerning your order, No. CU 1154/d which you placed four weeks ago. At that time we had expected to be able to complete the order well within the delivery date we gave you which was 18 June, but since then we have heard that our main supplier of chrome has gone bankrupt.

This means that we have to find another supplier who could fulfil all the outstanding contracts we have to complete. As you will appreciate this will take some time, but we are confident that we should be able to arrange to get our materials and deliver consignments to our customers by the middle of next month.

The units themselves have been assembled and simply now need completing.

We regret this unfortunate situation over which we had no control and apologize for the inconvenience. If you wish to cancel the order it would be quite understandable, but we stress that we will be able to complete delivery by next month and would appreciate it if you could bear with us till then.

Please let us know your decision as soon as possible. Thank you for your consideration.

Yours sincerely,

D. Panton

D. Panton
Managing Director

5.7
Specimen letters

5.7.1
Delay in delivery

Questions
1 Why haven't Panton completed the order?
2 How do they intend to overcome the problem?
3 When do they now expect the order to be completed?
4 Can Majid Enterprises cancel the order if they want to?
5 What is the 'decision' referred to in the last paragraph?
6 Which words in the letter correspond to the following: *with reference to*; *finish*; *complete*; *certain*; *put together*; *trouble*; *tolerate the situation*?

5.7.2
Refusing an order

Questions

1 Why is the order being refused?
2 How does Mr York generalize his refusal?
3 What is the implication of 'in this instance' in the last sentence?

SP Wholesalers PLC

Old Meadow Road, King's Lynn, Norfolk PE30 45W

Telephone: King's Lynn 60841   Cable: SPOLE   Telex: 351214

Mr E. van Gellen
131 Place Roget
B–1210 Brussels

Ref: DY/ML

7 May 19—

Dear Mr van Gellen,

Thank you for your order, No. HU14449, which we received today. Unfortunately, we do not feel that we can offer the trade discounts which you have asked for, viz. 35 per cent as we only allow a 25 per cent trade discount to all our customers regardless of the quantity they buy.

Our prices are extremely competitive and it would not be worthwhile supplying on the allowance you have asked for. Therefore, in this instance, I regret that we have to turn down your order.

Yours sincerely,

Ɗ. York

D. York

5.8
Points to remember

1 Even if you use an official order form when placing an order, send a covering letter confirming terms of payment, discounts, delivery, and packing.
2 Orders should be acknowledged as soon as received.
3 When sending an advice, explain how the goods are being sent and let your customer know how to identify the consignment.
4 If there are problems with delivery, tell your customer immediately what you intend to do to correct them. Apologize for the inconvenience.
5 If turning an order down, be polite, and generalize the terms you use so that the customer does not think this refusal only applies to him.

5.9
Words to remember

a trial order
a provisional order
a firm order
to place an order
to confirm an order
to acknowledge an order
to accept an order
to refuse/reject/turn down an order
to fill/fulfil/make up/complete/meet/
supply an order
to deliver an order
to cancel an order

an order form
a compliment slip
a covering letter
an invoice
a pro-forma invoice
an advice of despatch
a consignment note

terms of payment
trade discount
quantity discount
cash discount
banker's draft
sight draft
bill of exchange
to draw a bill on a customer
documents against acceptance
irrevocable letter of credit
quarterly statements
long-term credit facilities

shipping documents
air waybill
bill of lading
insurance certificate
commercial invoice

goods in stock
goods out of stock
to pack goods in crates
to ship goods
to arrange shipment
a forwarding agent
air freight
delivery date

Payment

6

*Invoices, pro-forma invoices, statements of account;
methods of payment (home trade and foreign trade),
advice of payment, acknowledgement of payment;
asking for more time to pay; replying to requests for
more time; first and second requests for payment; third
requests (Final Demands).*

6.1
Invoices and statements

6.1.1
Invoices

Invoices are not only requests for
payment but also records of
transactions which give both the buyer
and seller information about what has
been bought or sold, the terms of the
sale and details of the transaction. The
invoice may be accompanied by a short
covering letter offering any additional
information the customer might need.

*Please find enclosed our invoice
No. B1951 for £29.43. The plugs you
ordered have already been despatched
to you, carriage forward, and you
should receive them within the next few
days.*

*The enclosed invoice (No. D1167) for
£56.00 is for 2 'Layeazee' chairs at
£40.00 each less 33 per cent trade*
*discount. We look forward to receiving
your remittance and will then send the
chairs on carriage forward.*

*Our Invoice No. TR3351/6 for £400
net is attached. We look forward to
receiving your cheque from which you
may deduct 3 per cent cash discount if
payment is made within seven days.*

*Your Order No. H615D is at present
being processed and will be sent on to
you within the next few weeks. Thank
you for your order. We are sure you will
be pleased with the units when you
receive them.*

6.1.2
Pro-forma invoices

A pro-forma invoice is an invoice with
the words pro-forma typed or stamped
on it, and is used:

1 if the customer has to pay for the
goods before receiving them, i.e. he
pays against the pro-forma;

2 if the customer wants to make sure that a quotation will not be changed: the pro-forma will tell him exactly what and how he will be charged.
3 if goods are sent on approval, or on sale or return, or on consignment to an agent who will sell them on behalf of the principal;
4 as a customs document.

A covering letter may accompany a pro-forma invoice:

The enclosed pro-forma No. 1164 for £853.76 is for your order No. C1534, which is now packed and awaiting despatch. As soon as we receive your cheque we will send the goods which will reach you within a few days.

We are sending the enclosed pro-forma (No. H9181) for £3,160 gross, for the consignment of chairs you ordered on approval. We would appreciate your returning the balance of unsold chairs by the end of May as agreed.

Pro-forma invoice, No. PL7715, is for your order, No. 652 1174, in confirmation of our quotation. The total of £15,351 includes cost, insurance, and freight.

6.1.3
Statements of account

Rather than requiring immediate payment of invoices, a supplier may grant his customer credit (see also Unit 8 *Credit*) in the form of *open account facilities* for an agreed period of time, usually a month but sometimes a quarter (three months). At the end of the period a statement of account is sent to the customer, listing all the transactions between the buyer and seller for that period. The statement includes the balance on the account, which is brought forward from the previous period and listed as Account Rendered. Invoices and debit notes (see 7.5.1) are added, while payments and credit notes (see 7.5.2) are deducted.

Statements of account rarely have letters accompanying them unless there is a particular point that the supplier wants to make, e.g. that the account is overdue, or that some special concession is available for prompt payment. Note the expression *as at*, which means up to this date.

I enclose your statement as at 31 July. May I remind you that your June statement is still outstanding, and ask you to settle as soon as possible?

Please find enclosed your statement of account as at 31 May this year. If the balance of £161 is cleared within the next seven days, you can deduct a 3 per cent cash discount.

6.2
Settlement of accounts

6.2.1
Methods of payment: home trade

Here is a list of methods of payment which can be used in the home trade, which refers in this case to trade in the UK.

Postal Order
Postal Orders can be bought from the Post Office, usually to pay small amounts, and sent to the supplier direct. They can be crossed or closed, i.e. only to be paid into the supplier's account, or open for cash. Poundage, i.e. the cost of buying the Order itself, is expensive, so they would only be used for small amounts.

Stamps
It is possible to pay someone with postage stamps, but unusual in business.

Giro
This postal cheque system is run by the Post Office and allows customers to send payments to anyone whether they have a Giro account or not.

C.O.D. (cash on delivery)
The Post Office offers a service by which they will deliver goods and accept payment on behalf of the supplier.

Cheque
You must have a current account, or certain types of savings accounts, to pay by cheque (see Unit 9 *Banking*). Cheques take three working days to clear through the commercial banks, and can be open, to pay cash, or closed (crossed), to be paid into an account. Unlike in most countries, UK cheques are valid up to six months.

Bank transfer
Banks will transfer money by order from one account to another.

Credit transfer
The payer fills out a Bank Giro slip and hands it in to a bank with a cheque. The bank then transfers the money to the payee.

Bank draft
The payer buys a cheque from the bank for the amount he wants to pay and sends it to the payee. Banks usually require two of their Directors' signatures on drafts, and make a small charge.

Bill of exchange
The seller draws a bill on the buyer. The bill states that the buyer will pay the seller an amount within a stated time, e.g. 30 days. The bill is sent to the buyer either by post, or through a bank, and

the buyer signs (accepts) the bill before the goods are sent. If this is done through a bank, the bank will ask the buyer to accept the bill before handing over the shipping documents; this is known as a *documents against acceptance* (D/A) transaction. See 9.5 and 9.6 for bill of exchange transactions.

Letter of credit
This method of payment can be used internally, but is more common in overseas transactions. See 6.2.2 Documentary credit.

6.2.2
Methods of payment: foreign trade

Cheque
It is possible to pay an overseas supplier by cheque, but it takes a long time before the supplier gets his money. In a German/UK transaction, for example, the supplier could wait up to three weeks for payment.

International Giro
Payment by International Giro, which replaced Money Orders, can be made whether the buyer has an account or not, and to a supplier whether he has an account or not. The International Giro form is obtained from any Post Office, filled out, then handed to the Post Office who forwards the order to the Giro centre which will send the amount to a Post Office in the beneficiary's country where the supplier will receive a postal cheque. He can then either cash it, or pay it into his bank account. Giros are charged at a flat rate.

International Money Orders
International Money Orders can be bought at most banks in the UK and are paid for in sterling or dollars. The bank fills out the order for the customer, then

for a small charge, hands the IMO over, and the buyer sends it to the *beneficiary*, i.e. the person receiving the money. IMOs can be cashed or credited to the recipient's account.

Bank transfer

Payment can be made by ordering a home bank to transfer money to an overseas account. If telegraphed, the transfer is known as a telegraphic transfer (TT), and if mailed, a mail transfer (MT). The Society for Worldwide Interbank Financial Communications (SWIFT) offers facilities for a 24-hour transfer of money to a beneficiary on its computer systems.

International bankers draft

This is a banker's cheque which the bank draws on itself and sells to the customer, who then sends it to his supplier as he would an ordinary inland cheque. So if you have to pay your supplier £2,000, you purchase the cheque for that amount, plus charges. Usually the receiver's bank should either have an account with the sender's bank, or an agreement.

Promissory notes

A promissory note is not a method of payment but simply a written promise from a debtor to a creditor that the former will pay the stipulated amount either on demand or after a certain date. In effect a promissory note is an IOU (I owe you).

Bill of exchange

The procedure is the same as for the home trade, but shipping documents usually accompany bills when the bank acts as an intermediary in overseas transactions.

Documentary credit

This term is used to distinguish the normal letter of credit, used in business, from the circular letter of credit, formerly used by foreign travellers and now largely replaced by Eurocheques, traveller's cheques, and cash cheque credits. Documentary credits have to be applied for from the buyer's bank, by filling out a form giving details of the type of credit (i.e. revocable or irrevocable), the beneficiary (the person receiving the money), the amount, how long the credit will be available for (i.e. valid until . . .), the documents involved (bill of lading, insurance, invoice, etc.), and a description of the goods. The money will be credited to the supplier's account as soon as confirmation of shipment is made. This is done when the documents are lodged with the customer's bank. See 9.7–9.9 for documentary credit transactions.

6.2.3
Advice of payment

Letters advising payment, particularly in the home trade, tend to be short and routine.

We have pleasure in enclosing our Postal Order/Cheque/bank draft for £. . . in payment of your statement/ Invoice No. . . . dated . . .

I have instructed my bank, today, to transfer £161.00 to your account in payment of your 31 May statement.

We have drawn a postal cheque for £26.00 in payment of your Invoice No. L231 dated 2 August. This can be cashed at any Post Office, or paid into your account.

Letters confirming payment in foreign trade transactions may be more complicated if you want to take advantage of the letter to make certain points, but they can be as straightforward as the home trade letters.

*Thank you for your prompt delivery.
Please find enclosed our draft for
£2,341 drawn on Eastland City Bank,
Sommerville. Could you please
acknowledge receipt?*

*We would like to inform you that we
have arranged for a credit transfer
through our bank, the Hammergsbank,
Bergen. The transfer is for £3,120 in
payment of invoice No. Re1641. Could
you confirm the transfer has been
made as soon as the correspondent
bank advises you?*

*We have pleasure in enclosing our bank
draft for £5,141.53 as payment on pro-
forma invoice No. 5512. Please advise
us when the goods will be shipped and
are likely to reach Barcelona.*

*You will be pleased to hear that we have
accepted your bill and now have the
documents. We shall collect the
consignment as soon as it arrives in
Bonn and honour your draft at maturity.*

*Our bank informs us that they now have
the shipping documents, and will be
transferring the proceeds of our letter of
credit to your account.*

6.2.4
Acknowledgement of payment

Letters acknowledging payment also
tend to be short, whether in the home
trade or in foreign trade.

*Thank you for your Postal Order
Cheque/draft/credit transfer/postal
cheque for £... in payment of our
statement/invoice No. ... dated ...*

*Our bank advised us today that your
transfer of £761.00 was credited to our
account. Thank you for paying so
promptly, and we hope to hear from you
again soon.*

*We received your Giro slip today
informing us that you had paid £126.00
into our account in settlement of Invoice*

*No. L231. Thank you for letting us know,
and we look forward to hearing from you
in the near future.*

*Thank you for sending your draft for
invoice No. 11871 so promptly. We
hope you like the consignment and look
forward to your next order.*

*We received an advice from our bank
this morning that your transfer for
invoice No. RE1641 has been credited
to our account. We would like to thank
you, and ask you to contact us if you
need anything else in menswear, or any
information about fashions in this
country.*

*Our bank informed us today that you
accepted our bill (No. BE 2255) and the
documents have been handed to you.
We are sure you will be pleased with the
consignment.*

*The Nippon Bank in Tokushima have
told us that the proceeds of your letter of
credit have been credited to our
account. Thank you for your custom
and we hope you will write to us again.
We are enclosing our summer
catalogue which we are sure will
interest you.*

6.3
Specimen forms and letters

6.3.1
Invoice

This is a relatively simple invoice. Note the addition for Value Added Tax (VAT) and postage and packing (p. & p.). The letters E & OE at the bottom mean Errors and Omissions are Excepted; in other words, if there is a mistake on the invoice, the supplier has the right to correct it by asking for more money or giving a refund.

INVOICE **No.** B1951

D & R Electrical Ltd.

35 Hill Street, Seacroft, Leeds LS14 1ND
Tel: 0532 640181

Registered London No. 115662
VAT Reg. No. 154 6627 19

To: P. Gwent & Co. Ltd.
43 Ring Road
Leeds LS16 2BN

Date: 1 May 19—

Your order No. L57/5

Number	Description	Total
40	RVA 250 volt plugs @ 65p. each Add VAT 17½% " p & p	£26.00 4.55 1.35
		£31.90
E & OE		

INVOICE

GLASTON POTTERIES

Clayfield, Burnley BB10 1RQ

Tel: 0315 46125   Fax: 0315 63182   Telex: 8801773

No. 1096/A3

MacKenzie Bros. Ltd.
1–5 Whale Drive
Dawson
Ontario
CANADA

11 July 19—

Your order No. DR1432

Quantity	Description	Cat. No.	£ each		£
35	Earthenware	R 194	@ 25.00	set	875.00
10	Wedgwood	W 161	@ 37.50	"	375.00
15	Bone/Tea	T 21	@ 12.00	"	180.00
10	Staffordshire Red	S 73	@ 22.60	"	226.00
	c.i.f.	1656.00			1656.00
	Less Cost & Freight Liverpool/Dawson	147.00			
	Less Insurance	92.00			
	10% discount off net price	1417.00	Less Disc.		141.70
			Total		1514.30

E & O.E.   Registered No. 716481   VAT Reg No. 133 5341 08

6.3.2
Invoice

This invoice is rather more complicated. It is from Glaston Potteries to their Canadian customers MacKenzie Bros. It would be sent with copies and shipping documents to The Canadian Union Trust Bank via the Burnley Bank who are their agents in England. These documents prove that a shipment has been made from Glaston to MacKenzie so that the Canadian bank can now release the money that MacKenzie Bros. committed to pay in their Letter of Credit. There will also be additional charges that MacKenzie Bros. pay their bank for handling the transaction.

It might be helpful to refer back to letters 3.3.3, 4.3.3, 5.4.5, and 5.4.6 to remind yourself of the enquiry, reply, order, and advice that have been sent during the correspondence between MacKenzie's agents and Glaston Potteries.

You will see from the invoice that cost, insurance, and freight charges have been deducted from the gross price. This is because under UK law the customer must be told exactly what he is paying for. And in this case c.i.f. has also been deducted so that the 10% special discount can be taken off the net price.

Questions

1 What is the net total of the invoice?
2 How have Glaston explained they have the right to correct the invoice if there is a mistake?
3 What sort of transaction is this?
4 Which reference would MacKenzie use when referring to this invoice?
5 How are the items identified?
6 What does the sign @ mean?

6.3.3
Statement of account

This statement is an account of the transactions that took place over the month of May between Seymore Furniture Ltd. and their customer, C. R. Méndez. You will see that a debit note (D/N 311) and a credit note (C/N C517) are listed as well as the invoices they corrected. There are also two payments which are listed here as cash, although the word *cheque* is also used in this context.

Questions

1 Is there an allowance for payment within a certain time?
2 How much did C. R. Méndez owe at the beginning of this month?
3 How much was the error in Méndez' favour?
4 What did Méndez pay during the month?
5 How will his 1 June statement open?
6 What was the total amount of Méndez' purchases during May?

STATEMENT

SEYMORE FURNITURE Ltd.

Tib Street, Maidenhead, Berks. SL6 5D2
Telephone 0628 26755
Registered No. 18514391 London
VAT No. 231 6188 31

C.R. Méndez SA   31 May 19—
Avda del Ejército 83
E–48015 Bilbao

Date	Item	Debit	Credit	Balance
19—		£	£	£
1 May	Account Rendered			270.00
2 "	Inv. L 8992	60.00		330.00
8 "	D/N 311	12.00		342.00
12 "	Cash		100.00	242.00
14 "	Inv. L 8995	720.00		962.00
20 "	C/N C 517		40.00	922.00
25 "	Cash		600.00	322.00

E. & O.E.   Cash Disc. 3% if paid within 7 days

F. Lynch & Co. Ltd.

(Head Office), Nesson House, Newell Street, Birmingham B3 3EL

Telephone No. 021 236 6571   Fax: 021 236 8592   Telex: 341641

Satex S.p.A.   Your Ref: ——
Via di Pietra Papa   Our Ref: Order 14463
00146 Roma
ITALY   16 June 19—

Attn. Mr D. Causio

Dear Mr Causio,

Thank you for being so prompt in sending the documents for our last
order, No. 14463. We have accepted the sight draft, and the bank
should be sending you an advice shortly.

We have been dealing with you on a cash against documents basis for
over a year and would like to change to payment by 40-day bill of
exchange, documents against acceptance.

When we first contacted you last February you told us that you would
be prepared to reconsider terms of payment once we had established
a trading association. We think that sufficient time has elapsed for us to
be allowed the terms we have asked for. If you need references, we
will be glad to supply them.

As we will be sending another order within the month, could you
please confirm that you agree to these new terms of payment?

Yours sincerely,

L. Crane

L. Crane
Chief Buyer

6.3.4
Advice of payment

This letter continues the
correspondence at 3.3.4 (enquiry),
4.3.5 (reply and quotation), 5.4.1 (order)
and 5.4.3 (acknowledgement of order).
The customer, Mr Crane of F. Lynch
& Co., uses this confirmation of payment
to ask for the terms of payment to be
revised (see also 8.3); if you look back
to 4.3.5, you will see that Satex S.p.A.
did in fact say that they would review the
terms after a while. Notice how the letter
begins with confirmation of payment,
then states the present arrangement,
and finally makes the next order subject
to Mr Causio accepting the new terms.
The letter is firm, but still polite.

6.3.5
Advice of payment

This letter continues the correspondence at 3.3.3 (enquiry), 4.3.3 (reply), 5.4.5 (order), 5.4.6 (advice of despatch) and 6.3.2 (invoice). MacKenzie Bros. use the letter both to confirm payment and to make a complaint about the packing (see also Unit 7 *Complaints and adjustments*). Note that MacKenzie Bros. will accept either replacements for the broken crockery or a credit note. Glaston Potteries will claim on their insurance company for the breakages, although they might not get compensation as they have been negligent in their packing.

MACKENZIE BROS. LTD.

1–5 Whale Drive, Dawson, Ontario, Canada
Branches: Ottawa, Vancouver, New York, Chicago.
Tel: (613) 238 1492   Cable: MAKIE   Telex: 315515

Mr J. Merton   15 December 19—
Sales Manager
Glaston Potteries Ltd.
Clayfield
Burnley BB10 1RQ
UNITED KINGDOM

Dear Mr Merton,

We have instructed our bank to arrange for a letter of credit for £6,158.92 to be paid against your pro-forma invoice No. G1152/S, and the proceeds will be credited to you as soon as Canadian Trust receive the documents.

We usually ask you to wrap each piece of crockery individually and pack no more than ten sets into a crate to allow for easy and safe handling. This was not done with our last consignment and as a consequence there were breakages. Attached you will find a list and we would like either replacements to be included in our next shipment, or your credit note.

Yours sincerely,

R. Mackenzie

R. MacKenzie

Enc.

6.4
Delayed payment

6.4.1
Asking for more time to pay

If you are writing to a supplier to tell him why you have not cleared an account, remember that he is mainly interested in *when* the account will be paid. So, while you must explain *why* you have not paid, you must also tell him *when* and *how* you intend to pay.

Remember to begin the letter with your creditor's name (this should always be done once correspondence has been established, but it is essential in this case: if you owe someone money, you should know their name). Refer to the account and apologize in clear, objective language (i.e. do *not* use language like 'Please forgive me for not settling my indebtedness to you'). Notice the verbs *clear* and *settle the account* are used rather than *pay*.

I am sorry that I was not able to clear my July account.

We regret we were unable to send a cheque to settle our account for the last quarter.

Explain why you cannot clear the account. But do not be dramatic.

The dock strike which has been in operation for the past six weeks has made it impossible to ship our products, and as our customers have not been able to pay us, we have not been able to clear our own suppliers' accounts yet.

A warehouse flood destroyed the majority of the components that were to be fitted into Zenith 900. We are waiting for our insurance company to settle our claim so that we can renew our stock and pay our suppliers.

We were not able to settle the account because of the bankruptcy of one of our main customers, who we hoped would have cleared his balance with us. The debt was considerable and its loss has made it difficult for us to pay our suppliers.

Notice in the last example above that there is no reference to the bankrupt customer's name, nor how much he owed. It would be unethical to give this sort of information. Also notice how the debtor generalizes the situation, explaining that none of his suppliers have been paid yet.

Tell your supplier when you will pay him; as far as he is concerned, this is the most important piece of information in your letter. You may be able to pay some money *on account*, i.e. to offer some money towards settlement; this shows a willingness to clear the debt, and will gain your creditor's confidence.

We will try to clear your invoice within the next few weeks. Meanwhile the enclosed cheque for £200.00 is part payment on account.

If you cannot offer a part payment, give as precise a date of payment as you can.

Once the strike has been settled, which should be within the next few days, we will be able to clear the balance.

As soon as the insurance company sends us compensation we will settle the account. We expect this to be within the next two weeks.

6.4.2

Replying to requests for more time

There are three possible ways in which you might reply to a request from a customer for more time to settle his account: you may agree to his request, or refuse it, or suggest a compromise.

If you agree to the request, a short letter is all that is needed.

Thank you for your letter concerning the outstanding balance on your account. I sympathize with the problem you have had in clearing the balance and am willing to extend the credit for another six weeks. Would you please confirm that the credit will be settled then?

I was sorry to hear about the difficulties you have been experiencing in getting components to complete orders from other suppliers, and realize that without sales it is difficult to settle outstanding accounts. Therefore your account has been extended another month, but I will have to insist on payment by the end of July.

If you refuse the request, you will need to explain, politely, why you are refusing.

Thank you for your letter explaining why you cannot clear your January statement for £2,167.54. I certainly appreciate your difficulty but we ourselves have to pay our own suppliers and therefore must insist on payment within the next ten days. We look forward to receiving your remittance.

With reference to your letter of 6 August in which you explained why the outstanding invoice, No. YR88190 C, has not been cleared, we understand the problems you have been facing in the current recession. However, it was in consideration of the present economic climate that we allowed you a two-month period to settle, and while we

would like to offer you more time to clear the balance, our own financial position makes this impossible. Therefore we must ask you to settle the account within the next fortnight.

An offer of a compromise (e.g. part payment) will also need an explanation.

Thank you for writing and letting us know why the May account is still outstanding. Unfortunately, we cannot extend the credit any longer as we allowed considerable discounts in lieu of a prompt payment. Nevertheless, in view of the difficulties you have been having with your two major customers in clearing their accounts, we are prepared to compromise and suggest that you clear half the outstanding balance immediately by sending a cheque for £4,871.71 and clear the remainder by the end of next month. We look forward to your remittance and confirmation that the balance of the account will be cleared in July.

I regret to hear about the strike which has held up production in your plant for the past few weeks and can understand why you need more time to clear your account with us. Nevertheless, when we allowed open account terms, we emphasized this was only on the condition that balances were cleared promptly on due dates as credit facilities put a strain on our own cash flow situation. Because of this we cannot extend the credit by another two months. However, because of your previous custom with us we are quite willing to allow you to clear half the balance, viz. £5,189 by sending us a sight draft, see enclosed B/E No. 898101, and clear the outstanding amount by accepting the enclosed draft B/E No. 898108, drawn at 30 days. We look forward to receiving your acceptance and confirmation.

6.5
Requests for payment

6.5.1
First request

You should never immediately assume your customer has no intention of paying his account if the balance is overdue. There may be a number of reasons for this. He may not have received your statement. He may have sent a cheque which has been lost. He might have just overlooked the account. Therefore a first request is in the form of a polite enquiry. One of the ways of doing this is to make the letter as impersonal as possible. This can be done by using the definite article, e.g. *this* outstanding balance, instead of *your* outstanding balance. Use the passive voice, e.g. *to be cleared*, instead of *which you must clear*; and modifying imperatives, e.g. *should*, instead of *must*. The first example will give you an idea of this style.

We are writing concerning the outstanding October account for £3,171.63, a copy of which is enclosed and which should have been cleared last month. Please let us know why the balance has not been paid.

With reference to your invoice, No. 81 45316, for £1,710 (see attached copy) which we expected to be cleared three weeks ago, we still have not yet received your remittance. Would you please either let us have your cheque, or an explanation of why the invoice is still outstanding?

We think you may have overlooked invoice No. 5A 1910 for £351.95 (see copy) which was due last month. Please could you let us have your cheque to

clear the amount? If, however, you have already sent a remittance, then please disregard this letter.

6.5.2
Second requests

If a customer intends to pay, he usually answers a *first request* immediately, offering an apology for having overlooked the account, or an explanation. But if he acknowledges your request but still does not pay, or does not answer your letter at all, then you can make a second request. As with first requests, you should include copies of the relevant invoices and statements, and mention your previous letter. This will save time. You should also refer to previous correspondence.

We wrote to you on 3 March concerning our January statement which is still outstanding. Enclosed you will find a copy of the statement and our letter.

This is the second letter I have sent you with regard to your March account which has not been cleared. My first letter dated 21 April, asked why the account had not been paid, and you will see from the enclosed that . . .

State that you have not received payment if this was promised in the reply, or that no reply has been received.

Since I wrote I have not received either a reply or remittance from you.

I would like to know why you have neither replied nor sent a cheque to clear the outstanding balance.

In your reply to my letter of 21 April you promised that the account would be cleared by the end of May, yet I have not received your remittance or an explanation.

Insist that you receive payment or an answer within a certain time.

We must now insist that you clear this account within the next seven days, or at least offer an explanation for not paying it.

As we have traded for some time, we have not pressed for payment. However, we must now insist that either you settle the account or offer a reasonable explanation for not doing so.

I would like your remittance by return of post, or failing that, your reasons for not clearing this account.

6.5.3
Third requests (Final Demands)

Review the situation from the time the account should have been paid.

We have written you two letters on 22 September and 19 October, and have sent copies of the outstanding invoices with them, but have not received either a reply or remittance.

I have written to you twice, on 8 May and 4 June, concerning your balance of £934.85 which has been outstanding since April, but as yet, have not received a reply.

I am writing to you about your June account which I had hoped you would have cleared by now. On 5 July and 12 August, I sent letters with copies of invoices and statements, asking you to clear the balance or at least offer an explanation of why you have not sent a remittance.

Explain that you have been patient.

When we arranged terms, we offered you payment against monthly statements, yet it has been three months since you wrote promising the account would be cleared. We now assume that you have no intention of clearing the balance.

We had expected this matter to have been settled at least two months ago, but you have shown no indication of co-operating with us.

Let the customer know what you intend to do, but do not threaten legal action unless you intend to take it, as it will make you look weak and indecisive. In the two examples below legal action is not threatened.

We feel that you have been given sufficient time to clear this balance and now insist on payment within the next ten days.

We must now press you to clear this outstanding account. Please send your remittance immediately.

In the next two examples legal action *is* threatened. Notice the language used to do this. Do not use obscure language (e.g. 'We will take other steps' or 'We will use other methods to enforce payment'), and do not try to sound like a lawyer (e.g. 'Unless payment is forthcoming, we will have to take steps to enforce our claims'). A direct statement will produce better results.

We were disappointed that you did not bother to reply to either of our letters asking you to clear your account, and you have left us no alternative but to take legal action.

We are giving you a further seven days to send your remittance after which the matter will be dealt with by our solicitors.

D. van Basten SA

Heidelberglaan 2, Postbus 80.115, NL–3508 TC, Utrecht

Telephone: (31) 30–532 044 Telefax (31) 30–581 617

The Director
DVB Industries GmbH
Correnstrasse 250
D–4000 Münster

15 January 19—

Dear Mr Schubert,

I am sorry that we were not able to clear your November statement for $3,850 and December invoice, No. 7713 for $289. We had intended to pay the statement as usual, but a large cash shipment to one of our customers in Australia was part of the cargo destroyed in the fire on the SS Tippa when she docked in Bombay in late November.

Our insurance company have promised us compensation within the next few weeks, and once we have received this the account will be paid in full.

We know you will appreciate the situation and hope you can bear with us until the matter is settled.

Yours sincerely,

D van Basten (Ms)

D. van Basten
Director

6.6
Specimen letters

6.6.1
Request for more time

D. van Basten S.A. write to their suppliers to warn them that payment will be delayed.

Questions

1 What is the total outstanding balance?
2 What explanation is given for non-payment?
3 When does Ms van Basten intend to pay?
4 Why is she confident that she can clear the account?
5 What does the expression *hope you can bear with us* mean?
6 Which words in the letter correspond to the following: *pay*; *meant*; *goods*; *make up for loss*; *understand?*

6.6.2
Agreeing to more time

This is a reply to the previous letter at 6.6.1. Mr Schubert accepts the request and asks for payment as soon as possible.

DVB Industries GmbH

Correnstrasse 250
D-4000

Tel: (49) 251–86613
Fax: (49) 251–90271
Telex: 6125930

The Director
D. van Basten S.A.
Heidelberglaan 2
Postbus 80.115
NL–3508 TC
Utrecht

20 January 19—

Dear Ms van Basten,

Thank you for your letter of the 15 January regarding our November statement and December invoice No. 7713.

We were sorry to hear about the difficulties you have had, and understand the situation, but would appreciate it if you could clear the account as soon as possible, as we ourselves have suppliers to pay.

We look forward to hearing from you soon.

Yours sincerely,

D. Schubert
Director

L. Franksen PLC

Prince of Wales Road, Sheffield S9 4EX

Telephone: (0742) 24789
Fax: 0742 25193

Mr D. Bishkin   19 May 19—
Zenith S.A.
Haldenstrasse 118
3000 Bern 22
SWITZERLAND

Dear Mr Bishkin,

I am sorry to tell you that I will not be able to meet my bill, No. BE7714, due on 6 June.

My government has put an embargo on all machine exports to Zurimba, and consequently we have found ourselves in temporary difficulties as we had three major cash consignments for that country. However, I am at present discussing sales of these consignments with two large Brazilian importers, and am certain that they will take the goods.

Could you allow me a further 60 days to clear my account, and draw a new bill on me, with interest of, say 6% added for the extension of time?

I would be most grateful if you could help me in this matter.

Yours sincerely,

L. Franksen

L. Franksen

6.6.3
Request for an extension

In this letter the customer asks for his bill of exchange to be extended for another 60 days.

Questions

1 What expression does Mr Franksen use instead of *pay*?
2 What is an embargo?
3 How does he intend to get the money for the cargo he cannot sell?
4 What solution does he suggest to the problem?
5 How does he propose to compensate Mr Bishkin?
6 Which words in the letter correspond to the following: *paid for goods*; *make out a draft*?

6.6.4
Offer of a compromise

In this case Mr Bishkin, the supplier, has the legal right to present the bill to his bank for payment, then if the bill is not met, call a *notary public* (a lawyer) to protest the bill, i.e. prevent the *drawee* (the person who would pay) from denying the bill was presented for payment, or *dishonouring* (not paying) the draft. The costs of this procedure are paid by the customer. However, the customer in this case has not said he *will not pay*, but *cannot pay* at present. If the supplier forced his customer to pay, the result might be bankruptcy, and all Mr Bishkin will get is a percentage of his customer's debts like other creditors. This could be as small as 5% of the total debt. So Mr Bishkin would be reluctant to force the bill on Mr Franksen. On the other hand, he has waited long enough for his money, and cannot be expected to wait another 60 days, even with the interest offered. So in his reply to Mr Franksen he offers a compromise.

Questions

1 Is Mr Bishkin sympathetic to Mr Franksen's problem?
2 What compromise does he suggest?
3 Why does he say he cannot wait a further 60 days for payment?
4 Does he want the 6% interest added on?
5 How will he know that Mr Franksen has accepted his offer?

Zenith S.A.

Haldenstrasse 118, 3000 Bern 22, Switzerland

Tel: Bern 30172
Fax: Bern 82357

Mr L. Franksen   23 May 19—
L. Franksen PLC
Prince of Wales Road
Sheffield S9 4EX
UNITED KINGDOM

Dear Mr Franksen,

Bill No. BE 7714

I was sorry to learn about the embargo your country has placed on exports to Zurimba and of the problems this has created. However, the above bill has already allowed credit for 40 days, and although I appreciate your offer for an additional 6% interest on the £4,360 outstanding, it is financially impossible to allow a further 60 days credit as I myself have commitments.

I think the following solution might help us both.

You need not add interest on the present amount, but I have enclosed a new draft (BE 7731) for £2,180 which is half the outstanding balance, and will allow you 40 days to pay it. But I expect you to pay the remainder viz. £2,180 by banker's draft.

Please confirm your acceptance by signing the enclosed bill and returning it to me with your draft by return of post.

I wish you luck with your negotiations with the Brazilian importers and hope that this setback will soon be resolved.

Yours sincerely,

N. Bishkin

N. Bishkin

Encl. Bill BE 7731

HOMEMAKERS Ltd.

54–59 Riverside, Cardiff CF1 1JW

Telephone: (0222) 49721   Registered No. C135162
Telex: 38217

R. Hughes & Son Ltd.   20 November 19—
21 Mead Road
Swansea
Glamorgan 3ST 1DR

Dear Mr Hughes,

I am writing to ask why you have not settled our invoice No. H931 for
£519.63, a copy of which is enclosed.

I know that since we began trading you have cleared your accounts
regularly on the due dates. That is why I wondered if any problems
have arisen which I might be able to help you with. Please let me know
if I can be of assistance.

Yours sincerely,

R. Cliff

R. Cliff

6.6.5
First request

Below is an example of a first request.
See 3.3.5 and 4.3.6 for other examples
of correspondence between these two
firms.

6.6.6
Reply to first request

You will see from Mr Hughes' reply to Mr Cliff's letter (6.6.5) that the invoice had been paid, not by cheque, which was Mr Hughes' usual method of payment but by credit transfer. If Mr Cliff had looked at his bank statement, he would have seen that the money had been credited. On the other hand, if Mr Hughes wanted to change his method of payment, he should have informed his supplier, as banks may not always advise credit transfers. This is a good example of why you should not assume a reason for your customer not paying an account. There is a further example on 6.6.7 and 6.6.8.

R. Hughes & Son Ltd.

21 Mead Road, Swansea, Glamorgan 3ST 1DR

Telephone: Swansea 58441
Telex: 881821

VAT No. 215 2261 30

Mr R. Cliff,   24th November 19—
Homemakers Ltd.,
54–59 Riverside,
Cardiff CF1 1JW

Dear Mr Cliff,

I was surprised to receive your letter of the 20th November in which you said you had not received payment for invoice No. H931.

I instructed my bank, The Welsh Co-operative Bank, Swansea, to credit your account in Barnley's Bank, Cardiff, with the £519.63 some time ago.

As my bank statement showed the money had been debited to my account, I assumed that it had been credited to your account as well. It is possible that your bank has not advised you yet. Could you please check this with Barnley's, and if there are any problems let me know, so that I can make enquiries here?

Yours sincerely,

R. Hughes

R. Hughes

6.6.7
Second request

This is an example of a second request for payment, but you will see that, even though this is a second letter, Snr. Costello still uses a careful and friendly tone.

Ingenieros Industriales SA

Barrio de Ibaeta s/n
E–20009 San Sebastian

Tel: (34) 943 212800
Fax: (34) 943 618590
Telex: 302196
Fecha: 30 August 19—

Su ref: ——
Ns. ref: 613/02

The Accountant
Omega S.p.A.
Via Angello 2153
20121 Milano
Italy

Dear Mr Giordianino,

We wrote to you on 10 August and enclosed copy invoices which made up your June statement, the balance of which still remains outstanding.

Having dealt with you for some time, we were disappointed in neither receiving your remittance nor any explanation as to why the balance has not been cleared. Please would you either send us a reply or cheque to clear the account within the next seven days? Thank you.

Yours sincerely,

R. Costello
Credit Controller

6.6.8
Reply to second request

Here is Mr Giordianino's reply to the previous letter.

Questions

1 Why didn't Mr Giordianino receive the statement and letter?
2 What has he done about the outstanding account, and what will he do in future?
3 What has he asked Mr Costello to do to ensure that letters get to him?
4 Why do you think Mr Costello did not receive Mr Giordianino's letter?
5 There is no reference to it in either letter, but what could have happened for the letter to have been mislaid?

Omega S.p.A.

Viale Mortidio 61269 I–10125 Torino
Telefono: (39)–11–5981461 Telefax: (39)–11–628351 Telex: 7793105

Vs. rif.: 613/02   Ns. rif.:   Data: 1 September 19—

The Credit Controller
Ingenieros Industriales SA
Barrio de Ibaeta s/n
E–20009 San Sebastian

Dear Mr Costello,

First let me apologize for not having cleared your June statement or replying to your letter of 10 August. However, I am surprised that you did not receive our circular letter informing all our suppliers that we were moving from Milano to Torino. I have checked our post book, and find that a letter was sent to you on June 30.

As you will see from the copy enclosed, we warned suppliers that during the move there might be some delay in clearing accounts and replying to correspondence as the move would involve replacing more than half our staff with new people who needed time to get used to our accounts and filing systems.

You will be pleased to hear that we have now settled into our new offices and will have a fully trained staff by the end of next month. Meanwhile, I am enclosing a cheque for Lit. 300,000 on account, and will send a full settlement of your June statement within the next few days.

Could you please note our new address, which is on the heading of this letter, for future reference?

Yours sincerely,

D. Giordianino

D. Giordianino
Accountant

Enc. Bank Draft No. 427322 for Lit. 300,000

Delta Computers Ltd.

Bradfield Estate, Bradfield Road, Wellingborough, Northamptonshire NN8 4HB

Telephone: 0933 16431/2/3/4
Telex: 485881
Fax: 0933 20016

Reg. England 1831713
VAT 2419 62114

Your Ref: ———
Our Ref: TYG A/C

P. Theopolis SA
561 3rd September Street
GR–104 32
Athens

9 December 19—

Dear Mr Theopolis,

Account No. TYG 99014

I wrote to you on two occasions, 21 October and 14 November,
concerning the above account which now has an outstanding balance
of £1,541.46 and is made up of the copy invoices enclosed.

I have waited three months for either a reply to explain why the
balance has not been cleared, or a remittance, but have received
neither.

Although I am reluctant to take legal action to recover the amount, you
leave me no alternative. Therefore, unless I receive your remittance
within the next ten days, my solicitors will be instructed to start
proceedings to recover the debt.

Yours sincerely,

J. Millar

J. Millar (Mrs)
Accountant

Encl. invoice copies

6.6.9
Third request (Final Demand)

Questions

1 How many times has Delta written to
   Mr Theopolis?
2 How long has the balance remained
   unpaid?
3 Do Delta want to take any action?
4 What expression is used which
   means the same as 'legal action'?
5 What was included with the letter?

6.7
Points to remember

1 Invoices record goods that have been sold. The commercial invoice is one of the main documents used in trading. It may be accompanied by a short covering letter.
2 Pro-forma invoices are sent in the case of pre-payment, or to inform the customer of the price.
3 Statements of account are sent monthly or sometimes quarterly, and include details of all transactions within the period.
4 There are various methods of payment available through the Post Office and banks. Letters accompanying payments are usually short, giving information about the payment and what it refers to, but they can also be used to make further comments if necessary.
5 Letters advising and acknowledging payment tend to be short and routine, but they may be used to, say, propose new terms of payment or to make complaints.
6 If you are asking for more time to pay, you should apologize for not having cleared the account on the due date, explain why you have not paid, and when and how you intend to clear the balance. Remember, your creditor is more interested in when he gets his money, than good excuses.
7 As a supplier, three steps are usually taken to recover a debt. The first is to write a polite letter which allows for the fact that there may be a good reason why the account has not yet been cleared. The second is to send a more insistent request which refers to the letter you have already sent with enclosures of copies of invoices and statements. You can, in the second request, state that you expect payment, or a reply, within a reasonable time. A final demand must be handled with restraint. Review what has happened, explain the balance has been outstanding for a long period, and if necessary threaten legal action if the account is not paid within a specified period.

6.8
Words to remember

an invoice
a remittance
a pro-forma
a statement of account
a credit/debit note
a balance
a refund

open account facility
Account Rendered
due date
prompt payment
to clear/settle an account
overdue account
to extend credit
a first/second/third request
a final demand
to recover a debt

carriage forward
trade discount
cash discount
goods on approval/sale or return

a postal order
a Giro
COD (cash on delivery)
a cheque
a current account
a savings account
a bank transfer
a telegraphic transfer (TT)
a mail transfer (MT)

a bank draft
a sight draft
a bill of exchange
a letter of credit
a money order
a promissory note
documentary credit
Value Added Tax (VAT)
postage and packing (p&p)
errors and omissions are excepted (E&OE)
The Society for Worldwide Interbank Financial Telecommunications (SWIFT)

Complaints and adjustments

7

Unjustified complaints; writing general complaints (the language of complaints, explaining the problem, suggesting a solution); replying to letters of complaint (getting time to investigate, explaining the mistake, solving the problem, rejecting a complaint); accounting errors and adjustments (debit notes, credit notes).

7.1
Unjustified complaints

To have to complain is annoying, but to complain without good reason will also annoy your correspondent. If you complain, make sure you get your facts right. And if you have to answer an unjustified complaint, be polite and restrained, and remember that we can all make mistakes.

Below are two examples of unjustified complaints, with the replies to them. Notice how restrained the replies are.

Dear Sir,

I strongly object to the extra charge of £9.00 which you have added to my statement. When I sent my cheque for £56.00 last week, I thought it cleared this balance. Now I find . . .

Dear Mr Axeby,

We received your letter today complaining of an extra charge of £9.00 on your May statement. I think if you check the statement you will find that the amount due was £65.00 not £56.00 which accounts for the £9.00 difference. I have enclosed a copy of the statement and . . .

Dear Sir,

I could not believe it when I read that your prices have now been increased by £7.00. To have to pay £12.00 for an article that was £5.00 only a few months ago is outrageous! The government is fighting inflation . . .

Dear Mr Richardson,

Thank you for your letter. I checked the item you referred to, which is in fact the Scriva Pen catalogue No. G14 on our price-list. The pen has been increased to £7.00, not by £7.00, and I think you will agree that for a fountain pen this is not an unreasonable increase considering that the price of our materials has doubled in the past few months.

7.2
Writing general complaints

7.2.1
Opening

Do not delay and do not apologize. Complain as soon as you realize a mistake has been made; delay not only weakens your case, but can complicate the matter as the people you are dealing with might forget the details. And there is no need to open your letter by apologizing for the need to complain ('We regret to inform you . . .', 'I am sorry to have to write to you about . . .'); this also weakens your case. Begin simply:

We would like to inform you . . .

I am writing to complain about . . .

I am writing with reference to Order No. P32 which we received yesterday.

7.2.2
The language of complaints

Terms like 'disgusted', 'infuriated', 'enraged', 'amazed' have no place in business. You can express dissatisfaction by saying:

This is the third time this mistake has occurred and we are far from satisfied with the service you offer.

Unless you can fulfil our orders efficiently in the future we will have to consider other sources of supply.

Please ensure that this sort of problem does not arise again.

Do not be rude or personal. In most cases correspondence between firms takes place between employees in various departments. Nothing is gained by being rude to the individual you are writing to; you may antagonize someone who has probably had nothing to do with the error and, rather than getting the error corrected, s/he could become defensive and awkward to deal with. Therefore, do not use sentences like:

You must correct your mistake as soon as possible.

You made an error on the statement.

You don't understand the terms of discount. We told you to deduct discount from net prices, not c.i.f. prices.

Use the passive and impersonal structures mentioned in 6.5.1.

The mistake must be corrected as soon as possible.

There appears to be an error on the statement.

There seems to be some misunderstanding regarding terms of discount. Discount is deducted from net prices, not c.i.f. prices.

Do not use words like 'fault' ('your fault', 'our fault') or 'blame' ('you are to blame'); these expressions are not only rude, but childish. Therefore, do not write:

It is not our fault, it is probably the fault of your despatch department.

But:

The mistake could not have originated here, and must be connected with the despatch of the goods.

Never blame your staff, and finally, while writing the complaint remember that your supplier wants to help you and correct the mistake. He is not in business to irritate or confuse his customers but to offer them a service.

7.2.3
Explaining the problem

If you think you know how the mistake was made, you may politely point it out to your supplier. Sometimes when a mistake occurs several times, you may be able to work out why it is happening more quickly than the firm you are dealing with.

Could you tell your despatch department to take special care when addressing my consignment? My name is C. J. Schwartz, Bergstr. 101 Köln. But there is a C. Schwartz, Bergstr. 110 Köln who also deals in electrical fittings.

Could you ask your accounts department to check my code carefully in future? My account number is 246–642, and they have been sending me statements coded 642–246.

I think the reason that wrong sizes have been sent to me is because I am ordering in metric sizes, and you are sending me sizes measured in feet and inches. I would appreciate your looking into this.

7.2.4
Suggesting a solution

If you think you know how the mistake can be corrected, let your supplier know. (For the reference to 'debit note' and 'credit note' in these examples, see 7.5.)

If I send you a debit note for £18.00 and deduct it from my next statement that should put the matter right.

The best solution would be for me to return the wrong articles to you, postage and packing forward.

Rather than send a credit note, you could send six replacements which would probably be easier than adjusting our accounts.

7.3
Replying to letters of complaint

7.3.1
Opening

Acknowledge that you have received the complaint, and thank your customer for informing you.

Thank you for your letter of 6 August informing us that . . .

We would like to thank you for informing us of our accounting error in your letter of the 7 June.

We are replying to your letter of 10 March in which you told us that . . .

7.3.2
Getting time to investigate the complaint

Sometimes you cannot deal with a complaint immediately, as the matter needs to be looked into. Do not leave your customer waiting, but tell him what you are doing straight away.

While we cannot give you an explanation at present, we can promise you that we are looking into the matter and will write to you again shortly.

As we are sending out orders promptly, I think these delays may have something to do with the haulage contractors and I am making investigations at the moment.

Would you please return samples of the items you are dissatisfied with, and I will send them to our factory in Düsseldorf for tests.

7.3.3
Explaining the mistake

If the complaint is justified, explain how the mistake occurred but do not blame your staff; you employed them, so you are responsible for their actions.

The mistake was due to a fault in one of our machines, which has now been corrected.

There appears to have been some confusion in our addressing system, but this has been adjusted.

It is unusual for this type of error to arise, but the problem has now been dealt with.

7.3.4
Solving the problem

Having acknowledged your responsibility and explained what went wrong, you must, of course, put matters right as soon as possible and tell your customer that you are doing so.

We have now checked our accounts and find that we have indeed been sending you the wrong statement due to a confusion in names and addresses. The computer has been reprogrammed and there should be no more difficulties. Please contact us again if any similar situation arises, and once more thank you for pointing out the error.

The reason for the weakness in the units you complained about was due to a faulty manufacturing process in production. This is being corrected at the moment and we are sure you will be completely satisfied with the replacement units we will be sending you in the next few weeks.

The paintwork on the body of the cars became discoloured because of a chemical imbalance in the paint used in spraying the vehicles. We have already contacted our own suppliers and are waiting for their reply. Meanwhile we are taking these models out of production and calling in all those that have been supplied.

The material you complained about has now been withdrawn. Its fault was in the weave of the cloth and this was due to a programming error in the weaving machines themselves. This has been corrected and replacement materials are now being sent on to you.

7.3.5
Rejecting a complaint

If you think the complaint is unjustified, you can be firm but polite in your answer (see also 7.1). But even if you deny responsibility, you should always try to give an explanation of the problem.

We have closely compared the articles you returned with our samples and can see no difference between them, and in this case we are not willing to either substitute the articles or offer a credit.

Our engineer has examined the machine you complained about and in his report tells us that the machine has not been maintained properly. If you look at the instruction booklet on maintenance that we sent you, you will see that it is essential to take care of . . .

Our factory has now inspected the stereo unit you returned last week, and they inform us that it has been used with

the wrong speakers and this had overloaded the circuits. We can repair the machine, but you will have to pay for the repairs as misuse of the unit is not included under our guarantee.

7.3.6
Closing

It is useful when closing your letter to mention that this mistake, error, or fault is an exception, and it either rarely or never happens, and of course you should apologize for the inconvenience your customer experienced.

In closing we would like to apologize for the inconvenience, and also point out that this type of fault rarely occurs in the Omega 2000.

Finally, may we say that this was an exceptional mistake and is unlikely to occur again. Please accept our apologies for the inconvenience.

The replacements of the faulty articles are on their way to you and you should receive them within the week. We are sure that you will be satisfied with them and there will be no repetition of the faults. Thank you for your patience in this matter, and we look forward to hearing from you again.

7.4
Specimen letters

7.4.1
Complaint of wrong delivery

The answer to this letter, 7.4.2, will explain why complaints should be carefully written and the writer should not assume that the correspondent is responsible for the mistake.

R. Hughes & Son Ltd.

21 Mead Road, Swansea, Glamorgan 3ST 1DR

Telephone: Swansea 58441   VAT No. 215 2261 30
Telex: 881821

Mr R. Cliff,   3rd February 19—
Homemakers Ltd.,
54–59 Riverside,
Cardiff CF1 1JW

Dear Mr Cliff,

I have received a consignment of 6 dressing tables from you yesterday, my order No. 1695, which were ordered from your summer catalogue, Cat. No. GR154. But on unpacking them I found that six heavy mahogany-finished dressing tables had been sent, instead of the light pine-finish ones asked for.

As most of my customers live in small flats earning a moderate income it is doubtful that I will be able to find a market for larger more expensive products.

I also have firm orders for the goods asked for. Would you send someone with my consignment as soon as possible and at the same time pick up the wrongly delivered goods? Thank you.

Yours sincerely,

R. Hughes
R. Hughes

HOMEMAKERS Ltd.

54–59 Riverside, Cardiff CF1 1JW

Telephone: (0222) 49721   Registered No. C135162
Telex: 38217

Mr R. Hughes   5 February 19—
R. Hughes & Son Ltd.
21 Mead Road
Swansea
Glamorgan 3ST 1DR

Dear Mr Hughes,

Thank you for your letter of 3 February in which you said that you had received a wrong delivery to your order (No. 1695).

I have looked into this and it appears that you have ordered from an out-of-date catalogue. Our current winter catalogue lists the dressing tables you wanted under DR 189.

I have instructed one of my drivers to deliver the pine-finish dressing tables tomorrow and pick up the other consignment at the same time. Rather than sending a credit note, I will cancel invoice No. T4451 and include another, No. T4467, with the delivery.

There is also a winter catalogue on its way to you in case you have mislaid the one I originally sent you.

Yours sincerely,

R. Cliff

Enc. Invoice No. T4467

7.4.2
Reply to complaint of wrong delivery

Questions

1 Why did Mr Hughes receive a wrong delivery?
2 What will Mr Cliff do about it?
3 Why is Mr Cliff not going to send a credit note?
4 How is Mr Cliff ensuring that Mr Hughes will not make the same mistake again?
5 Which words in the letter correspond to the following: *investigated*; *seems*; *ordered*; *collect*; *lost*?

7.4.3
Complaint of damage

You have already seen a complaint about breakages in MacKenzie's letter to Glaston Potteries, 6.3.5. This letter deals with damage.

Questions

1 How had the damage occurred?
2 Why can't the garments still be sold?
3 What does Mr Crane intend to do with the damaged consignment?
4 Why does Mr Crane suggest Mr Causio has to deal with the documentary details of the complaint?
5 What is enclosed with the letter?
6 Which words in the letter correspond to the following: *during transportation*; *assess*; *clothes*; *make up for the loss*?

F. Lynch & Co. Ltd.

(Head Office), Nesson House, Newell Street, Birmingham B3 3EL
Telephone No.: 021 236 6571   Fax: 021 236 8592   Telex: 341641

Satex S.p.A.   Your Ref:
Via di Pietra Papa   Our Ref:
00146 Roma
ITALY   Date: 15 August 19—

Attn. Mr D. Causio

Dear Mr Causio,

Our Order No. 14478

I am writing to you to complain about the shipment of sweaters we received yesterday against the above order.

The boxes in which the sweaters were packed were damaged, and looked as if they had been broken open in transit. From your invoice No. 18871 we estimate that thirty garments have been stolen to the value of £150.00. And because of the rummaging in the boxes, quite a few other garments were crushed or stained and cannot be sold as new articles in our shops.

As the sale was on a c.i.f. basis and the forwarding company your agents, we suggest you contact them with regard to compensation.

You will find a list of the damaged and missing articles attached, and the consignment will be put to one side until we receive your instructions.

Yours sincerely,

L. Crane

L. Crane
Chief Buyer

Satex S.p.A.

Via di Pietra Papa, 00146 Roma

Telefono: Roma 769910
Telefax: (06) 481 5473
Telex: 285136

Mr L. Crane, Chief Buyer   Vs. rif.:   Order 14478
F. Lynch & Co. Ltd.   Ns. rif.:   D/1162
Nesson House
Newell Street   24 August 19—
Birmingham B3 3EL
UNITED KINGDOM

Dear Mr Crane,

Thank you for informing us about the damage to our consignment (Inv. No. 18871).

From our previous transactions you will realize that this sort of problem is quite unusual. Nevertheless, we are sorry about the inconvenience it has caused you.

Please would you return the whole consignment to us, postage and packing forward, and we will ask the shipping company to come and inspect the damage so that they can arrange compensation. It is unlikely that our insurance company needs to be troubled with this case.

If you want us to send you another shipment as per your order No. 14478, please let us know. We have the garments in stock and it would be no trouble to send them within the next fortnight.

Yours sincerely,

D. Causio

D. Causio

7.4.4
Reply to complaint of damage

Because Satex sells goods on a c.i.f. basis to their retailers, and in this case there was no special instruction to send the goods in a particular way, Satex will have to find out what happened and whether they can be compensated. Mr Causio could have asked Mr Crane to keep those items which were not damaged, and return the garments which could not be sold. However, he wants the shipping company to inspect the whole consignment in case they do not accept that the damage was caused by pilfering.

7.4.5
Complaint of bad workmanship

When bad workmanship is involved the customer can only complain as the faults arise. But they should still complain immediately. In the correspondence at 3.3.6 and 4.3.7, Superbuys, a supermarket, had asked Wembley Shopfitters to refit a shop they were going to open. The work was completed, but some months later faults began to appear.

SUPERBUYS Ltd.

Superbuy House, Wolverton Road, London SW16 7DN

Telephone: 081-327 1651
Telex: 303113
Fax: 081 327 1935

Reg. No.: 94116 London
VAT No. 516 8410 30

Mr P. Lane
Wembley Shopfitters Ltd.
Wycombe Road
Wembley
Middlesex HA9 6DA

Date: 7th July 19—

Dear Mr Lane,

'Superbuys' Wembley High Street

I am writing to you with reference to the above premises which you refitted last February.

In the past few weeks a number of faults have appeared in the electrical circuits and the flooring which have been particularly dangerous to our customers.

With regard to the electrical faults we have found that spotlights on the far wall have either failed to work, or flicker while they are on, and replacing the bulbs has not corrected the fault.

The Duraflooring which you laid has been showing signs of deterioration with some areas being worn through to the concrete creating a hazard to our customers.

Will you please come and inspect the damage and arrange for repairs within the next week? The matter is urgent as we can be sued if any of our customers are injured by falling over the cracks in the flooring. I would also take the opportunity to remind you that you have guaranteed all your fixtures and fittings for one year. I look forward to hearing from you soon.

Yours sincerely,

K. Bellon

K. Bellon
Managing Director

Wembley Shopfitters Ltd.

Wycombe Road, Wembley, Middlesex HA9 6DA

Telephone: 081 903 2323   Reg: London 481629   VAT: 314 6519 28

Mr K. Bellon   10 July 19—
Superbuys Ltd.
Superbuy House
Wolverton Road
London SW16 7DN

Dear Mr Bellon,

The manager of your Wembley supermarket has probably told you by now that I came down to inspect the damage you wrote to me about in your letter of 7 July.

I looked at the faulty electrical wiring and this appears to have been caused by dripping water from the floor above. My foreman, who put the wiring in in February, tells me that the wall was dry at the time he replaced the old wires. However, we will make the repairs and seal off that section.

Duraflooring is one of the most hardwearing materials of its kind on the market and I was surprised to hear that it had worn away within six months, so I made a close inspection. I noticed that the floor had been cut into and this seems to have been the result of dragging heavy sharp boxes across it, possibly the ones you use to store some perishable products in. The one-year guarantee we offer on our workmanship is against normal wear and tear, and the treatment the floor has been subjected to does not come under this category. I am quite willing to have the surface replaced, but I am afraid we will have to charge you for the materials and work involved. If I may, I would like to suggest that you instruct your staff to use trolleys when shifting these containers.

I am sorry about the inconvenience you have experienced and will tell my men to repair the damage as soon as I have your confirmation that they can begin work.

The floor repairs should not come to more than £490 and the work can be completed in less than a day. Perhaps we can arrange for it to be completed on a Sunday when the supermarket is closed.

Yours sincerely,

P. Lane

P. Lane
Director

7.4.6
Reply to complaint of bad workmanship

Questions

1 What does Mr Lane think caused the faulty wiring and what does he intend to do about it?
2 What does he think caused the problem with the flooring, and what does he say he will do about it?
3 When does he suggest the faults could be corrected and why does he choose that time?
4 Do you think his offer is fair?
5 How does Mr Lane suggest the damage can be avoided?
6 How long will repairs take?
7 What expression is used to explain *normal use*?
8 Which words in the letter correspond to the following: *look at*; *installed*; *effect*; *close*; *durable*; *sorry*; *finished*?

7.4.7

Complaint of non-delivery

The final example in this section is an illustration of a strong complaint to a supplier. In this case the customer, Forham Vehicles PLC, makes lorries for export. They placed an order with Baden, to supply them with 60 dynamos for an export shipment of lorries that were to be sent to Greece. Baden have neither delivered the order, nor answered Forham's previous letter urging them to make delivery.

FORHAM VEHICLES PLC

Lever Estate, Scarborough, Yorkshire YO11 3BS
Directors: M. Blackburn, M.H. Thomson

Telephone 0723 16952
Fax: 0723 81953
Telex: 437865

Reg. England: 8969135
VAT. 1462 321 17

Mr R. Zeitman
E.F. Baden AG
Zülpicher Str. 10–20
D–4000 Düsseldorf 11

Date: 20th June 19—

Dear Mr Zeitman

Order No. VC 58391

We are writing to you with reference to the above order and our letter of 22 May in which we asked you when we could expect delivery of the 60 dynamos (Artex model 55) you were to have supplied on 3 June for an export order.

We have tried to contact you by phone, but could not get anyone in your factory who knew anything about this matter.

It is essential that we deliver this consignment to our Greek customers on time as this was an initial order from them and would give us an opening in the Greek market.

Our deadline is 28 June, and the lorries have been completed except for the dynamos that need to be fitted.

Unless we receive the components within the next five days, the order will be cancelled and placed elsewhere. We should warn you that we are holding you to your delivery contract and if any loss results because of this late delivery we will be taking legal action.

Yours sincerely,

M. Blackburn

E. F. Baden AG

Zülpicher Str. 10–20, D-4000 Düsseldorf II
Tel: (0211) 38.34.06/09 Fax: (0211) 38.34.271 Telex: 032651

Mr M. Blackburn   29 June 19—
Forham Vehicles PLC
Lever Estate
Scarborough YO11 3BS

Dear Mr Blackburn,

Thank you for your letter of 20 June concerning your order (No. VC 58391) which should have been supplied to you on 3 June.

First let me apologize for your order not being delivered on the due date and for the problems you have experienced in getting in touch with us about it. But as you may have read in your newspapers we have experienced an industrial dispute which has involved both administrative staff and employees on the shop floor, and as a consequence has held up all production over the past few weeks.

I can tell you that the dispute has been settled and we are back to normal production. There is a backlog of orders to catch up on, but we are using associates of ours to help us fulfil all outstanding commitments; your order has been given priority, so we should be able to deliver the dynamos before the end of this week.

May I point out, with respect, that your contract with us did have a standard clause stating that delivery dates would be met unless unforeseen circumstances arose, and we think you will agree that a dispute is an exceptional circumstance. However, we quite understand your problem and will allow you to cancel your contract if it will help you to meet your own commitments with your Greek customers. But we will not accept any responsibility for any action they may take against you.

Once again let me say how much I regret the inconvenience this delay has caused, and emphasize that it was due to factors we could not have known about when we accepted your delivery dates.

Please phone or fax me letting me know if you wish us to complete your order or whether you would prefer to make other arrangements.

I look forward to hearing from you within the next day or so.

Yours sincerely,

R Zeitman

R. Zeitman
Managing Director

7.4.8
Reply to complaint of non-delivery

Note how this letter is both apologetic but firm. Though Baden accept responsibility for the problems Forham face in delivering their consignment to their Greek customers, Herr Zeitman rejects the threat of legal action by drawing Mr Blackburn's attention to a clause in their contract stating that the company will not be responsible for 'unforeseen circumstances that arise'. However, Herr Zeitman is flexible enough to realize he must not antagonize his customer, so he allows Mr Blackburn the opportunity to cancel the order if he can make other arrangements.

Therefore, the two main points this letter makes are – first, do not commit yourself to contracts unless you are absolutely certain they can be fulfilled. Second, always try and be as flexible as possible with customers or associates even if you are in a strong position; it will improve your business reputation.

7.5
Accounting errors and adjustments

As we have seen, many letters of complaint arise out of accounting errors, which can be put right by adjustments. Debit notes and credit notes are used for this purpose.

7.5.1
Debit notes

Debit notes are a second charge for a consignment and become necessary if a customer has been undercharged through a mistake in the calculations on the original invoice. An explanation is included on the debit note:

Undercharge on invoice C293. 10 Units @ £2.62 each = £26.20, NOT £16.20

Invoice No. P.32, one line omitted viz. 100 C90 cassettes at £1.40 each = £140

VAT should have been calculated at 17½%, NOT 15% Difference = £1.86

Debit notes are the result of carelessness and show that you should be careful when making up invoices as once a buyer has settled an account, it is annoying to be told that there is an additional payment. A letter of apology should always accompany a debit note.

We would like to apologize for the mistake on invoice No. C293, which was due to an oversight. Please could you send us the balance of £10.00? Thank you.

I am sorry to trouble you, particularly since you were so prompt in settling the account, but I would be grateful if you would let us have the additional amount of £140 as itemized on the enclosed debit note.

I regret that we miscalculated the VAT and must now ask you to forward the difference of £51.86.

7.5.2
Credit notes

Credit notes are sent because of accidental overcharges:

10 copies of 'International Commerce' @ £3.50 = £35.00 NOT £40.00.

Invoice L283. Discount should have been 12%, not 8%. Credit = £5.60.

A credit note may also be issued when a deposit is being refunded (e.g. on the cartons or cases which the goods were packed in) or when goods are returned because they were not suitable or had been damaged.

Received 3 returned cases charged on Invoice No. 1436 @ £2.00 each = £6.00.

Refund for 4 copies of 'International Commerce' @ £3.50 each (returned damaged) = £14.00.

As with a debit note, a covering letter of explanation and apology should be sent with a credit note in the case of mistakes.

I have pleasure in enclosing a credit note for £5.00. This is due to a miscalculation on our invoice dated 12 August. Please accept our apologies for the mistake.

Please find enclosed our credit note No. C23 for £5.60 which is a refund for the overcharge on invoice No. L283. As you pointed out in your letter, the trade discount should have been 12%, not 10%, of the gross price. We apologize for the inconvenience.

DEBIT NOTE   No. 311

SEYMORE FURNITURE Ltd.
Tib Street, Maidenhead, Berks. SL6 5D2   Telephone 0628 26755

Registered No. 18514391 London
VAT No. 231 6188 31

C.R. Méndez SA   31 May 19—
Avda del Ejército 83
E–48015 Bilbao

19— 5 May	Invoice No. L 8992. UNDERCHARGE. The extension should have read: 6 Chairs @ £12.00 each = £72.00 NOT 6 Chairs @ £10.00 each = £60.00 We apologize for the error and ask if you would please pay the difference viz. £12.00.	£12.00

7.6
Specimen forms and letters

7.6.1
Debit note

This note is necessary because the suppliers, Seymore Furniture Ltd., have made a mistake in their calculations and have undercharged their customers, C.R. Méndez.

7.6.2
Credit note

Seymore Furniture Ltd. have made a mistake on another invoice and must now send a credit note. Note that the form for a credit note is the same as that for a debit note, except for the heading. Credit notes, however, are often printed in red.

CREDIT NOTE	No. C517

SEYMORE FURNITURE Ltd.
Tib Street, Maidenhead, Berks. SL6 5D2   Telephone 0628 26755

Registered No. 18514391 London
VAT No. 236 6188 31

C.R. Méndez SA   20 May 19—
Avda del Ejército 83
E–48015 Bilbao

19— 20 May	Invoice No. L8995. OVERCHARGE. The invoice should have read: 15% off gross price of £800.00 = £120.00 NOT 10% off gross price of £800.00 = £80.00 Refund = £40.00. Please accept our apologies.	£40.00

M. LANCELOT SARL

703 rue Métairie de Saysset, F–34000 Montpelier

Tél: (33) 843 10312
Fax: (33) 1291037
Telex: 59612503

Mr K. Winford   5 August 19—
K. Winford & Co. Ltd.
Preston New Road
Blackpool
Lancashire FY4 4UL

Dear Mr Winford,

I have received your July statement for £3,280.64 but noticed that a number of errors have been made.

1.   Invoice Y 1146 for £256.00 has been debited twice.

2.   No credit has been listed for the wallpaper (Cat. No. WR 114) which I returned in July. Your credit note No. CN 118 for £19.00 refers to this.

3.   You have charged me for a delivery of paint brushes, Invoice No. Y 1162 for £62.00 but I never ordered or received them. Could you check your delivery book?

I have deducted a total of £337.00 from your statement and will send you a draft for £2,943.64, once I have your confirmation of this amount.

Yours sincerely,

M. Lancelot
Director

7.6.3
Complaint of accounting errors

M. Lancelot of M. Lancelot SARL (Builders' Suppliers) has received a statement in which several accounting errors have occurred.

K. Winford & Co. Ltd.

Preston New Road, Blackpool, Lancashire FY4 4UL

Telephone: 0253 61290/1/2

Reg. No. 31162531
VAT 831 4003 36

7 August 19—

The Director
M. Lancelot SARL
703 rue Métairie de Saysset
F–34000 Montpelier

Dear Mr Lancelot,

Thank you for your letter of 5 August in which you pointed out that three
mistakes totalling £337.00 had been made on your statement.

I apologize for the errors which were due to a fault in our computer
which has now been fixed. I have enclosed another statement for July
which shows the correct balance of £2,943.64.

Yours sincerely,

K. Winford

K. Winford

Encl. Statement

7.7
Points to remember

1 Before writing a letter of complaint, make sure you have got your facts right.
2 Complaints are not accusations; they are requests to correct mistakes or faults, and should be written remembering that the supplier will *want* to put things right.
3 Therefore, write calmly, clearly presenting all the relevant information and making any suggestions that might help put the matter right.
4 Never make the complaint personal (*your* mistake, *your* fault, *you* are to blame). Use an impersonal tone (*the* mistake, it must have happened because, *the* error).
5 When answering a complaint, apologize for the mistake, thank the writer for pointing it out to you, explain how it occurred (but don't blame your staff) and how you intend to deal with it.
6 If you need more time to investigate the complaint, tell your customer so.
7 If the complaint is unjustified, politely explain why, but sympathize about the inconvenience it has caused.
8 Remember that, whether your customer's complaint is right or wrong, he/she *is* your customer and his/her comments about you to other people in your trade or profession can either improve or damage your reputation.

7.8
Words to remember

a mistake
an error
a fault
a misunderstanding
a complaint
a delay
an inconvenience
a deadline
a guarantee
a dispute
a backlog
a commitment
a contract

a miscalculation
an overcharge
an undercharge
a debit/credit note
a refund

damage
deterioration
out-of-date
wear and tear
bad workmanship
compensation
repair
legal action

to be satisfied/dissatisfied
to investigate a complaint
to look into a matter
to deny/accept responsibility
to give an explanation
to solve a problem
to put matters right
to apologize
to cancel an order

Credit

8

Forms of credit; requirements for granting credit; asking for credit; replying to requests for credit; taking up references; asking about credit rating; using an Enquiry Agent; replying to enquiries about credit rating.

8.1
Forms of credit

Credit arrangements between trading firms take two forms:

Bills of exchange, or drafts, by which the seller gives credit to the buyer for the period specified on the bill, e.g. 30, 60, or 90 days.

Open account facilities by which the buyer is allowed to pay for his goods against monthly or quarterly statements.

8.2
Requirements for granting credit

Credit facilities will only be granted by a supplier if the customer can satisfy one or more of certain requirements.

1 *Reputation*
Credit may be given to firms which have an established reputation, i.e. are well-known nationally or internationally.

2 *Long-term trading association*
If a customer has been trading with a supplier over a period of time and has built up a good relationship with the supplier by, for example, settling accounts promptly, he may be able to persuade his supplier to grant him credit facilities on this basis alone.

3 *References*
Normally, however, when asking for credit, a customer will supply references, i.e. the names of concerns or companies which will satisfy the supplier that the customer is reputable and credit-worthy. Banks will supply references, though these tend to be brief, stating what the company's capital

is and who its directors are. Trade associations, i.e. organizations which represent the company's trade or profession, also tend to give brief references telling the enquirer how long the company has been trading and whether it is a large or small firm. References can also be obtained from the customer's business associates, the commercial departments of embassies, and so on.

8.3
Asking for credit

8.3.1
Opening

In the opening paragraph of a letter asking for credit facilities, it is best to go straight to the point and specify what form of credit you are looking for.

I am writing to ask if it would be possible for us to have credit facilities in the form of payment by 60-day bill of exchange.

Thank you for your catalogue and letter. As there was no indication of your credit terms could you let me know if you would allow us to settle on monthly statements?

We appreciate your answering our enquiry so promptly. As I pointed out in my letter to you, our suppliers usually allow us open account facilities with quarterly settlements, and I hope that this method of payment will be acceptable to you also.

8.3.2
Convincing your supplier

As mentioned above, your supplier will only grant credit if he is convinced that

you will not default. So mention your previous dealings with the supplier.

As we have been dealing with you for more than a year we feel that you know us well enough to grant our request.

We believe we have established our reliability with you over the past six months and would now like to settle accounts on a quarterly basis.

During the past few months of our transactions we have always settled promptly, and therefore we feel we can ask for better credit facilities from you.

Mention your reputation, and, of course, offer references.

We are a well-established firm and can offer references if necessary.

We can certainly pay on the due dates, but if you would like confirmation concerning our credit-worthiness then please contact any of the following who will act as our referees: . . .

We deal with most of our suppliers on a quarterly settlement basis and you may contact any of those listed below for a reference.

8.3.3
Closing

We hope you will consider our request favourably and look forward to your reply.

Please follow up the references we have submitted. We look forward to your confirmation that payment by 30-day bill of exchange is acceptable.

As soon as we receive your confirmation that you will allow the open account facilities we have asked for, we will send our next order.

8.4
Replying to requests for credit

8.4.1
Agreeing to credit

If the supplier does not think it necessary to take up references, he may grant credit immediately.

As we have been trading for over a year references will not be necessary and you may clear your accounts by 30-day bill of exchange which will be sent to Burnley's Bank (Queens Building, Cathays Park, Cardiff CF1 9UJ) with shipping documents for your acceptance.

We are pleased to inform you that the credit facilities you asked for are acceptable, and knowing the reputation of your company there will be no need for us to contact any referees. Just to confirm what has been agreed – settlement will be made against monthly statements. We look forward to receiving your next order.

If references are considered necessary, however, the supplier will acknowledge the request (see 8.4.4) and then reply in full when references have been received.

We have now received the necessary references and are pleased to say that from your next order payment can be made on a quarterly basis against statements.

The referees you gave us have replied and we are able to tell you that as from next month you may settle your account on a documents against acceptance basis by 60 d/s B/E.

8.4.2
Refusing credit

When refusing credit facilities, the writer must explain why he is turning the request down. There may be a number of reasons for this. It might be uneconomical for him to offer credit facilities; he may not trust the customer, i.e. the customer has a bad reputation for settling accounts; or it might just be a policy of his company not to give credit. Whatever the reason, the reply must be worded carefully so as not to offend the customer.

Thank you for your letter of 9 November in which you asked to be put on open account terms. Unfortunately, we never allow credit facilities to customers until they have traded with us for over a year. We really are sorry that we cannot be more helpful in this case.

We regret that we are unable to offer open account terms to customers as our products are competitively priced and with small profit margins it is uneconomical to allow credit facilities.

We are sorry that we cannot offer credit facilities of any kind at present owing to rising inflation. However, perhaps if things settle in future we may be able to reconsider your request.

We have considered your request for quarterly settlements, but feel that, with our competitive pricing policy which leaves only small profit margins, it would be uneconomical to allow credit on your present purchases. However, if you can offer the usual references and increase your purchases by at least fifty per cent perhaps we can reconsider the situation.

8.4.3
Negotiating

Sometimes a supplier will not offer as much credit as the customer wants but will negotiate a compromise.

I regret that we cannot offer you credit for as long as three months, since this would be uneconomical for us. However, I am prepared to offer you settlement against <u>monthly</u> statements. Perhaps you will let me know if this would be acceptable.

Though we do not usually offer credit facilities, we would be prepared to consider partial credit. In this case you would pay half your invoices on a cash basis, and the rest by 30-day bill of exchange. If this arrangement suits you, please contact us.

8.4.4
Reply while waiting for references

In some cases you will not be able to grant credit without making further investigations. In particular, you may want to take up the references your customer has offered. In these cases, your reply will be little more than an acknowledgement of the request.

Thank you for your letter in which you asked for credit facilities. At present we are writing to the referees you mentioned and will let you know as soon as we hear from them.

In reply to your letter of 8 June, we will consider your request to pay by 30-day bill of exchange and will contact you as soon as we have reached a decision.

I received your letter of 15 March, yesterday, in which you asked for open account facilities. As soon as the usual enquiries have been made, I will contact you.

As we have only just received your letter asking for credit facilities, please would you allow us a little time to consider the matter? We will be answering you within the next couple of weeks.

R. Hughes & Son Ltd.

21 Mead Road, Swansea, Glamorgan 3ST 1DR

Telephone: Swansea 58441   VAT No. 215 2261 30
Telex: 881821

Mr R. Cliff,   18th July 19—
Homemakers Ltd.,
54–59 Riverside,
Cardiff CF1 1JW

Dear Mr Cliff,

I have enclosed an order, No. B1662, for seven more 'Sleepcomfy' beds
which have proved to be a popular line here, and will pay for them as usual
on invoice. However, I wondered if in future you would allow me to settle
my accounts by monthly statement which would be a more convenient
method of payment for me.

As we have been dealing with one another for some time, I think you have
enough confidence in my firm to allow open account facilities, but of course
I can supply the necessary references.

Yours sincerely,

R. Hughes

R. Hughes

Encl. Order No. B1662

8.5
Specimen letters

8.5.1
Request for open-account facilities

Mr Hughes, whose correspondence we
looked at in previous units (3.3.5, 4.3.6,
6.6.5, 6.6.6, 7.4.1, 7.4.2), asks his
supplier if he will allow him open account
facilities. He makes his request while
sending an order rather than making his
next order conditional on Mr Cliff's
acceptance; compare this with the letter
of 6.3.4 when F. Lynch & Co. made their
next order conditional on revised terms.

8.5.2
Reply granting open-account facilities

In their reply to 8.5.1, Homemakers are prepared to give credit even though they feel it may not be in the best interests of their customer.

Questions

1 Why does Mr Cliff think it would be better for Mr Hughes to settle invoices within seven days?
2 Why doesn't Mr Cliff need any references from Mr Hughes?
3 When should Mr Hughes pay invoice DM 1113?
4 What form of open account facilities is Mr Cliff offering?

HOMEMAKERS Ltd.

54–59 Riverside, Cardiff CF1 1JW

Telephone: (0222) 49721   Registered No. C135162
Telex: 38217

Mr R. Hughes   24 July 19—
R. Hughes & Son Ltd.
21 Mead Road
Swansea
Glamorgan 3ST 1DR

Dear Mr Hughes,

Thank you for your order, No. B1662, which will be sent to you tomorrow. I have taken the opportunity to enclose the invoice, DM 1113, with this letter.

With regard to your request for open account facilities, settlement against monthly statement, I feel there would be more advantage for you in claiming the 3% cash discounts offered for payment within seven days of receipt of invoice. Nevertheless, I am quite prepared to allow monthly settlements, and there will be no need to supply references as you are a long-standing customer.

The enclosed invoice will be included in your next statement.

Yours sincerely,

R. Cliff

R. Cliff

Enc. Invoice DM1113

Disc SA

251 rue des Ramonières F–86000 Poitiers Cédex
Tél: (33) 99681031 Télécopie: (33) 102163

Réf: PG/AL   3 December 19—

The Sales Director
R. G. Electronics AG
Haumart 601
D–5000 Köln 1

Dear Herr Gerlach,

I intend to place a substantial order with you in the next few weeks and
wondered what sort of credit facilities your company offered.

As you know, over the past months I have placed a number of orders
with you and settled promptly, so I hope this has established my
reputation with your company. Nevertheless, if necessary, I am willing
to supply references.

Please let me know if I could settle future accounts on, say, quarterly
terms with payments against statements.

Yours sincerely,

P. Gérard

P. Gérard

8.5.3
Request for general credit facilities

8.5.4
Refusal of credit facilities

In this reply to 8.5.3, Southern Importers turn the request down, even though the two companies have traded for some time.

Questions

1 How does Herr Gerlach assure M. Gérard that his firm's reputation has nothing to do with the rejection?
2 Why is Herr Gerlach refusing credit facilities?
3 Is it only in M. Gérard's case that credit has been refused?
4 How does Herr Gerlach encourage further correspondence?

R. G. Electronics AG

Havmart 601
D-5000 Köln 1
Tel: (221) 32 4298
Fax: (221) 83 61 25
Telex: 6153291

Your ref:

P. Gérard
Disc S.A.
251 rue des Raimonières
F–86000 Poitiers Cédex

8 December 19—

Dear Mr Gérard,

Thank you for your letter of December 3 in which you enquired about credit facilities.

We appreciate that you have placed a number of orders with us in the past, and are sure that you can supply the necessary references to support your request. However, as you probably realize, our tapes and CDs are sold at extremely competitive prices which allow us only small profit margins, and this prevents us offering any of our customers credit facilities.

We are very sorry that we cannot help you in this case, but are sure you understand our reasons. Once again, thank you for writing, and we look forward to hearing from you soon.

Yours sincerely,

R. Gerlach

R. Gerlach
Sales Director

MacKenzie Bros. Ltd.

1–5 Whale Drive, Dawson, Ontario, Canada
Branches: Ottawa, Vancouver, New York, Chicago.
Tel: (613) 238 1492   Cable: MAKIE   Telex: 315515

Mr J. Merton   9 February 19—
Glaston Potteries Ltd.
Clayfield
Burnley BB10 1RQ
UNITED KINGDOM

Dear Mr Merton,

Our bank has advised us that the proceeds of our letter of credit against
your invoice, No. G1197/S, have now been credited to your account.

We have been paying you for some time on this basis, which does not
really suit our accounting system, and as we feel you know us well
enough by now, we think you would not object to our paying on
quarterly statements by international banker's draft.

If you require a reference, you can contact our other suppliers, Pierson
& Co., Louis Drive, Dawson, Ontario, who will vouch for us. Write to
either Mr M. Pierson or Mr J. Tane.

Please confirm that these new terms are acceptable.

Yours sincerely,

R. MacKenzie

R. MacKenzie

8.5.5
Request for a change in the terms of payment

MacKenzie Bros. of Canada, as we have seen in previous units, import chinaware from Glaston Potteries in England; they currently pay by letter of credit, but now want to pay on quarterly statements by international banker's draft. This involves fairly long-term credit, so they supply references.

8.5.6
Notification of taking up references

Glaston Potteries are sympathetic to MacKenzie Bros. request, but decide to take up the reference offered.

GLASTON POTTERIES Ltd.

Clayfield, Burnley BB10 1RQ

Tel: 0315 46125
Telex: 8801773
Fax: 0315 63182

Registered No. 716481
VAT Registered No. 133 5341 08

Mr R. MacKenzie   14 February 19—
MacKenzie Bros. Ltd.
1–5 Whale Drive
Dawson
Ontario
CANADA

Dear Mr MacKenzie

Thank you for your letter of 9 February in which you asked to change your terms of payment to settlement by banker's draft on quarterly statements.

We are taking up the reference you offered, and provided it is satisfactory you can consider the new arrangement effective from your next order.

Yours sincerely,

J. Merton

J. Merton
Sales Manager

8.6
Asking about credit rating

The guide below gives you an outline on how to take up references and to ask about a company's credit rating.

8.6.1
Opening

Say who you are and why you want the information. Make it clear that the name of the company you are writing to has been given to you as a reference by your customer. (If this is not the case, you are unlikely to get a reply – see 8.7.1.)

We are a furniture wholesalers and have been asked by L.R. Naismith & Co. Ltd. of 21 Barnsley Road, Sheffield to offer them open account facilities, with quarterly settlement terms. They have given us your name as a reference.

As you will see from the letter heading, we are a glass manufacturers and have recently begun to export to the UK. D.R. Mitchell & Son, who are customers of yours, have placed an order with us, but want to pay by 30-day bill of exchange, and informed us that you would be prepared to act as their referees.

Your branch of the Eastland Bank was given to us as a reference by I.T.S. Ltd. who have placed a substantial order with us, but want to settle by 40-day draft. As we are a Czech company, we have little knowledge of British companies and their credit ratings.

8.6.2
Details

Say exactly what you want to know.

We would like to know if the firm is credit-worthy and has a good reputation. We would be grateful if you could tell us if the firm is reliable in settling its accounts promptly.

Could you let us know if this firm is capable of repaying a loan of this size within the specified time?

Could you tell us if the firm has a good reputation in your country; whether they can be relied on to settle promptly on due dates; and what limit you would place or have placed on credit when dealing with them?

If the amount of credit is known, it is usually mentioned.

The credit will be about £2,000.

We do not expect the credit to exceed £500.00.

The draft is for £226.00.

It is unlikely that they will ask for more than a £1,000 credit at this stage.

8.6.3
Closing

Thank the firm in advance for giving you the information, and tell them you will reciprocate if the opportunity arises. Also let them know that whatever they say in their letter will be treated in the strictest confidence.

We would like to thank you in advance for the information and can assure you that it will be treated in the strictest confidence.

Your help will be appreciated, and the information will be held in confidence. We will return the service should the opportunity arise.

You can be sure that the information will not be disclosed. Thank you for your assistance, and we will reciprocate in a similar situation in the future.

8.6.4
Using an Enquiry Agency

We have seen that banks and trade associations will usually only give brief references. Business associates may give more information, but see below at 8.7. An Enquiry Agency will give much more detail about a firm's activities, and for a fee, will research the firm's financial background, its standing, credit-worthiness and ability to repay loans or fulfil obligations. When writing to an Enquiry Agency, therefore, you can ask for more.

We have been asked by D.F. Rowlands Ltd. of Milton Trading Estate, Peterborough, to allow them a credit of up to £5,000 in allowing them to settle by quarterly statements. As we have no knowledge of this firm, would it be possible for you to give us detailed information of their trading activities over, say, the past three years?

The firm named on the enclosed slip has written to us asking if we would allow them to settle by 60-day bill of exchange. Our trading with them so far has only been up to £500.00. But as we know nothing about them or their credit-worthiness, would it be possible for you to investigate their business activities over the past few years and give us a detailed report?

8.7
Replying to enquiries about credit rating

In most countries there are laws which protect a firm from having its reputation damaged by another company saying or writing things that could harm the firm's good name, and this should be considered when giving details of a company's credit-worthiness, or commenting on its standing.

8.7.1
Refusing to reply

There are a number of reasons why you may not wish to reply to an enquiry about one of your customers. If, for example, the company writing to you does not state that you have been named as a referee by their customer, and you do not want to risk offending them, it would be better not to make any comment.

Thank you for your letter concerning our customer, but we cannot give you any information until we get permission from the customer himself. So if you can get the person mentioned in your letter to write to us asking us to act as referees we will give you the necessary information.

As we have not been asked by the person mentioned in your letter to write a reference on their behalf we cannot supply any information about them.

If you do not know enough about the company to comment, then it is better to say so.

With reference to the company you mentioned in your letter of 9 October, we are sorry to say we know little about them as we have only supplied them on a couple of occasions. Therefore we cannot give you any details of their trading record or credit standing.

Thank you for your letter which we received today. Unfortunately, we know nothing about the firm you are enquiring about as our only dealings with them have been on a cash basis. We are sorry that we cannot be of help to you in this matter.

Sometimes you may simply not want to give any information about a customer whether you know their reputation or not. In this case a polite refusal, generalizing your statements, is the best course of action.

With reference to your letter of October 16 in which you asked about the credit standing of one of our customers, we are sorry to say that we never give any information about customers to inquirers, and as business associates of ours we are sure you will appreciate that confidence. Perhaps an enquiry agency could be of more help to you in this.

8.7.2
Replying unfavourably

If you have to write an unfavourable reply it is better not to mention the name of the company. Give only the few facts as they concern *you*. Do not offer opinions and remind the firm you are writing to, that the information is strictly confidential.

With reference to your letter of 19 April where you asked us to act as referees for the customer mentioned, we have only dealt with this firm on a few occasions but found they tended to delay payment and had to be reminded several times before their account was cleared. But we have no idea of their trading records with other companies. We are sure you will treat this information in the strictest confidence.

In reply to your letter of 14 September concerning the customer you enquired about, we are sorry to say that we cannot recommend the firm as being reliable in their credit dealings, but this

is only based on our own experiences of trading with them. We offer this information on the strict understanding that it will be treated confidentially.

8.7.3
Replying favourably

If giving a favourable reply it is still wise not to mention the customer's name if possible. You can quote that you have yourself allowed credit facilities and also mention that the customer has a good reputation within your trade. In the examples you will see that the reference should still be considered confidential and that the referee takes no responsibility as to how the information is used.

We are pleased to inform you that the firm mentioned in your letter of 7 November is completely reliable and can be trusted to clear their balances promptly on due dates. We find no reason at all for you not offering the facilities they have asked for. However, we take no responsibility as to how this information is used.

With regard to the company mentioned in your letter of 8 December, we are willing to assure you that they have an excellent reputation in dealing with their suppliers, and though we have not given them the credit they have asked you for, we would allow them those facilities if they approached us. Please treat this information in confidence.

8.8
Specimen letters

8.8.1
Letter to a referee

As notified in 8.5.6, Glaston Potteries take up the reference offered by MacKenzie Bros.

Questions

1 What do Glaston want Pierson to do?
2 Why would Pierson be chosen to do this?
3 How do Glaston reassure Pierson about this information they will give?
4 Find the words in the letter that correspond to the following: *every three months*; *supporters*; *assurance*; *worth*; *payments*?

GLASTON POTTERIES Ltd.

Clayfield, Burnley BB10 1RQ

Tel: 0315 46125
Telex: 8801773
Fax: 0315 63182

Registered No. 716481
VAT Registered No. 133 5341 08

Mr M. Pierson
Pierson & Co.
Louis Drive
Dawson
Ontario
CANADA

16 February 19—

Dear Mr Pierson,

We are suppliers to MacKenzie Bros. Ltd., 1–5 Whale Drive, Dawson, Ontario, who have asked us to give them facilities to settle their statements on a quarterly basis.

They told us that you would be prepared to act as their referees, and while we have little doubt about their ability to clear their accounts, we would just like confirmation that their credit rating warrants quarterly settlements of up to £6,000.

We would be extremely grateful for an early reply, and can assure you that it will be treated in the strictest confidence.

Yours sincerely,

J. Merton

J. Merton
Sales Manager

Pierson & Co.

Louis Drive, Dawson, Ontario, Canada.

Tel: (614) 295 1682   Cable: PIERCO   Telex: 383172

Mr J. Merton   Date: 28 February 19—
Glaston Potteries Ltd.
Clayfield
Burnley BB10 1RQ
UNITED KINGDOM

Dear Mr Merton,

I am replying to your enquiry of the 16 February in which you asked
about MacKenzie Bros. of Dawson, Ontario.

I contacted them yesterday and they confirmed that they wanted us to
act as their referees, and I am pleased to be able to do so.

The firm has an excellent reputation in North America for both service
and the way they conduct their business with their associates in the
trade.

We have given them credit facilities for years and always found that
they paid on due dates without any problems. I might also add that our
credit is in excess of the one mentioned in your letter.

I am sure that you can have every confidence in this firm and offer them
the facilities asked for.

Yours sincerely,

M. Pierson

8.8.2
Referee's reply

Questions

1 What did Mr Pierson do before he
   wrote the reference?
2 What does he think of MacKenzie
   Bros. as a firm?
3 How does he explain that they are
   credit-worthy?
4 What does he mean by 'they paid on
   due dates'?
5 Which words in the letter correspond
   to the following: *got in touch with*;
   assured; *supporters*; *trading
   partners*; *more than*; *trust*?

8.8.3
Letter to a referee

Here is another example of taking up references, this one from Satex, the Italian sweater manufacturer we met in previous units. In the letter at 6.3.4, their customer, F. Lynch & Co., asked to be allowed to settle their accounts by 40–day bill of exchange, documents against acceptance. Lynch & Co. offered references which Satex are taking up.

Satex S.p.A.

Via di Pietra Papa, 00146 Roma

Telefono: Roma 769910
Telefax: (06) 481 5473
Telex: 285136

Mr T. Grover   4 July 19—
Grover Menswear Ltd.
Browns Lane
Rugeley
Staffordshire WS15 1DR

Dear Mr Grover,

Your name was given to us by Mr L. Crane, the chief buyer of F. Lynch & Co. Ltd., Nesson House, Newell Street, Birmingham B3 3EL, who have asked us to allow them to settle their account by 40-day draft.

They told us that you would be prepared to act as their referee. We would be grateful if you could confirm that this company settles promptly on due dates, and are sound enough to meet credits of up to £3,000 in transactions.

Thank you in advance for the information.

Yours sincerely,

D. Causio

D. Causio

Grover Menswear Ltd.

Browns Lane, Rugeley, Staffordshire WS15 1DR

Telephone: 08894 31621   Telex: 246181

Mr D. Causio   9 July 19—
Satex S.p.A.
Via di Pietra Papa
00146 Roma
ITALY

Dear Mr Causio,

We have had confirmation from F. Lynch & Co. Ltd. that they want us to act as referees on their behalf, and can give you the following information.

We have been dealing with the firm for ten years and allow them credit facilities of up to £2,000 which they only use occasionally as they prefer to take advantage of our cash discounts. However, we would have no hesitation in offering them the sort of credit you mentioned, i.e. £3,000, as they are a large reputable organization and very well known in this country.

Of course, we take no responsibility for how you use this information, and would remind you to consider it as confidential.

Yours sincerely,

T. Grover

T. Grover

8.8.4
Referee's reply

Note how Mr Grover says he will take no responsibility for how the information is used, and reminds Satex that the letter is confidential.

Questions
1 What expression is used to mean *for them*?
2 How does Mr Grover explain he will not be liable for Satex's decision?
3 Why does F. Lynch & Co. not use the full credit facilities?
4 What did Mr Grover do before contacting Satex?
5 What word is used to say the information is private?

8.8.5

Negative replies to enquiries about credit rating

1 In this letter, the writer refuses to reply because he does not have the company's permission.

> Dear Mr Stevens,
>
> I am replying to your letter of 10 August in which you asked about one of our mutual business associates.
>
> I am afraid I cannot give you the information you asked for as it would be a breach of confidence, and you, as one of our customers would appreciate this. If however, you can get the firm to write instructing us to act as their referee, then we may be able to help you.
>
> Yours sincerely,

2 The reply in this case is unfavourable. Notice how the writer does not refer to the company by name.

> Dear Mr Scrutton,
>
> I am answering your enquiry about the company mentioned in your letter to me of 3 May.
>
> We have in the past allowed that company credit, but nowhere near the amount you mentioned, and we found they needed at least one reminder before clearing their account.
>
> This information is strictly confidential and we take no responsibility as to how it is used.
>
> Yours sincerely,

3 The writer of this letter is unable to reply because he has little knowledge of the company.

> Dear Mr Cox,
>
> In reply to your letter of 10 August, we cannot offer you any information concerning the firm you asked about in your letter.
>
> We have had very little dealing with them and they have never asked for credit of any kind. Therefore any information we gave would be of no relevance.
>
> Yours sincerely,

P. Marlow & Co. Ltd.

31 Goodge Street, London EC49 4EE

Telephone: 071 583 6119   Registered in England 221359
Fax: 071 583 7125   VAT 240 7225 03

Mr S. Spade   9 April 19—
Credit Investigations Ltd.
1 Bird Street
London E1 6TM

Dear Mr Spade

You were recommended to me by a previous client of yours, S. Greenstreet & Co. Ltd.

I would like information about Falcon Retailers Ltd. who have asked us to allow them open account facilities with quarterly settlements and credits of up to £5,000.

Would you please tell us if this firm has had any bad debts in the past; if any court action has been taken against them to recover overdue accounts; what sort of reputation they have amongst suppliers in the trade; whether they have ever traded under another name, and if they have, whether that business has been subject to bankruptcy proceedings?

Please would you make the necessary enquiries, and let us know your fee, so that we can send you a cheque?

Yours sincerely,

P. Marlow

P. Marlow

8.8.6
Letter to Enquiry Agent

Checking on a customer's credit rating with an Enquiry Agency allows the seller to be more specific about the details he wants concerning his customer.

Questions

1 What credit does the buyer want?
2 Why would the supplier want to know if the firm traded under another name?
3 How does he ask if the firm owed money before?
4 Who told Mr Marlow to contact Mr Spade?
5 Which expressions are used to mean *late payments*; *legal action to close the business*?

8.8.7
Enquiry Agent's reply

Questions

1 Which figure represents Falcon's yearly sales?
2 Have legal proceedings ever been taken against Falcon?
3 Have Falcon ever gone out of business?
4 How many people run that company?
5 Do Falcon pay their debts on due dates?
6 What does Mr Spade think Falcon's problem is?
7 Which words in the letter correspond to the following: *research*; *asked*; *yearly income*; *regain money owed*; *held up*?

CREDIT INVESTIGATIONS Ltd.

1 Bird Street, London E1 6TM

Telephone: 071 623 1494
Fax: 071 623 1965
Reg. London 3121561

Mr P. Marlow   26 April 19—
P. Marlow & Co. Ltd.
31 Goodge Street
London EC49 4EE

Dear Mr Marlow,

We have completed our investigation into Falcon Retailers Ltd, who you enquired about in your letter dated 9 April 19—.

The firm is a private limited company with a registered capital of £1,000 and consists of two partners, David and Peter Lorre. It has an annual turnover of £50,000 and has been trading since October 1971. As far as we know neither the company nor its directors have ever been subject to bankruptcy proceedings, but the firm was involved in a court case to recover an outstanding debt on the 17 January 19—. The action was brought by L.D.M. Ltd. and concerned the recovery of £2,150 which Falcon eventually paid. But we ought to point out that L.D.M. broke a delivery contract which accounted for the delayed payment.

From our general enquiries we gather that some of Falcon's suppliers have had to send them second and third reminders before outstanding balances were cleared, but this does not suggest dishonesty so much as a tendency to overbuy which means the company needs time to sell before they can clear their accounts.

We hope this information proves useful, and if you have any further enquiries, please contact us.

You will find our account for £175.00 enclosed.

Yours sincerely,

S. Spade
Credit Investigations Ltd.

Encl. Account

8.9
Points to remember

1 Credit is only given if the supplier knows his customer well, has a reference from a bank or business associate of his customer, or his customer has an excellent reputation.

2 When asking for credit, say why you want it and convince your supplier that you will pay on due dates. State how long you have been dealing with the company. Offer references to support you.

3 When agreeing to credit, your letter can be short and simple.

4 When refusing credit, you must give reasons and convince your customer that the refusal does not discriminate against him in particular. Using generalizations can help, e.g. *we usually/as a rule/normally/do not offer credit facilities*.

5 When taking up a reference, tell the firm who you are and who you are enquiring about. Tell them the type of credit involved, e.g. bill of exchange, monthly settlements, and let them know how much the credit is for. Assure them that the information will be in confidence and that you will reciprocate should the occasion arise.

6 When writing a favourable reference, let the firm know you are pleased to offer a reference, and tell them why you think the credit should be offered, e.g. that you have been trading with the firm for a long time and have allowed them credit. Tell the firm the information is given in confidence and without responsibility.

7 When writing an unfavourable reply, if you are not sure what you want to say, simply write that you cannot give information about any of your customers. Or, alternatively, be brief, stating only the facts as they concern you, but do not give opinions.

8.10
Words to remember

credit
credit facilities/terms
credit-worthy
credit rating
to ask for credit
to grant credit

a reference
a referee
to offer/take up references
to treat something in confidence
confidential
a reputation
reputable
reciprocate

a due date
to settle an account
settlement against monthly statements
to clear a balance
to default
a bad debt
court action
bankruptcy proceedings

a bill of exchange
a banker's draft
open account facilities
documents against acceptance
profit margins
turnover

Banking

9

Banks in the UK; commercial bank facilities (current accounts, deposit accounts, credit cards, standing orders, loans and overdrafts); international banking; bills of exchange; documentary credits.

9.1
Banks in the UK

These can be divided into two groups: merchant banks and commercial banks.

Merchant banks tend to encourage larger organizations to use their services, and while the facilities they offer are similar to those of the commercial banks, the former specialize in areas of international trade and finance, discounting bills, confirming credit status of overseas customers through confirming houses, acting in the new issue market (placing shares), and in the bullion and Euro-bond market. They are, in addition, involved in shipping, insurance, and foreign exchange markets. Brown Shipley, Hambros, Keyser Ullmann, Schroders, etc. are merchant banking houses.

Commercial banks offer similar services but are particularly interested in private customers' accounts, encouraging them to use their current account, deposit account, savings account, and credit facilities. They will lend money, against securities, in the forms of overdrafts and loans, pay accounts regularly by standing orders, and transfer credits through the bank Giro system. Essentially the difference between the merchant and commercial banks is the latter's availability to customers with their numerous branches throughout the UK, their low charges, and the laws which govern the way each organization handles its affairs. The 'big four' commercial banks are Barclays, Lloyds, Midland, and National Westminster.

9.2
Commercial bank facilities in the UK

9.2.1
Current accounts

Current accounts can be used by anyone in the UK provided they can supply a reference or references. The advantages of this account include cheque payments, if there are funds in the account. As a matter of extra security the customer, when paying by cheque, is required to provide a *cheque card*, which makes the bank responsible for the cheque passed, up to the limit stated on the card.

The card also acts as a *cash card* allowing money to be drawn from *cash dispensers* even when the bank is closed.

Although cheques can be drawn immediately, they will take three working days before the amount is debited or credited to an account.

When depositing cash or cheques, a *paying-in slip* is used to record the deposit, its *counterfoil*, with the bank's stamp and cashier's initials, being proof that the deposit was made.

It is possible to *overdraw* an account, i.e. take out more money than there is in credit, but this can only be done with the bank manager's agreement, otherwise the customer's cheque may not be honoured. However, many banks offer special current accounts where overdraft facilities are automatically included, for an extra charge.

As a rule interest is not paid on current account credit balances and charges are made for transactions. However, there are special current accounts, which have certain requirements, e.g. a minimum balance, and minimum amount for cheques being passed, which offer interest.

Many firms have more than one current account, e.g. a No. 1 account for paying wages and overheads, and a No. 2 account for paying suppliers.

9.2.2
Deposit accounts

Deposit accounts do pay interest to a maximum established by the bank, but the customer can be asked to give notice of withdrawal, and can only withdraw on a *withdrawal slip* handed in at the branch where the account is kept. No cheque book is supplied, and there are no overdraft facilities.

Banks offer various types of other accounts, e.g. a budget account, where the bank will pay a customer's bills spread over a twelve-month period. And there are numerous savings accounts on which interest is paid according to the credit balance in the account and the period it is left for. With some of these accounts there are penalties for withdrawing money before the agreed date.

9.2.3
Credit cards

Credit cards offer credit facilities to customers making purchases in shops, and for a basic charge plus interest, calculated monthly, the customers can buy goods up to a limit on most cards, but with, say, a *Barclay's Premier Card*, the limit can be over £7,000. *Access,*

Barclaycard, and *Visa* are internationally recognized. Some of these cards, such as *Barclay's Connect* act as a cheque and cash card, and can be used for automatic debiting when a customer pays for goods in a shop. this card is also internationally recognized.

9.2.4

Standing orders and direct debits

Customers making regular payments, such as rent, or mortgage repayments, can ask the bank to transfer the money to the payee on a particular day every month. A standing order or direct debit is one method of doing this. In the latter case, however, once the instructions are given, for, say a period of a year, the order cannot be cancelled unless the payee agrees.

9.2.5

Loans and overdrafts

Loans and overdrafts for large amounts are usually allowed on a formal agreement. A loan will usually be covered by a *negotiable security*, e.g. shares, with repayment specified on the agreement. Interest in the UK is not controlled by law, but market forces. The money for a loan is immediately deposited in the customer's account. With an overdraft, however, the customer is given permission to overdraw an account up to a certain limit.

Since the early 1980s, banks have had more freedom in lending and investing. *Mortgages*, for example, once the privilege of the Building Societies, who specialized in lending money to customers to buy houses, are now

offered by banks, with the bank buying the property for the customer and the customer repaying over a twenty/ twenty-five-year period. In addition, there is a wide range of other financial and investment services the banks offer. However, unlike most banks in the world, the UK banks do not generally act as *brokers/dealers* on the Stock Market for customers, but will use their own broker to buy securities on a customer's behalf.

The other services the banks offer include acting as trustees and executors, offering insurance, foreign exchange, and discounting services, and negotiating documents.

9.3
Specimen letters

9.3.1
Administrative letters

A *Opening a current account*
The owner of a fashion shop applies to open a current account. The bank manager will acknowledge the letter, telling the customer that the account has been opened and the money credited, and either enclose a cheque book or let her know that one is being made up for her.

Dear Mr Day,

I am writing to you with reference to our conversation three days ago when we discussed my opening a current account with your branch.

I would appreciate it if you could open a current a/c for me under my trading name R & S Fashions Ltd., 915 East Street, Brighton, Sussex. Enclosed you will find two specimen signatures, my own and my partner's, Miss Catherine Sidden. Both signatures will be required on all cheques. I have included a reference from Mr Young, who banks with your branch, a cheque for £57.00 from a customer, and a paying-in slip which I picked up in the bank the other day.

Yours sincerely,

B *Change of signature*
The bank must be informed of any change of address and, as here, of a change in the signatures required on cheques.

Dear Mr Winston,

Will you please note that as from 11 August 19— the two signatures that will appear on cheques for our number 1 and 2 accounts will be mine and that of our new accountant Mr Harold Lloyd, who is taking over from Mr David Story

I enclose a specimen of Mr Lloyd's signature and look forward to your acknowledgement.

Yours sincerely,

C *Request for a standing order*

Dear Sir,

Account No. 33152 110 9501

We have just moved to new premises at the above address and would like to pay our monthly rent of £574.00 to our landlords, Richards & Long, 30 Blare Street, London SW7 1LN, by standing order.

Would you please arrange for £574.00 to be transferred from our No. 2 account to their account with Dewlands Bank, Leadenhall Street, London EC2, on the 1st of every month, beginning 1 May this year?

Please confirm that the arrangement has been made.

Yours faithfully,

Dear Sir,

Please would you cancel cheque No. 17892165001 for £1,672 in favour of B. Gelt Ltd? The cheque appears to have been lost in the post and I am sending another in its place.

Yours faithfully,

D *Cancellation of a cheque*
Cancelling a cheque must be done in writing, not on the phone. Banks are obliged to pay cheques if the payer has funds in his current account, so the bank will want written proof to protect them.

E *Transfer of money from current account to deposit account*

Dear Mr Collis,

Please would you transfer £2,500 from my current account to my deposit account? The account numbers and details are on the enclosed transfer slip, and I would be grateful if you could stamp the counterfoil and return it to me.

Yours sincerely,

9.3.2
Advice of an overdrawn account

Banks prefer not to stop payments because of the embarrassment it can cause the customer, but if there has not been an arrangement for overdraft facilities, and the cheque, in the bank manager's opinion, is too large, he will stop it. In the case of Mr Hughes, however, the bank manager lets the credit transfer go through.

Questions

1 Why has the bank manager passed Mr Hughes' cheque although it led to an overdraft?
2 What does he advise Mr Hughes to do if he wants an overdraft in future?
3 How does he suggest Mr Hughes corrects the overdraft?

Welsh Co-operative Bank

Chairman: A.C.M. Conway   Directors: R.M. Lloyd, C.R. Gymre A.I.S.
Seaway House, Glendower Road, Swansea, Glamorgan 8RN 1TA

Reg. No.: Swansea 385 1623

Telephone: (0792) 469008 (10 lines)
Telex: 84903
Fax: (0792) 431726

Mr R. Hughes   8 August 19—
R. Hughes & Son Ltd.
21 Mead Road
Swansea
Glamorgan 3ST 1DR

Dear Mr Hughes,

Account No. 0566853 01362

I am writing to inform you that you now have an overdraft of £158.63 on your current account.

I allowed your last credit transfer to Homemakers Ltd. to pass as you have a large credit balance on your deposit account. But I would point out that we cannot allow overdraft facilities unless you make a formal arrangement with the bank. If you would like to do this, please contact me and we can discuss it. Alternatively, would you make sure that your current account is in credit? Thank you.

Yours sincerely,

D. Collis
Manager

R. Hughes & Son Ltd.

21 Mead Road, Swansea, Glamorgan 3ST 1DR

Telephone: Swansea 58441   VAT No. 215 2261 30
Telex: 881821

The Manager   10th August 19—
Welsh Co-operative Bank
Seaway House
Glendower Road
Swansea
Glamorgan 8RN 1TA

Dear Mr Collis,

Thank you for your letter of 8th August. Please allow me to apologize for my oversight in not realizing I had a debit balance on my current account.

The reason I did not realize I had overdrawn my account was because I had received a post-dated cheque for £300.00 from a customer which had not been cleared. However, to avoid a repetition I have transferred £500.00 from my deposit account and this should ensure against overdrawing in future.

Thank you for allowing the credit transfer to Homemakers to go through despite the debit balance it created.

Yours sincerely,

R. Hughes

9.3.3
Reply to advice of an overdrawn account

Mr Hughes is aware that the credit transfer could have been stopped, which would have been embarrassing to him, especially as he had arranged monthly settlements with Homemakers only recently (see 8.5.1 and 8.5.2) and there had earlier been a problem over a credit transfer (see 6.6.5 and 6.6.6).

Questions

1 Why had Mr Hughes overdrawn his account?
2 How does he make sure it won't happen again?
3 What does 'oversight' mean?
4 Why hadn't the £300.00 cheque been cleared?

9.3.4
Request for an overdraft or loan

In this letter Mr Cliff of Homemakers Ltd. wants to obtain either an overdraft or loan to expand his furniture factory. He asks for an appointment to discuss the matter, and explains why he needs the money.

Questions

1 What new line does Mr Cliff want to put on the market?
2 Why does he need the loan or overdraft?
3 Why is he sure he can repay the loan?
4 What evidence does he offer to show his company is in a healthy state?
5 What security is he offering?
6 What is a balance sheet?
7 Which words in the letter correspond to the following: *talk about*; *enlarge*; *put together*; *gone further*; *meet (orders)*; *assess*; *checked (by an accountant)*?

HOMEMAKERS Ltd.

54–59 Riverside, Cardiff CF1 1JW

Telephone: (0222) 49721
Telex: 38217

Registered No. C135162

The Manager   18 September 19—
Barnley's Bank Ltd.
Queens Building
Cathays Park
Cardiff CF1 9UJ

Dear Mr Evans,

I would like to make an appointment to see you to discuss either a loan or overdraft to enable me to expand my business.

Over the past year I have been testing the market with a new line – furniture assembly kits – and have found that demand for these kits, both here and overseas, has exceeded my expectations. In the past six months alone I have had over £60,000 worth of orders, half of which I could not fulfil because of my limited resources.

I will need a loan for about £8,000 to buy additional equipment and raw materials. I can offer £2,000 in IBM ordinary shares, and £3,000 in local government bonds as part security for the loan, which I estimate will take me about nine months to repay.

I enclose an audited copy of the company's current balance sheet, which I imagine you will wish to inspect, and I look forward to hearing from you.

Yours sincerely,

R. Cliff

Encl.

BARNLEY'S BANK Ltd

Chairman: B. Davenport F.I.D.	Telephone: (0222) 825316	Head Office:
Directors: B.R. Lewin V.C., D.F.C., C.I.S.	Telex: 841132	Queens Building
A.L. Brodwin A.I.C.A.	Fax: (0222) 613625	Cathays Park
N. CHARDIS	Reg. No: Cardiff 3516614	Cardiff
		CF1 9UJ

Mr R. Cliff   Date: 27 September 19—
Homemakers Ltd.
54–59 Riverside
Cardiff CF1 1JW

Dear Mr Cliff,

With reference to our meeting on 23 September, I am pleased to tell you that the credit for £8,000 which you requested has been approved.

I know we discussed an overdraft, but I think it would be better if the credit were given in the form of a loan at the current rate of interest which is 15 per cent, and which will be calculated on half-yearly balances.

The loan must be repaid by June 19— and we will hold the £2,000 IBM ordinary shares and £3,000 local government bonds you pledged as security. We agreed that the other £3,000 was to be guaranteed by Mr. Y. Morgan, your business associate, and I would appreciate it if you could ask him to sign the enclosed guarantor's form, and if you would sign the attached agreement.

The money will be credited to your current account and available from September 30 subject to your returning both forms by that time.

I wish you luck with the expansion of your business and look forward to hearing from you.

Yours sincerely,

I. Evans
Manager

Encls.

9.3.5
Grant of a loan

The bank manager has now seen Mr Cliff and checked his accounts to make sure that the business has been doing as well as the owner said. He has considered the matter of the overdraft or loan, and is now replying.

Questions

1 Is the bank manager going to give Mr Cliff an *overdraft?*
2 If he is not giving him an overdraft what has he suggested?
3 What does the bank manager propose to do as there is not sufficient security to cover the credit?
4 Who is Mr Y. Morgan?
5 How is the interest on the credit to be charged?
6 When will the credit be available from?
7 Which account will the loan be paid into?
8 Which words used in the letter correspond to the following: *paid back*; *promised*; *someone known in business*; *contract?*

9.3.6
Refusal of an overdraft

Mr Ellison's company owns a chain of petrol stations and garages. He is also a customer of Barnley's Bank and has also asked for an overdraft, but in his case the bank is not willing to lend him the money.

Questions

1 What two things have influenced the bank manager's decision not to allow a credit in this case?
2 Why did Mr Ellison want the credit?
3 Was the bank manager sympathetic?
4 Did he offer an alternative which might help Mr Ellison raise the money?

BARNLEY'S BANK Ltd

Chairman: B. Davenport F.I.D.
Directors: B.R. Lewin V.C., D.F.C., C.I.S.
A.L. Brodwin A.I.C.A.
N. CHARDIS

Telephone: (0222) 825316
Telex: 841132
Fax: (0222) 613625
Reg. No: Cardiff 3516614

Head Office:
Queens Building
Cathays Park
Cardiff
CF1 9UJ

Mr P. Ellison
Ellison & Co. Ltd.
Bridgend Road
Bridgend IF31 3DF

Date: 19 November 19—

Dear Mr Ellison,

I am sorry to inform you that we will not be able to offer the credit you asked for in your letter of 14 November.

You have had an overdraft in the past year which partly influenced our decision, but there is also a credit squeeze at present which has particularly affected loans to the service sector of the economy. I sympathize with you when you say that you have been offered a rare opportunity to expand your business if you can secure the £15,000 additional capital. With regard to this, may I suggest that if there are no other possibilities for you to raise the money, perhaps you could approach a Finance Corporation who might be willing to help.

I am sorry that we have to disappoint you in this matter, and hope that we may be of more help in the future.

Yours sincerely,

I. Evans
Manager

9.4
International banking

At 6.2.2 we looked at various methods of payment used in foreign trade. In this section we look in detail at two methods of payment, bills of exchange and documentary credits, and the way in which they involve banks at home and abroad.

9.5
Bills of exchange

A bill of exchange is an order sent by the *drawer* (the person asking for the money) to the *drawee* (the person paying) stating that the drawee will pay on demand or at a specified time the amount shown on the bill. If the drawee accepts the bill, he will sign his name on the face of it and date it. See 9.6.2.

The bill can be paid to a bank named by the drawer, or the drawee can name a bank he wants to use to clear the bill, as happens at 9.6.2. If this is the case, the bill will be kept in the drawer's bank until it is to be paid. When the bill is due it is presented to the paying bank. Such bills are said to be *domiciled* with the bank holding them.

A *sight draft* or *sight bill* is paid on presentation. In a *documents against payment* (D/P) transaction, the sight draft is presented to the importer with the shipping documents, and the importer pays immediately, i.e. 'on presentation' or 'at sight'.

A bill paid 'after date' or 'after sight' can be paid on or within the number of days specified on the bill. Therefore, '30 days after sight' means that the bill can be paid 30 days after it has been presented.

Overseas bills in the UK are known as *foreign bills*, and those used within the UK as *inland bills*. A *clean bill* is one that is not accompanied by shipping documents.

The advantage for the exporter of payment by bill is that the draft can be *discounted*, i.e. sold, to a bank at a percentage less than its value, the percentage being decided by the current market rates of discounting. So even if the bill is marked 90 days, the exporter can get his money immediately. The advantage for the importer is that he is given credit, provided the bill is not a sight draft. The bank, however, will only discount a bill if the buyer has a good reputation.

Bills can be negotiable if the drawer *endorses* the bill. If Mr Panton, the *beneficiary* of the bill at 9.6.2, wanted to pay another manufacturer, he could write on the back of the bill, i.e. endorse it, and the bill would become payable to the person who owned it. Mr Panton can *endorse* it *specifically*, i.e. make it payable only to the person named on the bill.

It is possible to send the bill direct to the importer, if he is well known to the exporter, or if not, to his bank which will hand it to him with the documents for either acceptance or payment.

A *dishonoured* bill is one that is not paid on the *due date*. In this case the exporter will *protest* the bill, i.e. he will go to a *notary*, a lawyer, who will, after a warning, take legal action to recover the debt.

The abbreviations B/E for bill of exchange and d/s for days after sight are often used. And you are now familiar with D/P, documents against payment and D/A, documents against acceptance.

9.6
Specimen letters and
form: bill of exchange
transactions

9.6.1
Letter advising despatch of a bill

Panton Manufacturing Ltd. have
completed an order for a Dutch
customer. They now advise him that the
agreed bill of exchange has been sent
off.

Questions

1 Where has the b/e been sent?
2 When should the bill be paid?
3 How can Mrs Haas get the shipping
documents?

Panton Manufacturing Ltd.

Panton Works, Hounslow, Middlesex, TW6 2BQ

Tel: 081 353 0125   Registered No. England 266135
Telex: 21511
Fax: 081 353 6783

Mrs B. Haas,   2nd March 19—
B. Haas B. V.,
Heldringstraat 180–2,
Postbus 5411,
Amsterdam 1007,
NETHERLANDS

Dear Mrs Haas,

<u>Order No. 8842</u>

Thank you for your order which has now been completed and is being sent
to you today.

As agreed we have forwarded our bill, No. 1671 for £860.00 with the
documents to your bank, Nederlandsbank, Heldringstraat, Amsterdam.
The draft has been made out for payment 30 days after sight, and the
documents will be handed to you on acceptance.

Yours sincerely,

D. Panton

D. Panton
Managing Director

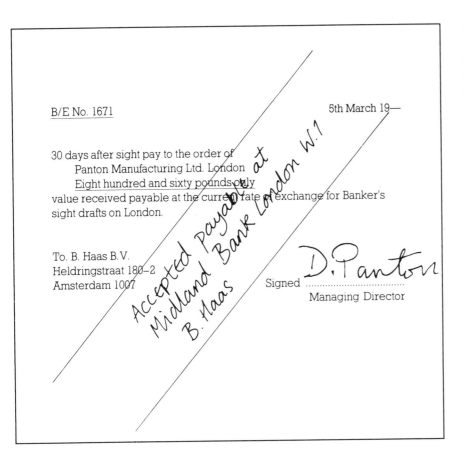

B/E No. 1671   5th March 19—

30 days after sight pay to the order of
    Panton Manufacturing Ltd. London
    Eight hundred and sixty pounds only
value received payable at the current rate of exchange for Banker's
sight drafts on London.

To. B. Haas B.V.
Heldringstraat 180–2
Amsterdam 1007

Signed ....
                                        Managing Director

Accepted payable at Midland Bank London W.1
B. Haas

D. Panton

9.6.2
Bill of exchange

Here is the bill mentioned in the previous
letter. The bill has already been
accepted by the drawee, who has
named a bank in London which she
wants to use to clear the bill.

Questions

1 What type of draft is this?
2 How much is it for?
3 Who is the payee?
4 When must the draft be paid?
5 What is the rate of exchange?

9.6.3
Letter advising despatch of a sight draft

The bill at 9.6.2 was for payment 30 days after sight. If the supplier wants immediate payment or does not have time to check the customer's credit-worthiness, he may send a sight draft, as in this example.

Panton Manufacturing Ltd.

Panton Works, Hounslow, Middlesex, TW6 2BQ

Tel: 081 353 0125
Telex: 21511
Fax: 081 353 6783

Registered No. England 266135

Mr J. Lindquvist,   10th June 19—
Lindquvist A.S.,
Vestergade 190–2,
DK 1171,
Copenhagen K,
DENMARK

Dear Mr Lindquvist,

We have made up your order, No. 8540, which is now aboard the <u>SS Leda</u> which sails for Copenhagen tomorrow.

We are sure you will be pleased with the selection of items that we were able to get from stock. As there was no time to check references, we have drawn a sight draft which will be sent to Nordbank, Garnes Vej, Copenhagen, and will be presented to you with the documents for payment.

If you can supply two references before placing your next order, we will put the transaction on a documents against acceptance basis with payment 30 days after sight.

Yours sincerely,

D. Panton

D. Panton
Managing Director

Panton Manufacturing Ltd.

Panton Works, Hounslow, Middlesex, TW6 2BQ

Tel: 081 353 0125
Telex: 21511
Fax: 081 353 6783

Registered No. England 266135

The Manager,
Midland Bank Ltd.,
Portman House,
Great Portland Street,
London W1N 6LL

4th July 19—

Dear Sir,

Please would you send the enclosed draft on J.K.B. Products Pty. and documents to the National Australian Bank, 632 George Street, Sydney, Australia, and tell them to release the documents on acceptance.

Yours faithfully,

D. Panton

D. Panton
Managing Director

Encl.

9.6.4
Request to a bank to forward a bill

Exporters sometimes ask their banks to forward bills to importers' banks.

9.6.5
Request to a bank to accept a bill

The Australian importer mentioned in the previous letter now writes to his bankers to tell them to accept the bill.

J.K.B. Products Pty.

President: D. Bruce   Managing Director: L. Thompson   Directors: I.R. Marsh, T.L. Bradman
Bridge House, 183–9 Kent Street, Sydney NSW 2000

Telephone: 02 279611
Telex: 212160

Date: 18 July 19—

The Manager
National Australian Bank
632 George Street
Sydney NSW 2000

Dear Sir,

You will shortly be receiving a bill of exchange for £2,163 and relevant documents from Panton Manufacturing Ltd., England. Would you please accept the draft on our behalf, send us the documents, and debit our account?

Yours faithfully,

L. Corey

L. Corey
J.K.B. Products Pty.

Panton Manufacturing Ltd.

Panton Works, Hounslow, Middlesex, TW6 2BQ

Tel: 081 353 0125   Registered No. England 266135
Cables: PANMAN
Telex: 21511
Fax: 081 353 6783

Mrs B. Haas,   10th April 19—
B. Haas B. V.,
Heldringstraat 180–2
Postbus 5411
Amsterdam 1007
NETHERLANDS

Dear Mrs Haas,

B/E No. 1671

The above bill for £860.00 was returned to us from our bank this morning marked 'Refer to Drawer'.

The bill was due on the 5th April and appears to have been dishonoured. We are prepared to allow you a further three days before presenting it to the bank again, in which time we hope that the draft will have been met.

If the account is still not settled, we will have to make a formal protest, which we hope will not be necessary.

Yours sincerely,

D. Panton

D. Panton
Managing Director

9.6.6
Non-payment of a bill

If a customer cannot pay a bill, he must inform his supplier immediately; there is an example of this at 6.6.3. When a bill is not paid and no notice has been given, the supplier usually writes to the customer before protesting the draft, as here. Note the expression 'Refer to Drawer' which means the bank is returning the bill to the drawer. (This expression is also used when a dishonoured cheque is returned.) Also notice that a formal protest is to be made, which means that the drawer will contact a lawyer to handle the debt, if payment is not made within the specified time.

9.7
Documentary credits

A bill of exchange might not be honoured, as we saw at 9.6.6, or the order might be cancelled. But a letter of credit is a more binding method of payment.

Letters of credit (L/C) have been used for centuries in one form or another to enable travellers to obtain money from overseas banks. The process begins with the traveller asking his bank to open a letter of credit in his favour, i.e. for him, for a specific amount which is debited to his account. The bank then drafts a letter which will allow him to draw money on overseas banks with whom the home bank has an agreement. The foreign banks will then draw on the home bank to recover their payments.

This method of obtaining money has now generally been replaced by Euro cheques, traveller's cheques, and credit cards. But documentary credits – *letters of credit accompanied by documents* – are widely used in the import/export trade.

There are two types of documentary credit: *revocable*, i.e. those that can be cancelled, and *irrevocable*, i.e. those that cannot be cancelled. The second type is more common in overseas business transactions.

The stages in an irrevocable documentary credit transaction are as follows:

1 The *importer* agrees to pay by documentary credit, and tells his bank that he will do so by completing an application form (see 9.8.2) which names the exporter and states: the amount to be paid; the documents concerned; what the consignment consists of; whether the shipment is c.i.f., f.o.b., etc.; details of despatch and any other documents involved, e.g. certificate of origin, consular invoice, certificate of quality; and the length of time the credit will be available. The availability of the credit should take account of how much time it will take to prepare and ship the goods.

2 The *importer's bank* will then select a bank in the exporter's country to act as its *agent*, and will notify them that the credit has been opened.

3 The *agent bank* will notify the exporter that a credit has been opened, and they may add their own confirmation, i.e. they will promise to see that the conditions of payment against the documents will be fulfilled. If they confirm the letter, the L/C is known as a *confirmed credit* and the agent bank as the *confirming bank*.

4 The *exporter* ships the goods before the credit expires and sends the shipping documents (bill of lading, insurance certificate, invoice, etc.) to the *agent bank* who check the documents against the conditions and pay him; or they may have asked him to draw a bill of exchange on them, and will discount the bill for him so that he can get his money immediately.

5 The *agent bank* will then send the documents and debit the importer's bank with the cost and charges, which are calculated as a percentage of the total amount of the invoice, plus an extra charge if the letter is confirmed.

6 The *importer's bank* then checks the documents, pays the agent bank, and sends the documents to the importer so that he can claim the goods.

N. Z. Business Machines Pty.

100, South Street, Wellington
Directors: C.M. Perimann, L.F. Drozin

Telephone: 444 8617
Telex: 60184 BUSMAC
Fax: 444 3186

The Manager
New Zealand Bank
Takapuna House
Takapuna Street
Wellington 8

Date: 3 May 19—

Dear Sir,

Please open an irrevocable documentary credit for £22,000 in favour of
Delta Computers Ltd., England. I have enclosed your application form with
all the relevant details completed.

Please inform me when you have made arrangements with your agents in
London.

Yours faithfully,

M. Tanner

M. Tanner
N.Z. Business Machines Pty.

Encl. Application for documentary credit

9.8
Specimen letters and forms: a documentary credit transaction (1)

This section contains the correspondence and forms in a documentary credit transaction of the type described in 9.7.

9.8.1
From the importer to his bank

The importer writes to his bank opening the credit.

9.8.2

Application form for documentary credit

Here is a specimen application form. The form filled in by Mr Tanner for his bank in New Zealand will have been similar to this.

APPLICATION FOR DOCUMENTARY CREDIT—WITHOUT FULL CASH COVER Date

To

FOR BANK USE ONLY

	Branch Reference
BARCLAYS BANK PLC Branch	

BARCLAYS BANK INTERNATIONAL LIMITED		Branch
Customer	Customer's Reference	International Ref.

Beneficiary(ies)   NAME
                   ADDRESS

To be advised through/established with your Correspondents in

Please request Barclays Bank International Limited to open on *my/our behalf their *revocable/irrevocable credit by (a) air-mail/cable with *brief/full details at   rate, in favour of the above named beneficiary(ies) for *up to/about
say

available against *his/their drafts drawn on Barclays Bank International Limited or their Correspondents at
sight for   per cent. of the (b)   invoice value and
accompanied by the following documents:

Signed INVOICES (c)

Full set of clean on board blank endorsed Shipping Company's BILLS OF LADING, marked notify:

Short Form Bills of Lading *are/are not acceptable

*INSURANCE will be arranged by me/us and I/we engage on demand to place in your hands duly endorsed in blank a Policy or Certificate of Insurance approved by you.

*INSURANCE Policy or Certificate (in duplicate) endorsed in blank for the invoice value of the goods plus   per
cent. covering Marine and War Risks (d):

OTHER DOCUMENTS

covering the following GOODS

To be shipped from   to
not later than
Partshipments *permitted/prohibited   Transhipments *permitted/prohibited
Documents to be presented within   days of *shipment/despatch/taking in charge
This credit to be available for negotiation or payment abroad until   inclusive.
FURTHER INSTRUCTIONS

In consideration of your so doing I/we hereby authorise you at maturity of such draft(s), or on presentation if drawn at sight, to debit my/our account and hereby engage to provide you with the funds to meet such draft(s) on presentation to you at sight or three days before maturity in the case of acceptances.

IF APPLICABLE PLEASE INDICATE

☐ Forward Contract: Rate _____ Maturity _____ Total Amount _____
☐ C.F.C. Account

SUBJECT TO UNIFORM CUSTOMS AND PRACTICE FOR DOCUMENTARY CREDITS (1974 REVISION). INTERNATIONAL CHAMBER OF COMMERCE BROCHURE No. 290.

To provide you with your margin of security you are authorised to debit *my/our account with £   to be accounted to me/us when all your claims in respect of the above credit have been satisfied

It is understood that where any drafts are drawn in a currency other than in English sterling, your demand on me/us for reimbursement will be calculated, unless you shall previously agree to the contrary, at your selling rate of exchange for the currency concerned on the day you effect payment or receive advice from your branch or correspondent that payment has been made, and that interest, where applicable, from the date of payment by your branch or correspondent, until the reimbursement currency is at your disposal will be for my/our account

The Bank and its Correspondents are not to be responsible for the genuineness, correctness or form of any document or documents or any endorsement thereon, nor in the event of any misrepresentation as to the quantity, quality or value of any goods comprised therein nor for the Shippers' charges on any such goods

In the case of the insurance not being arranged to the satisfaction of the Bank the Bank is authorised to effect such insurance, the cost of which insurance I/we engage to pay and the amount insured is to be held as available to the Bank until payment of your disbursement(s) under this credit

It is understood that after due payment of such disbursement(s) with the cost of insurance and any other expenses incurred by the Bank in connection with

the shipment concerned, the relative documents as and when received by you are to be given up to me/us provided all other disbursement(s) due, cost of insurance and expenses shall have been paid. In the event of my/our failing to provide for such disbursement(s) and of the Bank selling the relative goods, which it is hereby fully authorised to do I/we undertake to pay on demand the amount of any deficiency on such sale, together with *all usual commission, charges and expenses whether incidental thereto or otherwise

If the above instructions request you to establish the credit by cable I/we shall feel obliged by your transmitting such instructions entirely at my/our risk, through your Correspondents or otherwise, either literally or in cypher, it being understood that the choice as to the most suitable method of transmitting the instructions lies in your discretion and that you are not to be held liable for any irregularity, delay, mistake or omission which may occur in the transmission of the message, or for its non-receipt, or for its misinterpretation when received, and that in case of either incorrect payment or over payment by reason of any such error, you will hold me/us responsible for the amount thus paid in excess or otherwise

SIGNATURE OF CUSTOMER

Registered in London, England, Reg. No. 4883v Reg. Office. 54 Lombard Street, London, EC3P 3AH

NOTES

*Delete as appropriate; all deletions and alterations to be initialled.
(a) Unless otherwise stated sent by airmail.
(b) Insert C.I.F., C. & F., F.O.B., etc. as required.
(c) Import licence number should be quoted when relevant.
(d) Insert other risks and/or clause required, eg. S.R. & C.C., warehouse to warehouse, etc.

N. Z. Business Machines Pty.

100, South Street, Wellington
Directors: C.M. Perimann, L.F. Drozin

Telephone: 444 8617
Telex: 60184 BUSMAC
Fax: 444 3186

Mr G. James
Delta Computers Ltd.
Bradfield Estate   Date: 5 May 19—
Bradfield Road
Wellingborough
Northamptonshire NN8 4HB
UNITED KINGDOM

Dear Mr James,

Thank you for replying to our enquiry of 19 April and letting us know that
the C2000 computers, Cat. No. D16 are available.

The terms you quoted are quite satisfactory, and you will find our order,
8815, enclosed. We have instructed our bank, New Zealand Bank,
Takapuna Street, Wellington, to open an irrevocable letter of credit for
£22,000 in your favour. This should cover c.i.f. shipment and bank charges,
and the credit is valid until 10 June 19—.

You will receive confirmation from our bank's agents Eastland Bank Ltd.,
401 Aldgate, London EC1, and you may draw on them at 60 days for the
amount of the invoice. When submitting your draft, would you please
enclose the following documents?

Bill of lading (6 copies)
Invoice c.i.f. Wellington (4 copies)
A.R. Insurance Policy for £24,200

Please fax or telex us as soon as you have arranged shipment.

Yours sincerely,

M. Tanner

M. Tanner
N.Z. Business Machines Pty.

Encl: Order 8815

9.8.3
From the importer to the exporter

At the same time as opening the credit
at his bank, who will notify their agents
in London, the importer writes to his
supplier.

Questions

1 Which words are used to mean *for
  you*, and *hand over*?
2 When does the credit expire?
3 What should the beneficiary do to get
  the money?
4 What sort of shipment is this?
5 Who is the confirming bank?

9.8.4

From the agent bank to the exporter

Eastland Bank, London, who are the agents for the New Zealand Bank, now inform Delta Computers that the credit has been opened for them. The documents listed in the letter are the essential shipping documents. But they could also have included a *customs form*; a *certificate of origin*, i.e. a certificate stating that the goods or their materials are of a particular origin, and used to claim preferential duty or special allowances; a *consular invoice*, which is an invoice, or sometimes a stamp on the commercial invoice, issued by the importing country's consul giving permission for the goods to be imported; *a certificate of inspection*, i.e. a certificate signed by agents to ensure the customer is getting goods of the type and quality he ordered; *a health certificate.*

Eastland Bank

401 Aldgate, London EC1
Telephone: 071 635 2217 (10 lines)
Fax: 071 635 2226

Chairman: Lord Seaforth
Managing Director: I.P. Raimer
Directors: R. Lichen M.Sc., B.A., S.D. Harrisman O.B.E., P.R. Akermann B.Sc., N.L. Renut

Delta Computers Ltd.   15 May 19—
Bradfield Estate
Bradfield Road
Wellingborough
Northamptonshire NN8 4HB

Dear Sir,

Please find enclosed a copy of the notification we received yesterday from the New Zealand Bank, Wellington, to open an irrevocable letter of credit in your favour for £22,000 which will be available until 10 June 19—.

You may draw on us at 60 days against the credit as soon as you provide evidence of shipment. Would you include with the draft the following documents?
Bill of lading (six copies)
Commercial invoice c.i.f. Wellington (four copies)
A.R. Insurance certificate for £24,200.

Your draft should include our discount commission which is five per cent, and our charges listed on the attached sheet.

Yours faithfully,

P. Medway

P. Medway
Documentary Credits Department

Enc. Irrevocable Credit No. 2/345/16

BARCLAYS International

Barclays Bank International Limited
168 Fenchurch Street, London, EC3P 3HP.

date 20th July 19..

DOCUMENTARY CREDITS DEPARTMENT

SPECIMEN

IRREVOCABLE CREDIT No:- FDC/2/6789
To be quoted on all drafts and correspondence.

Beneficiary(ies)	Advised through
Speirs and Wadley Limited, Adderley Road, Hackney, London, E.8.	
Accreditor Woldal Incorporated, PO Box 666, Broadway Hong Kong	To be completed only if applicable Our cable of Advised through — Refers

Dear Sir(s)

In accordance with instructions received from The Downtown Bank & Trust Co.
we hereby issue in your favour a Documentary Credit for £4108
(say) Four thousand, one hundred and eight pounds sterling available by your drafts
drawn on us

at sight
for the 100% c.i.f. invoice value, accompanied by the following documents:-

1. Signed Invoice in triplicate.
2. Full set of clean on board Shipping Company's Bills of Lading made out to order and blank endorsed, marked "Freight Paid" and "Notify Woldal Inc., PO Box 666, Broadway, Hong Kong."
3. Insurance Policy or Certificate in duplicate, covering Marine and War Risks up to buyer's warehouse, for invoice value of the goods plus 10%.

Covering the following goods:-

400 Electric Power Drills

To be shipped from London to Hong Kong c.i.f.

not later than 10th August 19..

Partshipment not permitted Transhipment not permitted

The credit is available for presentation to us until 31st August 19..

Documents to be presented within 21 days of shipment but within credit validity.

Drafts drawn hereunder must be marked "Drawn under Barclays Bank International Limited 168 Fenchurch Street London branch, Credit number FDC/2/6789"

We undertake that drafts and documents drawn under and in strict conformity with the terms of this credit will be honoured upon presentation.

Yours faithfully,

Co-signed (Signature No. 9347) Signed (Signature No. 10247)

CRE 202 (replacing CRE 83, 606 series) PLEASE SEE REVERSE

Subject to Uniform Customs and Practice for Documentary Credits (1974 Revision,) I.C.C. Publication No. 290

9.8.5

Notification of documentary credit

The notification forwarded to Delta Computers by Eastland Bank will have been similar to this one. Note that many banks will have their customers application forms (9.8.2) faxed to them and write the letter of credit on a word processor to suit the customer's requirements.

Questions

1. Who will receive the money?
2. Which documents are involved besides the L/C?
3. What special clause is mentioned in the insurance policy?
4. Can the goods be moved from one ship to another?
5. What is the value of the credit?
6. When is the L/C valid till?
7. Who is the issuing bank?
8. Who opened the L/C?
9. Can the exporters ship the consignment in different lots?
10. What does the consignment consist of?

9.8.6

From the exporter to the agent bank

The exporter will now acknowledge the agent bank's letter, and send them the documents they asked for and their draft.

Delta Computers Ltd.

Bradfield Estate, Bradfield Road, Wellingborough, Northamptonshire NN8 4HB

Telephone: 0933 16431/2/3/4
Telex: 485881
Fax: 0933 20016

Reg. England 1831713
VAT 2419 62114

Your Ref: ———

Our Ref: ———

Mr P. Medway
Eastland Bank Ltd.
401 Aldgate,
London EC1

24 May 19—

Dear Mr Medway,

Thank you for your advice of the 15 May. We have now effected shipment to our customers in New Zealand and enclose the shipping documents you asked for and our draft for £23,100 which includes your discount, commission, plus charges.

Will you please accept the draft and remit the proceeds to our account at the Midland Bank, Oxford Street, London W1.

Yours sincerely,

N. Smith

N. Smith
Senior Shipping Clerk

Enc. Bill of lading (6 copies)
    Commercial invoice c.i.f. Wellington (four copies)
    A.R. Insurance certificate for £24,200
    Draft 2152/J

Delta Computers Ltd.

Bradfield Estate, Bradfield Road, Wellingborough, Northamptonshire NN8 4HB

Telephone: 0933 16431/2/3/4	Reg. England 1831713
Telex: 485881	VAT 2419 62114
Fax: 0933 20016	Your Ref:
	Our Ref:

Mr M. Tanner   25 May 19—
N.Z. Business Machines Pty.
100 South Street
Wellington
New Zealand

Dear Mr Tanner,

We are pleased to inform you that your order, No. 8815, has been shipped today on the SS Northern Cross which is due in Wellington in four weeks.

The shipping documents, including bill of lading, invoice, and insurance have been passed to the Eastland Bank, London, and will be forwarded to the New Zealand Bank, Wellington, who will advise you.

As agreed, we have drawn on the Eastland Bank at 60 days for the net amount of £23,100 which includes the bank's discount commission and charges.

We are sure that you will be pleased with the consignment, and look forward to hearing from you soon.

Yours sincerely,

N. Smith

N. Smith
Senior Shipping Clerk

9.8.7
From the exporter to the importer

Delta Computers notify their customers in New Zealand that the consignment is on its way to them.

Questions

1 When will the consignment arrive?
2 What has happened to the shipping documents?
3 How has the bank earned money on the transaction?
4 Who is the agent bank in this transaction?
5 What do the letters *SS* stand for?
6 What expressions are used to mean: *arrive*; *sent*; *made out a b/e*; *notify*?

9.8.8
From the importer's bank to the importer

The New Zealand Bank now advises NZ Business Machines that their account has been debited, and that the documents are ready for collection. When he has picked up the documents, Mr Tanner will be able to take delivery of his goods.

New Zealand Bank

Chairman: Sir Francis Tuckman   Directors: L.N. Bowman, P.O. Shearing, L.D. Nesterman
Takapuna House, Takapuna Street, Wellington 8

Telephone: 448135/6/7/8
Telex: Newban NZ 28131
Fax: 806358

29 May 19—

Mr M. Tanner
N.Z. Business Machines Pty.
100 South Street
Wellington

Dear Mr Tanner,

In accordance with your instructions of 3 May our agents, Eastland Bank, London, accepted a draft for £23,100 drawn by Delta Computers Ltd. on presentation of shipping documents for a consignment sent to you on 24 May.

We have debited your account with the amount plus our charges of $280 NZ. The documents are now with us and will be handed to you when you call.

Yours sincerely,

I. Close
Manager

International Crafts Ltd.

Thameside, Walworth, London SE3 2EL
Chairman: B. Valour

Telephone: 081 834 2179, 081 834 2710   Cable: INTERCRA   Telex: 315620   Fax: 081–834 4431

Lee Boat Builders Ltd.   9 April 19—
Dock 23
Mainway
HONG KONG

Dear Sirs,

We spoke to your representative, Mr Chai, at the Earls Court Boat Show in London last week, and he showed us a number of dinghies which you produce, and informed us of your terms and conditions.

We were impressed with the craft, and have decided to place a trial order for ten of them, your Cat. No. NR17. The enclosed order, No. 90103, is for delivery as soon as possible as the summer season is only a few weeks away.

As Mr Chai assured us that you could meet any order from stock, we have instructed our bank, Northern City Ltd., to open a confirmed irrevocable letter of credit for £7,300 in your favour, and valid until 1 June 19—.

Our bank informs us that the credit will be confirmed by their agents, Cooper & Deal Merchant Bank, Pekin Road, Hong Kong, once you have contacted them, and they will also supply us with a certificate of quality once you have informed them that the order has been made up and they have checked it.

You may draw on the agents for the full amount of the invoice at 60 days, and your draft should be presented with the following documents:

> Six copies of the bill of lading.
> Five copies of the commercial invoice, c.i.f. London
> Insurance certificate for £7,140 (A.R.)
> Certificate of origin
> Certificate of quality

The credit will cover the invoice, discounting, and any other bank charges. Please cable us confirming that the order has been accepted and the craft can be delivered within the next six weeks.

Yours faithfully,

B Valour

B. Valour
International Crafts Ltd.

Enc. Order No. 90103

9.9
Specimen letters: a documentary credit transaction (2)

9.9.1
From the importer to the exporter

This letter, from the buyer (importer) in London to the seller (exporter) in Hong Kong, is the first step in our second example of a documentary credit transaction. Note that International Crafts ask for a certificate of origin, which they need since they intend to re-export the dinghies to France, which is an EEC country. Note also that they will use their bank's agents to verify the quality of the boats.

9.9.2

From the exporter to the importer

Northern City Ltd., who are International Crafts' bankers, have now notified their agents in Hong Kong, Cooper & Deal, who have in turn advised Lee Boat Builders that the credit is available. Meanwhile Lee have cabled International Crafts confirming that they have accepted the order, and can deliver within six weeks. They follow this by sending this letter, advising shipment.

Questions

1 When will the consignment arrive in London?
2 How have the dinghies been packed?
3 What documents were required by International Crafts Ltd.?
4 What does '60 d/s' mean?
5 Who are Cooper & Deal, and what role do they play in the transaction?
6 What will the Northern City Bank advise International Crafts?
7 What restrictions do Lee Boat Builders put on their guarantee?
8 What must International Crafts do once they have received the consignment?
9 Which words in the letter correspond to the following: *should arrive*; *small boats*; *boxes*; *pays for*; *send*; *warranty*?

Lee Boat Builders Ltd.

Dock 23, Mainway, Hong Kong
Telephone: 385162   Telex: 349512   Fax: 662553   Cable: LEBATS

International Crafts Ltd.,   6 May 19—
Thameside,
Walworth,
London SE3 2EL
UNITED KINGDOM

Dear Mr Valour,

Order No. 90103

We are pleased to inform you that the above order has been loaded on to the SS Orient which sails tomorrow and is due in Tilbury (London) on 3 June.

The dinghies and their equipment have been packed in polystyrene boxes in ten separate wooden crates marked 1–10, and bearing our brand ⚠.

The shipping documents (see list attached) have been handed to Cooper & Deal, Hong Kong, with our draft for £7,293.50 at 60 d/s. This covers all charges and discounting. Cooper & Deal will forward the documents to Northern City Bank Ltd. who will advise you within the next few weeks.

We are sure you will be extremely pleased with the consignment. We noticed that you require a certificate of origin, and have supplied one. However, we wondered if this was for re-exporting purposes. We should point out that your customers will have the same guarantee as yourself only if the boats are not modified in any way, as this will be outside the terms of the guarantee.

Thank you for your order, and we hope you will contact us again in the future. Meanwhile, please confirm delivery, when you receive the consignment.

Yours sincerely,

J. Lee

J. Lee
Director

9.10
Points to remember

1 Merchant banks and commercial banks in the UK offer similar services, but commercial banks encourage private account holders to use their facilities, as well as commercial concerns.
2 Commercial bank facilities include current accounts, deposit accounts, credit cards, standing orders, loans, and overdrafts.
3 The two main methods used in settling overseas accounts – bills of exchange and documentary credits – involve banks at home and abroad.
4 Bills of exchange can be *at sight*, i.e. payable on presentation, or *after sight*, payable at a stipulated date in the future. The exporter can send the bill to the importer direct, or to his bank with the documents and will obtain either payment on presentation, or acceptance against the bill. The advantage of a bill is that the exporter can get money immediately if the bill is discounted, and the importer can obtain credit if the bill is not a sight draft. The disadvantage is that the bill can be cancelled, or not paid on the due date.
5 A *confirmed irrevocable documentary credit* cannot be cancelled (unlike a revocable credit), and the importer's bank and its agent can guarantee payment. The importer is protected by the bank checking documents and can get a certificate of quality to ensure that the goods are up to standard. The exporter is assured of payment, and, with discounting facilities, does not have to wait for his money if the bank agrees that he can draw against the credit.

9.11
Words to remember

a commercial bank
a merchant bank
to open an account
a current/deposit/savings/budget account
a specimen signature
a balance
a transaction
Giro system
a cheque/Eurocheque/traveller's cheque
a cheque card
cash card
cash dispenser
a credit card
to honour a cheque
to cancel a cheque
to stop a cheque
a paying-in/withdrawal/transfer slip
notice of withdrawal
a counterfoil
a cashier

negotiable securities
a guarantor
a loan
an overdraft
to overdraw
overdraft facilities
to call in an overdraft
interest
Base Rate
inflation
bank charges
a standing order
a direct debit

overseas customer
credit status
confirming houses
new issue/bullion/Euro-bond market
shipping/insurance/foreign exchange market

a bill of exchange
a drawer
a drawee
a sight draft/bill
days after sight (d/s)
documents against payment (D/P)
documents against acceptance (D/A)
a foreign bill
an inland bill
a clean bill
to discount a bill
to endorse a bill
a dishonoured bill
to protest a bill

a letter of credit (L/C)
a revocable/irrevocable letter of credit
an importer
an exporter
an agent
confirmed credit
commission
confirming bank

Agents and agencies

10

Types of agencies (brokers, buying and selling agents); finding an agent; offering an agency (convincing the agent, exclusive or non-exclusive agency, area to be covered, commission, settlement of accounts, support from the principal, delivery, duration of the contract, disagreements and disputes, special terms); asking for an agency (convincing the manufacturer, suggesting terms).

10.1
Types of agencies

Agents and agencies are appointed by firms to represent them. There is a wide range of activities concerning representation and although in this unit we will mainly be dealing with buying and selling agencies, it would be useful to look at other areas where companies act on behalf of their clients, as they will be referred to later.

10.1.1
Brokers

Brokers usually buy or sell goods for their *principals* (the firms they represent) and sometimes never handle the consignments themselves. There are various types of brokers, and the list below will give you an idea of the sort of broking facilities that exist.

Brokers/dealers on the Stock Exchange buy and sell shares for their clients, who cannot go on to the 'floor' of the Exchange and deal for themselves if they are not members. The client asks the broker/dealer to buy or sell shares for him, and the broker takes a commission on the purchase or sale.

Ship brokers arrange for ships to transport goods for their clients. The brokers operate mainly from the Baltic Exchange or one of its branches, and we will look at this in more detail in Unit 11 Transportation and shipping.

Insurance brokers arrange insurance cover with underwriters who pay

compensation in the event of a loss.
See Unit 12 Insurance.

The Commodity Markets. In these
markets brokers buy and sell
commodities, e.g. cocoa, tea, coffee,
rubber, etc., on behalf of their clients.

The Metal Exchange, i.e. the market for
buying and selling ores and metals in
bulk, also employs brokers to deal on
behalf of companies.

There are other Exchanges where
companies use brokers to represent
them, either because the company does
not have membership of that Exchange,
or they want to use the broker's
specialized knowledge of the market.

Contact between buyers and brokers is
done by phone, cable, fax, or telex, as
prices in the markets tend to fluctuate
quickly, even by the minute in the case
of bullion and foreign currency.

10.1.2
Confirming houses

These agents often receive orders from
abroad, place them, arrange for
packing,shipment,insurance,and
sometimes finance or purchase the
goods themselves, then resell them to
the client. They may act on a
commission, but if buying on their own
account will make a profit on the
difference between the ex-works price
and the resale price they quote the
importer.

10.1.3
Export managers

If a firm does not have a branch in the
country it is exporting to, they can
appoint an export manager. He will deal

under his own name, but use the
address of the company he represents.
His job is primarily to develop the
market for the exporter, and for his
services he may charge a fee, or
arrange for a profit-sharing scheme
between himself and the exporter.

10.1.4
Factors

These agents can buy and sell in their
own names, i.e. *on their own account*,
receive payment, and send accounts to
their principals. They often represent
firms exporting fruit or vegetables.

Note: 'Factoring' is the process in which
the firm buys the outstanding invoices
of a manufacturer's customers, keeps
the accounts, then obtains payment.
'Non-recourse factoring' involves the
buying up of outstanding invoices and
claiming the debts. If the buyer (the
manufacturer's customer) goes
bankrupt, the factor has no claim,
whereas in 'recourse factoring', the
factor will claim from the manufacturer
if the customer cannot pay.

10.1.5
Manufacturer's agents

This agent represents a manufacturer
and obtains goods, then resells them.
The agent may work on a commision,
i.e. buying the goods *on consignment*,
or, if described as a *merchant*, he will
buy the goods from the manufacturer on
his own account, that is to sell them for
his own profit. If he is a *sole agent*, he
agrees only to sell his principal's
products, and not those of a competitor,
and the manufacturer would probably
agree not to supply the sole agent's
rivals in his country.

10.1.6
Buying agents

Buying agents, or buying houses, buy products on behalf of a principal and receive a commission. The agency is employed to get the best possible terms for their principal, and will try to find the most competitive rates in shipping and insurance for them. Buying houses often act on behalf of large stores.

The orders sent to buying agents are called *indents* and are of two types: *open indents*, where the agent chooses his/her supplier, and *closed* or *specific indents*, where the supplier is named by the principal.

10.2
Finding an agent

It is possible to find an agent through a number of sources: advertising; in Trade Journals; contacting government departments of trade in your own country or the country you wish to export to; consulting Chambers of Commerce, Consulates, Trade Associations, and banks. Letters to these organizations are routine, and the guide below gives you an indication of how these letters are laid out.

10.2.1
Opening

Tell the organization who you are.

We are a large manufacturing company specializing in . . .

We are one of the leading producers of . . .

You probably associate our name with the manufacture of chemicals/ textiles/business machines/heavy engineering . . .

10.2.2
Explaining what you want

We are looking for an agent who can represent us in . . .

We would like to appoint a sole agent in Scotland to act on our behalf selling . . .

We are trying to find an established firm to represent us in selling our products.

10.2.3
Closing

Close by saying that you would be grateful for any help that can be given.

We would be grateful if you could supply us with a list of possible agents.

We hope you can help us, and look forward to hearing from you.

Thank you in advance for your help, and we look forward to receiving your recommendations.

10.3
Offering an agency

Once you have found out the names and addresses of prospective agents, you can write to them direct. Below is a guide for manufacturers offering terms to a prospective agent.

10.3.1
Opening

Tell the agent how you obtained his name.

You were recommended to us by the Saudi Trade Commission in London.

Mr Milos Petric of the Jugobank Export Department wrote to us telling us that . . .

Explain who you are.

We are an established company manufacturing . . .

We are the leading exporters of . . .

We are one of the main producers of chemicals/steel/kitchenware/furniture/ chinaware/industrial equipment, etc.

10.3.2
Convincing the prospective agent

Convince the agent that the products you make are worth taking and will sell in his market.

As you can see from our catalogue, we can offer a wide range of products which have attractive designs, are hard-wearing, light, easy to use, and fully guaranteed for one year.

You will notice that the prices quoted are extremely competitive for a product of this quality. We know there is a growing demand for this product in your country and are sure that once our brand is established, it will lead the market.

The Zenith 2000 is the result of many years' research and development, and we know that once it is put on the Scottish market, it will overtake sales of all competitive brands.

10.3.3
Exclusive or non-exclusive agency

There are two types of agency: a *sole* or *exclusive agency*, when your agent will only be supplied by you in a particular area, and when he will not sell products that compete with yours; and a *non-exclusive agency* where there is no

such undertaking. The agency contract explains the conditions on which the agency will be operated and what the rights and obligations of the agent and principal are.

We will not restrict the agent by offering a sole agency as we have found that this limits our own sales, and is sometimes awkward for the agent himself.

We are offering a sole agency which will mean that you will not have competition from our products in the area specified in the contract.

We cannot offer an exclusive agency for Zambia at present. However, if the agency is successful we may reconsider a sole agency in the future.

It should be established whether you are going to deal with your agent on a *consignment basis*, when the agent will not own the products you send, but will sell them on a *commission basis*; or whether you want to supply the agent for him to re-sell to customers *on his own account*, in which case he will decide on resale prices and take the profits from his sales.

We generally do not deal on a consignment basis, but prefer our agents to buy our products on their own account. They usually prefer this method as it proves more profitable for them and allows them greater freedom in determining prices.

Note that the use of the term 'generally' in the above example leaves the offer open to negotiation.

10.3.4
Area to be covered

Make it clear what region or area the agency is for.

You will have sole distribution rights for the whole of France, which will give you an excellent opportunity to establish a wide range of customers.

Initially, we will give you a sole agency for the Lazio region, but if sales are successful, we will extend that to other regions.

As sole agents you will have no competition from our products in Northern Germany, therefore with effective selling you would be able to get a large return.

10.3.5
Commission

Some firms offer terms in an initial enquiry, others wait until they have had a reply from the prospective agent. If offering terms, however, you should make them sound as inviting as possible.

The agency we are offering will be on a commission basis, and as we are very interested in getting into the French market, we are prepared to offer a 15% commission to our agent, plus a substantial advertising allowance.

As the agency will be a sole agency, to prevent a competitive product being sold, we are prepared to offer a generous commission as compensation, and a reasonable allowance for expenses.

As an inducement to the agent we appoint, we will be offering a 12 per cent commission on net prices.

10.3.6
Settlement of accounts

Orders should be sent to us direct for shipment, and we will arrange for customers to pay us. You may issue us with quarterly/monthly statements of account which will be paid by sight draft at the bank of your choice.

We would expect you to supply orders from your stock, or we will ship consignments as soon as you send the order to us.

Customers should pay us direct by letter of credit, on each sale, and we will remit your commission by bill once you have submitted your monthly/quarterly account. Credit is not to be offered without our express consent.

10.3.7
Support from the principal

The prospective agent will want to know what support you will give him in his efforts to sell your goods.

Our products of course carry a one-year guarantee and we will replace any faulty item carriage paid.

As you know, our company offers a full after-sales service, which is essential in establishing the reputation of our brands, and your customers need have no worries about spare parts or maintenance.

We will offer you additional expenses of £5,000 per annum for any advertising that you think will help sell the products. This will be increased after a year if we think sales warrant it.

10.3.8
Delivery

Providing there are no unforeseen delays we will be able to deliver six weeks from receipt of order.

We would hope that you will keep large stocks of our three main ranges. However, we will be able to deliver within a month of receiving orders.

Delivery should not take longer than three weeks providing we have the items in stock.

10.3.9
Duration of the contract

The length of time for the contract is usually discussed after the agency has been agreed. Nevertheless, it would be stated as follows.

The contract will be from 1 March for one year, and, provided both parties agree, will be renewed for a further year.

We feel that nine months should be enough time to decide whether it is worth continuing with sales, and will make out the first contract accordingly.

Subject to our mutual agreement, the contract will be renewed annually.

10.3.10
Disagreements and disputes

A provision is usually made for disagreements and disputes. This too, would not usually appear in an opening letter, but in correspondence confirming the agency.

In the case of disagreement over conditions or payments, the matter will be settled by arbitration.

As a rule we follow American law to determine legal disputes over contracts.

Note: Arbitration is when a neutral organization settles problems between the principal and agent. A Chamber of Commerce or Trade Association often acts in cases of arbitration.

10.3.11
Special terms

In some cases agents are offered special terms if they are prepared to hold themselves liable (responsible) for their customers' debts. These agents receive a 'del credere commission', which is a special commission to compensate them for the risk they take.

We are prepared to offer an extra 2½% del credere commission if you are willing to be responsible for customers' debts.

In addition to the 12% commission on net sales, we will offer a further 3% del credere commission, if you are willing to deposit £5,000 as a security to guarantee all customers' debts.

10.4
Asking for an agency

Here is a guide to the kind of letter you should write if you want to offer your services as an agent to a manufacturer.

10.4.1
Opening

Explain who you are and how you saw or heard of the manufacturer's product.

You were recommended to us by our associates Lindus Products Ltd., of Lagos, who told us that you were looking for an agent to represent you in oil-drilling equipment in Nigeria.

We are contacting suppliers of medical equipment in your country with a view to acting as their representatives here in Saudi Arabia. Your name was given to us by the British Consul in Jeddah. We already import medical supplies from a number of different countries, but are particularly interested in the E.E.G. machines and scanners you manufacture.

10.4.2
Convincing the manufacturer

You have to convince the supplier first that there is a market for his product in your country or area, and second that you are the best person to develop the market and sell his goods.

As you know, Germany is extending its farming areas with the aid of government grants to farmers and this expansion is creating a demand for all forms of agricultural machinery, particularly with regard to your products. We have many contacts in the government who will direct us to large-scale farms and enterprises which are in the market for your products.

We have an established reputation in Nigeria for supplying oil companies here with excavation and drilling equipment and are quite willing to offer you references. We can also assure you of excellent sales prospects as the oil industry is rapidly expanding.

Because we have already established business relationships with hospitals and clinics here in Saudi Arabia we are sure that we would be the best company to represent you here. And as you are probably aware, the development of the health service here means that generous grants to clinics and hospitals have increased the demand for the more sophisticated equipment that you manufacture.

10.4.3
Suggesting terms

You may want to leave discussion of terms until after you know that the supplier is interested in your request. But there is no harm, even at this stage, in describing the terms on which you normally operate and asking if they would be acceptable in the present case.

May we suggest the terms we usually operate on to give you an idea of the sort of agency contract we are considering? We generally represent our principals as sole agents for Germany, buying products on our own account, with an initial contract to run for one year, renewable by mutual agreement. We expect manufacturers to offer advertising support in the form of brochures – in German and English – and catalogues, and in return we promise our customers a full after-sales service and two-year guarantees on all products. Therefore we would expect a first class spare-parts service with delivery for both manufactures and spare parts within six weeks of receipt of order. We would pay you direct by 40-day bill of exchange, documents against acceptance. If this type of agency interests you, please contact us so that we can draw up a draft agreement.

10.5
Specimen letters and forms

10.5.1
Offer of an agency

In this set of three specimen letters, the manufacturer offers an agency, the prospective agent discusses terms, and the manufacturer replies by adding more details and sending a copy of an agency agreement.

Questions

1 Who recommended the agency to British Crystal?
2 Where does British Crystal export to at present?
3 What type of agency are they offering?
4 What commissions could the prospective agent earn?
5 Are they offering the prospective agent any additional help?
6 What does Mr Jay mean by a 'unique opportunity' and 'resources to handle a sole agency'?
7 What is the condition for the agent offering his customers credit terms?
8 Which words are used to mean: *a wide range* and *unusual damage*?

BRITISH CRYSTAL Ltd.

Glazier House, Green Lane, Derby DE1 1RT
Telephone: 0332 45790   Telex: 901614   Fax: 0332 51977

S.A. Importers Ltd.   4 May 19—
Al Manni Way
Riyadh
SAUDI ARABIA

Dear Sirs,

Mr Mohammed Al Wazi, of the Saudi Arabian Trade Commission in London, informed us that you may be interested in acting as our agent in your country.

As you will see from the catalogue enclosed, we are manufacturers of high quality glassware and produce a wide selection of products from moderately-priced tableware in toughened smoked glass to ornate Scandinavian and Japanese-designed light coverings.

We already export to North and South America and the Far East, and would now like to expand into the Middle Eastern market where we know there is an increasing demand for our products.

The type of agency we are looking for will have resources to cover the whole area of Saudi Arabia in selling our products, and we are offering a 10% commission on net list prices, plus advertising support. There would be an additional 2½% del credere commission if the agent is willing to guarantee his customer's accounts, and he may offer generous credit terms once we have approved of the account.

This is a unique opportunity for someone to start in an expanding market and grow with it. Therefore, if you believe you have the resources to handle a sole agency covering the area mentioned, and feel that you can develop this market, please write to us as soon as possible.

Yours faithfully,

N. Jay
Director

Enc. Catalogue

S.A. Importers Ltd.

Al Manni Way, Riyadh

Telephone: 4356698   Telex: 991546   Cable: SAIL Riyadh   Fax: 3134981

Mr N. Jay	Your ref: 4 May 19—
British Crystal Ltd.	Our ref: SA/8016
Glazier House	
Green Lane	Date: 17 May 19—
Derby DE1 1RT	
UNITED KINGDOM	

Dear Mr Jay,

Thank you for your letter of 4 May in which you offered us a sole agency for your products in Saudi Arabia.

First, let me say that we can handle an agency of the type you described, and that we agree that the demand for Western goods here is increasing. However, there are some points we would like answered before we make a decision.

Payment of accounts. Would customers pay you direct in the UK or will they pay us, and we in turn would settle with you deducting our commission? How would payment be arranged? Bill of exchange, letter of credit, or bank draft?

Delivery. Would we be expected to hold stocks or will you supply from stock? If you supply the customers direct, how long will it take an order to be made up and shipped once it has been received?

Advertising. You mentioned that you would be willing to help with advertising. We would like more details about the type of assistance you would give us.

Disputes. If a disagreement arises over the terms of the contract, who would be referred to in arbitration?

Length of contract. Finally, how long would the initial contract run? I think three years would allow us to see how your products sell in this market.

If you can send us this information, and possibly enclose a draft contract, we could give you our answer within the next few weeks.

Yours sincerely,

M. Kassim

M. Kassim

10.5.2
Agent's reply, asking for more details

Mr Kassim, of S.A. Importers Ltd., is interested but wants more information.

Questions

1 What sort of agency was offered?
2 How long does Mr Kassim want the agency to run?
3 Does Mr Kassim suggest a method of payment?
4 What does he mean when he says: *arbitration*; *initial contract*; *disagreement arises*; *make up an order*?
5 Is he confident about selling the product in his country?
6 What is a draft contract?

10.5.3
Manufacturer's reply, giving more details

Mr Jay provides the information and encloses a draft contract.

Questions

1 How will customers pay British Crystal unless Mr Kassim accepts a del credere commission?
2 Would customers be supplied from Mr Kassim's warehouse?
3 What sort of advertising will Mr Jay offer?
4 How long will the agency run initially?
5 What does 'mutual agreement' and 'disputes' mean?
6 Which words in the letter correspond to the following: *remit*; *fulfil*; *distributed*; *press*; *conditional*?

BRITISH CRYSTAL Ltd.

Glazier House, Green Lane, Derby DE1 1RT
Telephone: 0332 45790   Telex: 901614   Fax: 0332 51977

Mr M Kassim   6 June 19—
S.A. Importers Ltd.
A1 Manni Way
Riyadh
SAUDI ARABIA

Dear Mr Kassim,

Thank you for your letter which we received today. As you requested, we have enclosed a draft contract of the agency agreement.

You will see that we prefer our customers to pay us direct, and usually deal on a letter of credit basis, unless we can obtain references or your guarantee if you take the del credere commission.

You would not be required to hold large stocks of our products, but a representative selection of samples, and we can meet orders from the Middle East within four weeks of receipt.

Leaflets and brochures will be sent to you to hand out to your customers as one method of advertising, but we will also allow £3,000 in the first year for publicity which can be spent on the type of advertising you think suitable for glassware. We find that newspapers and magazines are the best media.

The initial contract will be for one year, subject to renewal by mutual agreement, and that disputes will be settled with reference to Dutch law, as our relative legal systems are different.

If you have any further questions with regard to the contract, or anything else, please contact me. I look forward to hearing from you.

Yours sincerely,

N. Jay

N. Jay

Enc: Draft contract

Allison & Locke Importers Ltd.

Rooms 21–8, Rothermede House, Eastgage Street, London WC1 1AR.
Directors: M. Allison, B. Locke

Telephone: 071 636 9010/1/2/3/4 Reg. No.: London 897032
Telex: 9816172 VAT No.: 232 6165 73
Fax: 071 636 9271
Cable: ALLOCK London

Mr F. Iglasis 17 October 19—
Iglasis Leather Manufacturing SA
Enrique Granados 109
Barcelona
Spain

Dear Mr Iglasis,

We are interested in the offer you made to us in your letter of 8 October to act as sole agents for your leather goods in this country.

We think that the annual turnover you suggested was rather optimistic, and while we agree that there is a demand for leather cases and bags here, we think that half the figure you quoted would be more realistic. In view of this, the commission you offer, six per cent, is rather low, and we would expect a minimum of ten per cent on net invoice totals.

As sole agents, the territory you offer, i.e. London, would be too restrictive for sales, and this would have to be extended to the home counties. We also feel it would be better for customers to settle with us direct, and we would remit quarterly account sales deducting our commission, but we are prepared to leave this matter open for discussion.

Finally, we will hold the stock you suggested, but if there is a rush of orders, as there may be now we are nearing Christmas, you would have to shorten the delivery date you quoted, from six weeks to three weeks from receipt of order.

If these conditions are suitable, then we would certainly accept an initial one-year contract to act as your agents.

Yours sincerely,

M. Allison

M. Allison

10.5.4
Reply to an offer of an agency

This letter is a reply to an offer of an agency, but the prospective agent is asking for the terms to be changed.

Questions

1 What sort of agency is Mr Iglasis offering?
2 Why does Mr Allison think a six per cent commission is rather low?
3 Which matter is he prepared to negotiate?
4 Why are delivery dates a problem?
5 How long will the initial contract run?
6 What did Mr Allison mean by saying that the annual turnover Mr Iglasis suggested was optimistic?
7 If you were Mr Iglasis, what concessions do you think you could make to meet Mr Allison's terms?
8 Which words in the letter correspond to the following: *exclusive*; *too hopeful*; *at least*; *limited*; *send*; *pay*; *first*?

10.5.5
Request for an agency

In this letter a British retailer is asking an American manufacturer if he can represent him in the UK. Notice that he explains who he is; tells the manufacturer where he saw the product; convinces him that there is a market; and suggests terms.

Glough & Book Motorcycles Ltd.

31–37 Traders Street, Nottingham NG1 3AA
Directors: B. Glough, T. Book

Telephone: 0602 77153 (6 lines)
Telex: 45513
Fax: 0602 48865

Registration: 733152
VAT Registration: 878 5662 74

Sales Manager
Hartley-Mason Inc.
618 West and Vine Street
Chicago
Illinois
U.S.A.

1 March 19—

Dear Sir,

We are a large motorcycle retail chain, with outlets throughout the UK, and are interested in the heavy touring bikes displayed on your stand at the Milan Trade Fair recently.

As you are probably aware there is an increasing demand in this country for machines of this type due to increasing traffic congestion, environmental problems and the acceptance of the motorcycle as a common means of transport, rather than just a teenage phase. And sales of larger machines have increased by more than 70 per cent in the last two years.

We are looking for a supplier who will offer us a sole agency to retail heavy machines. At present we represent a number of manufacturers, but only sell machines up to the 600cc range, which would not compete with the 750cc, 1000cc, and 1200cc models you make.

We operate on a 10% commission basis on net list prices, with an additional 3% del credere commission if required, and we think you could expect an annual turnover of more than £2,000,000. With an advertising allowance we could probably double this figure.

Our customers usually settle with us direct, and we pay our principals by bill of exchange on a quarterly basis.

You can be sure that our organization will offer you first class representation and excellent sales to guarantee the success of your products in this country.

We look forward to hearing that you are interested in our proposal.

Yours faithfully,

B. Glough

Hartley-Mason Inc.

President: J.R. Mason D.F.A.   Directors: P. Hartley Snr., A. Hartley Jnr.
618 West and Vine Street, Chicago, Illinois
Telephone: 216 818532   Telex: 67712   Fax: 216 349076

Mr B. Glough   14 March 19—
Glough & Book Motorcycles Ltd.
31–37 Traders Street
Nottingham NG1 3AA
ENGLAND

Dear Mr Glough,

We were pleased to receive your letter of March 1 and to see that you
were interested in the machines we produce.

The United States, like Great Britain, has also experienced an increase in
motorbike sales, and like you we think that there is a vast market to be
tapped for the heavy touring bike.

With regard to your offer, I should tell you straight away that we never use
sole agencies anywhere in the world, but rely on merchants buying our
products on their own account, then retailing them at market prices in their
country. We, of course, offer a 30% trade discount off net list prices and a
further 5% quantity discount for sales above $100,000. We have found
sole agencies tend to be rather restrictive both for ourselves and our
customers.

As far as advertising is concerned, you will be pleased to hear that we have
arranged for an extensive campaign which begins next month and features
our heavy machines. We are sending dealers throughout Europe
brochures, leaflets, and posters to hand to their customers, and this will be
followed up by television advertising in May.

Our terms of payment are 60 d/s bills, documents against acceptance if the
customer can provide references.

Once again, thank you for writing to us, and please contact us if you have
any more enquiries.

Yours truly,

J.R. Mason
President

10.5.6
Reply to a request for an agency

The American manufacturer is
interested in Mr Glough's proposal,
but does not agree to the terms.

Questions

1 How does Mr Mason encourage
Mr Glough's view that there is an
increase in motorcycle sales?
2 How does he explain that it is not only
Mr Glough's firm that would not be
offered a sole agency, and why
doesn't Mr Mason's company offer
sole agencies?
3 What sort of campaign is Hartley-
Mason planning to help sales?
4 What are Hartley-Mason's usual
terms of payment?
5 Which words in the letter correspond
to the following: *exploit a market*;
agents acting on their own account;
depend; *selling direct to the public*;
large programme; *give*?

10.5.7
Request from a buying agent

This letter is from a buying agent in the UK asking a French store if he could represent them. Buying agents have a first-class knowledge of the country, its products, the most competitive prices on the market for goods, freight, and insurance, and that is why they often take a commission on c.i.f. invoice values rather than *net* invoice values.

L. Dobson & Co. Ltd.

Royal Parade, Plymouth PL1 4BG

Telephone: 0752 31261   Reg. No.: 81 561771
Telex: 110753

Vivas S.A.R.L.   8 June 19—
138 rue Cimarosa
F–75006 Paris

For the attention of the Chief Buyer

Dear Sir,

I am replying to your advertisement in the trade magazine *Homecare* in which you said you were looking for a buying agent in the UK to represent your group of stores in France.

My company already acts for several firms in Europe and America and we specialize in buying domestic appliances and other household goods for these markets. We have contacts with all leading brand manufacturers so we are able to obtain specially reduced export prices for their products and we can offer excellent terms for freight and insurance.

Our usual commission is 5 per cent on c.i.f. invoiced values, and we make purchases in our principals' names, sending them accounts for settlement.

We will keep you well informed of new products that come on to the market, sending you any information or literature that we think will be helpful.

I have enclosed our usual draft contract for you to consider, and if you are interested, I would be pleased to hear from you.

Yours faithfully,

L. Dobson

Enc.

Vivas S.A.R.L.

138 rue Cimarosa, F–75006 Paris
Tél: (1) 46 0313 09   Telex: 621593   Fax: (1) 46 0319 31

L. Dobson & Co. Ltd.
Royal Parade
Plymouth PL1 4BG
UNITED KINGDOM   23 June 19—

Dear Mr Dobson,

Thank you for your letter in reply to our advert in *Homecare*. Although
we are interested in your proposition, the five per cent commission you
quoted on c.i.f. invoice values is higher than we considered paying.
However, the other terms quoted in your draft contract are quite
suitable.

We accept that you can get competitive rates in freight and insurance.
Nevertheless, we do not envisage paying more than three per cent
commission on net invoice values, and if you were willing to accept this
rate we would sign a one-year contract to be effective as from 1 August.
We can assure you that the volume of business would make it worth
accepting our offer.

Yours sincerely,

Marie Varenne

Marie Varenne (Mme)

10.5.8
Reply to a buying agent's request

The French company is not happy with
Mr Dobson's proposal to charge 5%
commission on c.i.f. invoiced values.

Questions

1 Does Mme Varenne concede that
  Dobson's rate is justified?
2 If Mme Varenne's counter-proposal
  is accepted, what sort of contract
  would be offered?
3 What is a 'draft contract'?
4 How does Mme Varenne explain that
  her offer is worth considering?

10.5.9
Agent's report

Here is a report from an agent who is sending an account sales to an English publisher for books he has sold on his behalf in South East Asia. The Agent takes advantage of the letter to make an enquiry.

International Trading Co. Ltd.

511, Silom Road, Bangkok, Thailand

Telex: 885173   Cable: Intrad

Mr J. Trevor   Your Ref: ———
Educational Books Ltd.   Our ref: 93/2
187 Springfield Road
Chatham   Date: 4 April 19—
Kent ME4 6SN
UNITED KINGDOM

Dear Mr Trevor,

We are submitting our account sales for the consignment delivered ex-SS Orianna. You will find our draft for £1,190.80 enclosed, which is for the total sales, less our commission at 10 per cent and charges.

A number of booksellers here have been asking us if they could get scientific text books, or classic fiction which is written in a simplified form of English and would be suitable for students of an intermediate level in English.

If you produce a series like this, would you send us a list? If not, could you put us in touch with a company that specializes in these books?

Yours sincerely,

L Chailing

L. Chailing

Encl. account sales and draft.

ACCOUNT SALES

By International Trading Co. Ltd.
511 Silom Road, Bangkok, Thailand

4 April 19—

In the matter of books ex-S.S. Oriana, sold for the account of Educational Books Ltd., Chatham, Kent, England.

					£
100	Copies	English Dictionary	@ 9.00	each	900.00
50	"	Adv. Eng. Stud. by P. Bowles	@ £6.00	"	300.00
100	"	Int. Eng. by M. Nash	@ £5.00	"	500.00
80	"	Eng. for Proficiency by V. Roberts	@ £7.00	"	560.00
70	"	Eng. for First Cert. by T. Cubitson	@ £5.60	"	392.00
90	"	Beginning English by U. Vickers	@ £3.40	"	306.00
					————
					2958.00

Less Charges	£
Ocean Freight	146.00
Dock Dues etc.	61.00
Marine Insurance	31.60
Customs Tariff	42.00
Commission @ 10% on 2958.00	295.80

	576.40
	2381.60

Signed....................................

E. & O. E.   INTERNATIONAL TRADING CO.

10.5.10
Account sales

This shows the amount International Trading Co. Ltd. received for selling books on behalf of Educational Books Ltd., less charges and commission.

10.6
Points to remember

1 If you are offering an agency to someone, convince him that your products are worth selling and will find a market in his area.
2 Be clear about the type of agency you are offering: exclusive or non-exclusive, on a consignment basis or a sale and retail basis.
3 Offer terms and suggest methods of settlement of accounts. Be positive about the support that you, the principal, can provide for your agent.
4 If you are asking for an agency, make sure the manufacturer appreciates the standing of your company and convince him that his products will be well represented.

10.7
Words to remember

an agent
an agency
a broker
a principal
a client
an importer
an exporter
a competitor
a rival

to offer an agency
sole/exclusive agency
non-exclusive agency
consignment basis
commission basis
'del credere' commission
own account basis
c.i.f. invoice values
net invoice values

a reference
Trade Journals
departments of trade
Chambers of Commerce
consulates
Trade Associations

a broker/dealer
the Stock Exchange
shares

commodity markets
the Metal Exchange
bullion
foreign currency

insurance brokers
insurance cover
underwriters
compensation

indents – open/closed/specific
a confirming house
an export manager
a manufacturer
a supplier
a factor
non-recourse factoring
recourse factoring
a manufacturer's agent
a buying agent/house

to develop a market
to create a demand
to renew a contract

Transportation and shipping

11

Road, rail and air transport and documentation; shipping (types of vessels, shipping organizations, shipping documentation and insurance, forwarding agents); container services and documentation; chartering ships.

11.1
Road, rail, and air

The three main methods of transporting goods, besides shipping which we will deal with in a separate section, are road, rail, and air.

11.1.1
Road transport

Road transport tends to be comparatively cheaper and more direct than rail, and in the past few years haulage (trucking) has doubled in the UK. The reasons for this include the increased capacity for lorries to carry goods, particularly with the introduction of containers (large steel boxes which allow for bulk transportation), faster services, with road improvements (motorways), and accessibility abroad with ferries (boats crossing the Channel) offering rolling-on and rolling-off facilities, i.e. trucks can drive on to a Channel ferry, cross, then drive off without unloading.

11.1.2
Rail transport

Rail transport is faster than road, which is necessary especially when transporting perishable goods, i.e. fish, fruit, meat, etc., and can haul bulk commodities (oil, grain, coal) in greater volume than road transporters.

There is a link between road and rail through companies such as Freightliners, but transhipment (transferring goods from train to truck) can still be a problem. Special ferries are available to take trains across the Channel to link up with European rail services, and British Rail also has container facilities. Nevertheless, rail transport tends to be comparatively more expensive than road haulage.

11.1.3
Air transport

Some goods lose value over time, e.g. newspapers, or deteriorate, e.g. flowers; therefore, air transport is used for speed, particularly over long distances. Insurance tends to be cheaper as consignments spend less time in transit. However, with bulk consignments, air is much more expensive, and can be uneconomical.

The main document used is the *Air Waybill* (AWB), which consists of 12 copies distributed to the airline, exporter, importer, and customs, see 11.2.9. Unlike the *bill of lading*, 11.3.3, the Air Waybill is only a receipt and cannot be transferred to another person.

11.1.4
Documentation

Consignment notes are used in road and rail transportation, see 11.7.7, and like the AWB they are not *documents of title* so ownership of the document does not mean ownership of the goods. They are not negotiable, i.e. they cannot be bought, sold, transferred by the *consignor* (the exporter), or the *consignee* (the importer).

Consignment notes and *waybills* are obtained by the consignor filling out an instructions for despatch form, and

paying the freight charges (the cost of sending the goods). These charges are calculated in size (volume), weight, or value, and sometimes risk, particularly if special precautions have to be taken.

Most freight companies are private carriers, which means they are only responsible for negligence (not taking proper care of the goods).

In the Economic Community, and European Free Trade Area (EFTA) *movement certificates* are used especially for container shipments, see 11.5, if the consignment is taken through different customs posts to member countries.

Since the late 1980s many of these customs forms have been included in one document, the *Single Administrative Document* abbreviation: (SAD). This is an eight-part set of forms for export declarations. In addition the *Simplified Clearance Procedure* abbreviation: (SCP) is also used to make documentation easier for exports and agents.

Correspondence in transport is generally between the sellers and freight firms, or sellers and forwarding agents, who send goods on behalf of the seller. The customers are kept informed by *advice notes* which give details of packing and when goods will arrive.

HOMEMAKERS Ltd.

54–59 Riverside, Cardiff CF1 1JW

Telephone: (0222) 49721   Registered No. C135162
Telex: 38217

Transport Manager   10 November 19—
Cartiers Ltd.
516–9 Cathays Park
Cardiff CF1 9UJ

Dear Sir,

Would you please quote for collecting, from the above address, and
delivering the following consignment to R. Hughes & Son Ltd., 21 Mead
Road, Swansea?

  6 divans and mattresses 700cm × 480cm
  7 bookcase assembly kits packed in strong cardboard boxes,
  measuring 14 cubic metres each
  3 coffee table assembly kits, packed in cardboard boxes, measuring 10
  cubic metres each
  4 armchairs, 320 × 190 × 260cm

The divans and armchairs are fully protected against knocks and scratches
by polythene and corrugated paper wrapping, and the invoiced value of
the consignment is £1,660.50.

I would appreciate a prompt reply, as delivery must be made before the
end of next week.

Yours faithfully,

R. Cliff

R. Cliff

11.2
Specimen letters

11.2.1
Request for a quotation for delivery by road

In this letter the furniture manufacturer
we met in earlier units, Homemakers
Ltd., is writing to a road haulage firm
asking them for an estimate to deliver
furniture to his customer, Mr Hughes;
he describes the packing (note that size
rather than weight will be the main
concern of the carrier in this case),
states the value of the consignment,
and mentions a delivery time.

11.2.2
Quotation for delivery by road

In the reply to Mr Cliff's letter, note how the writer refers to the consignment note as a 'receipt'. He also quotes for 'picking up and delivering' the consignment; carriers may quote for delivery, as here, or on a time basis, i.e. how long it will take to load or unload the lorry or van.

CARTIERS Ltd.

516–9 Cathays Park, Cardiff CF1 9UJ
Directors: P.R. Barry, T. Griffiths A.C.A.

Reg. No: 31883512
VAT No: 96 4218792

Telephone: (0222) 821597/8/9
Telex: 421639 CARTEL G
Fax: (0222) 498315

12 November 19—

Mr R. Cliff
Homemakers Ltd.
54–59 Riverside
Cardiff CF1 1JW

Dear Mr Cliff,

In reply to your letter of 10 November, we can quote £72.20 for picking up and delivering your consignment from your address to the consignee's premises. This includes loading and unloading, plus insurance.

If you fill out the Despatch Note enclosed, and let us know two days before you want the delivery made, our driver will hand you a receipt when he calls to collect the consignment.

Yours sincerely,

H. Weldon
H. Weldon
Supervisor

Enc.

HOMEMAKERS Ltd.

54–59 Riverside, Cardiff CF1 1JW

Telephone: (0222) 49721
Telex: 38217

Registered No. C135162

Mr R. Hughes
R. Hughes & Son. Ltd.
21 Mead Road
Swansea
Glamorgan 3ST 1DR

13 November 19—

Dear Mr Hughes,

Order No. B1517

As our own driver is ill, I have arranged for Cartiers Ltd. to deliver the above order on Wednesday 18 November. Before signing the delivery note, could you please check that the consignment is complete and undamaged?

I have enclosed the invoice, No. DM2561, and will add it to your monthly statement as usual.

Yours sincerely,

R. Cliff

Enc. Invoice No. DM2561

11.2.3
Advice of delivery
Homemakers Ltd. now advise their customer.

11.2.4
Complaint of damage in delivery by rail

Delivery notes are sent with consignments and can be signed stating that the 'contents have been examined'; which means the consignee has seen the goods and is accepting them in good condition, or 'contents not examined' as a precaution against receiving damaged goods. In this letter, the goods were sent by road, at the consignee's request, and were received damaged. Disc S.A., the customer, is writing to their supplier complaining about the consignment.

Questions

1 How does M. Gérard describe the damage?
2 Were all the boxes damaged?
3 Is there any chance of selling the goods?
4 Is M. Gérard going to return the consignment?

Disc SA

251 rue des Raimonières F–86000 Poitiers Cédex
Tél: (33) 99681031 Télécopie: (33) 102163

Réf: PG/AL   15 August 19—

The Sales Director
R.G. Electronics AG
Havmart 601
D–5000 Köln 1

Dear Mr Gerlach,

Consignment Note 671342 158

Yesterday we received the above consignment to our order, No. T1953, but found on opening boxes 4, 5, and 6 that the CDs and tapes in them were damaged.

Most of the CDs were either split or warped, in boxes 4 and 5, and the majority of cassette cases in box 6 were smashed, with tape spilling out of the cassettes themselves.

The goods cannot be retailed even at a discount and we would like to know whether you want us to return them, or hold them for inspection.

Yours sincerely,

P. Gérard

P. Gérard

R. G. Electronics AG

Havmart 601
D–5000 Köln 1
Tel: (221) 32 42 98
Fax: (221) 83 61 25
Telex: 6153291

Your Ref: JA/MR

P. Gérard
Disc S.A.
251 rue des Raimonières
F–86000 Poitiers Cédex

20 August 19—

Dear Mr Gérard,

I was sorry to hear about the damage to part of the consignment (No. T1953) that we sent you last week.

I have checked with our despatch department and they tell me that the goods left here in perfect condition. There should be our checker's mark on the side of each box, which is a blue label with a packer's number and date on it.

As you made the arrangements for delivery, I am afraid we cannot help you. However, I suggest you write to Gebrüder Bauer Spedition and if the goods were being carried at 'carrier's risk' I am sure they will consider compensation.

I have enclosed a copy of their receipt from their goods depot at Köln, and you can have any other documents that we can supply to help you with your claim.

Yours sincerely,

R. Gerlach

R. Gerlach
Sales Director

Enc.

Questions

1 What does Herr Gerlach quote in the letter?
2 Why will he not take responsibility for the consignment?
3 Why is he sure the goods were in perfect condition when they left his company?
4 What help does he offer M. Gérard?
5 Which words in the letter correspond to the following: *goods*; *send*; *transported*; *make up for loss*?

11.2.6

Complaint to the carrier

Disc S.A. write to the railway company.
On receipt of this letter, the railway
company will inspect the goods and
decide whether the damage was due to
negligence. If it was, the customer will
receive compensation.

Questions

1 What did the consignment consist of?
2 What sort of condition were the goods
  in when delivered to the sender's
  station?
3 How does M. Gérard think the
  damage was caused?
4 What compensation is M. Gérard
  asking for?
5 Why does M. Gérard feel he has the
  right to claim compensation?
6 What is being sent with the letter?
7 Which words used in the letter
  correspond to the following: *brought*;
  place of business; *left*; *believe*;
  breakable; *retain*?

Disc SA

251 rue des Raimonières F–86000 Poitiers Cédex
Tél: (33) 99681031 Télécopie: (33) 102163

Réf: PG/Al   14 September 19—

Gebrüder Bauer Spedition
Mainzerstrasse, 201–7
D–5000 Köln 1

Dear Sirs,

Consignment Note 671342 158

The above consignment was delivered to our premises, at the above
address, on September 6. It consisted of eight boxes of records and
cassettes, three of which were badly damaged.

We have contacted our suppliers, and they inform us that when the goods
were deposited at your depot, they were in perfect condition. Therefore
we assume that damage occurred while the consignment was in your care.

The boxes were marked FRAGILE and KEEP AWAY FROM HEAT, but
because of the nature of the damage to the goods (CDs warped, cassette
cases split), the consignment appears to have been roughly handled and
left near a heater.

We estimate the loss on invoice value to be F 6,720, and as the goods were
sent 'carrier's risk' we are claiming compensation for that amount.

You will find a copy of the consignment note and invoice enclosed, and we
will hold the boxes for your inspection.

Yours faithfully,

P. Gérard

P. Gérard

BRITISH CRYSTAL Ltd.

Glazier House, Green Lane, Derby DE1 1RT

Telephone 0332 45790   Telex: 901614   Fax: 0332 51977

Cargo Manager   15 June 19—
Universal Airways Ltd.
Palace Road
London SW1

Dear Sir,

We would like to send from Heathrow to Riyadh, Saudi Arabia, twelve
boxes of assorted glassware, to be delivered within the next fortnight.

Each box weighs 40 kilos, and measures 0.51 cubic metres. Could you
please quote charges for shipment and insurance?

Yours faithfully,

N. Jay
Director

11.2.7
Request for a quotation for delivery by air

British Crystal Ltd. write to an airline to find out how much it will cost to send glassware to their agents in Saudi Arabia. (See 10.5.1/2/3 for original correspondence.)

11.2.8
Quotation for delivery by air

Here is the airline's reply to Mr Jay. We saw before that airlines calculate freight charges on weight or volume; in this case both will have been taken into account. Note also that there are twelve copies of an air waybill: when the document is made out for this shipment, one will go to the airline, one to the consignor, and one to the consignee, each being accepted as originals; the other copies go to customers and handling.

Questions

1 What other charges are there besides the freight charges?
2 Are there daily flights to Saudi Arabia?
3 Why should an invoice be included in the parcel?
4 Who will arrange insurance?

Universal Airways Ltd.

Airline House, Palace Road, London SW1
Directors: Sir Bernard Hullings, E.M. Marchant FCA, D.L. Owen ACA, B. Friens MA

Telephone: 071 638 4129   Reg. No: London 281395
Telex: 381215   VAT No: 85 116259 15
Cable: UNIWAY
Fax: 071 638 5551

Mr N. Jay   18 June 19—
British Crystal Ltd.
Glazier House
Green Lane
Derby DE1 1RT

Dear Mr Jay,

Thank you for your enquiry of 15 June.

We will be able to send your consignment to Riyadh within two days of your delivering it to Heathrow. The cost of freight Heathrow/Riyadh is £3.60 per kilo, plus £1.50 air waybill, and £14.00 customs clearance and handling charges. But you will have to arrange your own insurance.

There are three flights a week from London to Saudi Arabia, Monday, Wednesday, and Saturday.

Please fill in the enclosed Despatch Form and return it to us with the consignment and commercial invoices, one of which should be included in the parcel for customs inspection.

Yours sincerely,

R. Laden

R. Laden
Cargo Manager

Enc.

| 125- | LHR | -8815 0635 | | | | 125-8815 0635 |

Shippers Name and Address

WADLEY Ltd.,
ADDERLEY ROAD
HACKNEY   LONDON E 8

Shippers account Number

Not negotiable
Air Waybill
(Air Consignment note)
Issued by
British Airways London
Member of IATA

British airways

Copies 1, 2 and 3 of this Air Waybill are originals and have the same validity

Consignee's Name and Address

WOLDAL INCORPORATED
BROADWAY
NEW YORK USA

Consignee's account Number

It is agreed that the goods described herein are accepted in apparent good order and condition (except as noted) for carriage SUBJECT TO THE CONDITIONS OF CONTRACT ON THE REVERSE HEREOF. THE SHIPPER'S ATTENTION IS DRAWN TO THE NOTICE CONCERNING CARRIERS' LIMITATION OF LIABILITY. Shipper may increase such limitation of liability by declaring a higher value for carriage and paying a supplemental charge if required.

Issuing Carrier's Agent Name and City

BRUNSWICK AIR
ASHFORD ROAD
HOUNSLOW MIDDX

Accounting Information

Agent's IATA Code 93-7-3031 **Account No.** 70- 3476/83

Airport of Departure (Addr. of first Carrier) and requested Routing
LONDON BA

to	By first Carrier	Routing and Destination	to	by	to	by	Currency	CHGS Code	WT/VAL PPD COLL	Other PPD COLL	Declared Value for Carriage	Declared Value for Customs
JFK	BRITISH AIRWAYS						UKL		X	X	N V D	

Airport of Destination NEW YORK   **Flight/Date** BA175/14   **For Carrier Use only** **Flight/Date**

Handling Information Also notify Mr R Smith, PO Box 178 New Jersey USA

10 Drums/ ADDR/ Nos 0011 – 0020   To be kept upright

No of Pieces RCP	Gross Weight	kg lb	Rate Class / Commodity Item No.	Chargeable Weight	Rate / Charge	Total	Nature and Quantity of Goods (incl. Dimensions or Volume)
10	480.0	K	Q –	500.0	0.55	275.00	Abrasive Paste (Not Restricted) Dims (10 x) 30x30x40 cm
						275.0	

Prepaid 275.00 **Weight Charge** **Collect**   **Other Charges** Handling 6.50 (C)

Valuation Charge   AWB 1.50 (A)

Tax

Total other Charges Due Agent 1.50

Shipper certifies that the particulars on the face hereof are correct and that insofar as any part of the consignment contains restricted articles, such part is properly described by name and is in proper condition for carriage by air according to the International Air Transport Association's Restricted Articles Regulations.

Total other Charges Due Carrier 6.50

K Westnott Brunswick Air

Signature of Shipper or his Agent

Total prepaid 283.00 **Total collect**

14 December 1983 Ashford Middx.   KJW

Currency Conversion Rates **cc charges in Dest. Currency**   Executed on   (Date)   at   (Place)   Signature of Issuing Carrier or its Agent

For Carrier Use only at Destination **Charges at Destination** **Total collect Charges**

125-8815 0635

M. 197-1 st.   Original 3 - (For Shipper)

Air Waybill

See 11.1.3.

Questions

1 Can the Air Waybill be transferred to another person?
2 Who is the exporter here?
3 How much is the handling charge on the bill?
4 How many copies would the shipper get?
5 Does the consignee have an account with the airline?
6 What is the gross charge for delivery?
7 What is the size of each parcel?

11.3
Shipping

11.3.1
Types of vessels

There are a variety of vessels available for exporters to use when shipping goods:

Passenger liners are ships that follow scheduled routes and concentrate on passenger services, but also carry cargo.

Passenger cargo vessels concentrate on cargoes, offer more facilities for loading and unloading, but carry few passengers.

Tramps travel anywhere in the world on unscheduled routes, picking up any cargo and delivering it.

Tankers are usually oil carriers, and are like *bulk carriers* which transport bulk consignments such as grain, wheat, and ores.

Container vessels offer facilities to move containers from one country to another, and have special lifting gear and storage space for the huge steel boxes they transport.

Roll-on roll-off ferries are vessels which allow cars and trucks to drive on at one port and off at another without having to load and unload their freight.

There are also *barges*, large flat-bottomed boats, which transport goods inland along canals and waterways, and *lighters* which may do the same work as a barge, or are used for taking goods from a port out to a ship, or vice versa.

Note that before the name of the ship, which is usually underlined in correspondence, the letters SS are used. These stand for Steam Ship and show it is a British Merchant vessel. MV, Motor Vessel, and MS, Motor Ship, are also used.

11.3.2
Shipping organizations

The exporter also has a choice as to whether he uses a company which is a member of the *Shipping Conference* group, or one that is listed on the *Baltic Exchange*.

The Shipping Conference is an international organization of ship owners who have agreed to fix prices for transporting goods or passengers. They meet periodically to set costs for hiring their vessels. The advantage for their customers is that the costs of shipment are steady, i.e. do not fluctuate over a short period, and universal, i.e. the same price is quoted by all members. They can also claim rebates (discounts) by shipping in bulk. A similar body to the Shipping Conference can be found in airlines – IATA, International Air Transport Association.

The Baltic Exchange has a number of functions, but its freight market offers facilities to exporters to charter (hire) ships and planes through brokers, who work on a commission and are specialists with a knowledge of the movement of ships and the most competitive rates available at any one time. See 11.6 *Chartering ships* for more details of this.

11.3.3
Shipping documentation

We have seen in Unit 9 Banking, that there are a number of documents used in overseas trade. Now we can look at the main documents used in shipping.

A *freight account* is an invoice sent by the shipping company to the exporter stating their charges. Once the goods are received on the dock, a *shipping note*, with a receipt, is handed to the Superintendent of the docks, advising him that the goods are to be shipped. A *dock receipt*, (sometimes called a *wharfinger's receipt*) will be returned to the consignor confirming that the goods are stored and awaiting shipment. Once the goods are on board the ship, a *mate's receipt* may be sent, acknowledging that the goods have been loaded. The mate's receipt is often sent when the consignment is loaded directly, and serves as a document of title until the bill of lading is ready.

The *bill of lading* (b/l or blading) (see 11.4.3) is the most important document in shipping as it is a document of title, i.e. gives ownership of the goods to the person named on it. If the words 'to order' are written on it, it means that it is a negotiable document and can be traded. In this case it will be endorsed on the back (the exporter will sign it), and if the endorsement is blank, there will be no restrictions on ownership. In an l/c transaction the confirming bank will usually ask for the b/l to be made out to them when they pay the exporter, then transfer it to the customer.

A *shipped bill of lading* means that the goods have been loaded on to the ship. Sometimes the words 'shipped on board' are used to mean the same thing. In c.i.f. and c. & f. transactions the words 'freight prepaid' are used to signify that the costs of shipment have been paid. Bills are also marked 'clean' to indicate that the goods were taken on board in good condition, or 'dirty/claused' to indicate that on inspection there was found to be something wrong with the consignment, e.g. packing, or the goods were damaged. This statement protects the shipping company from claims that they were responsible for the damage or bad condition of the consignment.

Usually two copies of the b/l are sent to the buyer or his bank, by air and sea for security.

11.3.4
Shipping liabilities

The *Hague Rules* signed at the Brussels Convention in 1924 govern liability for loss or damage to cargo carried by sea under a bill of lading, and state that the carrier will not be responsible under the following conditions:
Acts of war, riots, civil disturbances;
Force majeure, i.e. exceptional dangers such as storms, abnormal disturbances, or unusual hazards;
Negligence, i.e. when the goods have not been properly packed, or were in a bad condition when packed;
Inherent vice, i.e. when goods are subject to deterioration because of their content or nature. For example, fish can go bad, wood can carry insects, metal can oxidize.

The *Hamburg Rules* of 1978 have extended the shipping companies' liability for damage or delay to 'goods in their charge' unless they can prove they took all measures to avoid problems.

To be safe, most companies insure their consignments under *all risk* cover, which protects them against most contingencies, but special 'war insurance' is necessary for particularly dangerous zones.

11.3.5
Forwarding agents

Forwarding agents are used by exporters to arrange both import and export shipments. In the case of the former, their services include collecting the consignment, arranging shipment, and if required, packing and handling all documentation, including making out the bill of lading, obtaining insurance, sending commercial invoices and paying the shipping company for their clients. They also inform the importer's forwarding agent that the shipment is on its way by sending an advice note, and he, in turn, will inform his client, send the goods on to him, or arrange for them to be stored until collected. Many forwarding agents in importing countries also act as *clearing agents*, ensuring that the goods are cleared through the customs and are sent to the importer.

Because forwarding agents handle many shipments they can collect consignments for the same destination and get competitive 'groupage rates' for sending a lot of consignments in one shipment. However, many exporters find it more convenient to deal direct with the forwarding agents in the importer's country, and some importers prefer to deal with their supplier's forwarding agent.

11.4
Specimen letters

11.4.1
Request for freight rates and sailings

Lee Boat Builders of Hong Kong write to Far Eastern Shipping Lines to ask about freight rates and sailings to London. See the letter at 9.9.1 for the beginning of this transaction.

Lee Boat Builders Ltd.

Dock 23, Mainway, Hong Kong

Telephone: 385162   Telex: 349512   Fax: 662553   Cable: LEBATS

Far Eastern Shipping Lines
31–4 Park Road
Hong Kong

21 April 19—

Dear Sirs,

We intend to ship a consignment of dinghies and their equipment to London at the beginning of next month. The consignment consists of ten boats which have been packed into wooden crates marked 1–10, each measuring 4 × 2 × 2.5 metres and weighing 90 kilos.

Could you inform us which vessels are available to reach London before the end of next month, and let us know your freight rates?

Yours faithfully,

J. Lee
Director

Far Eastern Shipping Lines

31–4 Park Road, Hong Kong
Directors: S. Chung, M. Whang, L. Grover

Telephone: 421897
Cable: FREAST
Telex:879216
Fax:602135

Mr J. Lee   24 April 19—
Lee Boat Builders Ltd.
Dock 23
Mainway
Hong Kong

Dear Mr Lee,

Thank you for your enquiry of 21 April. Enclosed you will find details of
our sailings for the end of this month and the beginning of next, from
Hong Kong to Tilbury.

You will see that the first available vessel we have will be the SS Orient
which will accept cargo from 3 May to 7 May, when she sails. She is
due in Tilbury on 3 June.

Our freight rate for crated consignments is £31.00 per tonne, and I
have attached our Shipping Instructions to the enclosed itinerary.

Yours sincerely,

M Whang

M. Whang (Mrs)

Enc. (2)

11.4.2
Reply to request for freight rates and sailings

If Mr Lee is satisfied with this reply and decides on shipment, the shipping company will send him a freight account (their invoice) and a bill of lading to complete. When the goods have been loaded, Mr Lee will send an advice to his customer informing him of shipment (see the letter at 9.9.2).

Questions

1 When will Mr Lee's cargo leave Hong Kong?
2 How much does the shipping company charge?
3 What is sent with the letter?
4 Which words in the letter correspond to the following: *information*; *ship*; *arrive*; *shipping charges*?

11.4.3
Bill of lading

See 11.3.3 for details of this document.

Questions

1 Can the b/l be transferred?
2 Which word is used for the sender of the cargo?
3 What expression is used for the place where cargo is unloaded?
4 Where would you write the name of the ship carrying the cargo?
5 Who needs to sign a b/l?
6 How do we describe a b/l when goods taken on board are damaged?
7 What does freight prepaid mean?
8 How many copies of the b/l are usually issued?

Bill of lading specimen form.

Delta Computers Ltd.

Bradfield Estate, Bradfield Road, Wellingborough, Northamptonshire NN8 4HB

Telephone: 0933 16431/2/3/4
Telex: 485881
Fax: 0933 20016

Reg. England 1831713
VAT 2419 62114

Your Ref:

Our Ref:

Mr J.D. Simpson
Kent, Clarke & Co. Ltd.
South Bank House
Borough Road
London SE1 0AA

11 May 19—

Dear Mr Simpson,

Could you please pick up a consignment of 20 C2000 computers and make the necessary arrangements for them to be shipped to Mr M. Tanner, N.Z. Business Machines Pty., 100 South Street, Wellington, New Zealand?

Would you please handle all the shipping formalities and insurance, and send us seven copies of the bill of lading, five copies of the commercial invoice, and the insurance certificate? We will advise our customers of shipment ourselves, and would appreciate it if you could treat the matter as urgent. Your charges may be sent to us in the usual way.

Yours sincerely,

N. Smith

N. Smith
Senior Shipping Clerk

11.4.4
Instruction to a forwarding agent

This letter is from Delta Computers to their forwarding agents, Kent, Clarke & Co. Ltd., instructing them to pick up twenty machines which is a consignment to be sent to their customers NZ Business Machines Pty., Wellington. (Refer back to 9.8.1–9.8.8 for previous correspondence.)

Questions

1 What types of documents are involved in this shipment?
2 Who will pay the charges?
3 What does the consignment consist of?
4 Who will advise the customer of shipment?
5 Which words in the letter correspond to the following: collect; deal with; inform; handle; transported?

11.4.5
Forwarding agent's enquiry for freight rates

Kent, Clarke & Co. write to an international shipping line.

Kent, Clarke & Co. Ltd.

Chairman: Lord Matherson   Directors: B. Kent ACA, C.D. Clarke HND, R.P. Diller
South Bank House, Borough Road, London SE1 0AA

Reg No: London 3395162   Telephone: 071 928 7716
VAT No: 41 61823159   Telex: 988153
                                                 Fax: 071 928 7111

International Shippers Ltd.   12 May 19—
City House
City Road
London EC2 1PC

Dear Sirs,

We have packed and ready for shipment 20 C2000 computers which our clients, Delta Computers, Wellingborough, want us to forward to Wellington, New Zealand.

The consignment consists of 4 wooden crates, each containing 5 machines and their cases. The weight of each crate is 210 kilos and measures 94 × 136 × 82 cm.

Would you let us know by return of post the earliest vessel leaving London for New Zealand, and let us have your charges and the relevant documents?

Yours faithfully,

J.D. Simpson

J.D. Simpson
Supervisor

International Shippers Ltd.

Chairman: Sir Donald Low   Directors: P.R. Castle, D.S.M. Bracking, R.T. Kitson
City House, City Road, London EC2 1PC

Reg No: England 4513869   Telephone: 071 312 5038
VAT No: 12 631541 23   Telex: 951363 INTHIP G
                                                     Fax: 071 312 6117

Mr J.D. Simpson   14 May 19—
Kent, Clarke & Co. Ltd.
South Bank House
Borough Road
London SE1 0AA

Dear Mr Simpson,

In reply to your letter of May 12, the earliest vessel due out of London for
New Zealand is the SS Northern Cross which is at present loading at No. 3
Dock, Tilbury, and will accept cargo until May 18 when she sails. She is due
in Wellington on June 25, and the freight rate for cased cargo is £112.00 per
ton or 10 cubic metres.

I have enclosed our shipping form and bill of lading for you to complete
and return to us.

Yours sincerely,

Y. Pollard

Y. Pollard (Miss)

Enc. (2)

11.4.6
Shipping company's reply

Questions

1 Is the *SS Northern Cross* the only
  vessel leaving for Wellington?
2 Which two documents will Mr
  Simpson receive, and what should he
  do with them?
3 What is the closing date for cargo?
4 What should Mr Simpson do with the
  enclosures?
5 What are the shipping charges?
6 What other words could be used
  instead of *due out* and *due in*?

11.4.7
Confirmation of shipment

The forwarding agents have telexed or phoned Delta Computers informing them that there is a vessel available and quoting the cost of shipment, and Delta have confirmed that the sailing time and rate is acceptable. Kent, Clarke now return the completed shipping note and bill of lading to International Shippers with this covering letter.

Kent, Clarke & Co. Ltd.

Chairman: Lord Matherson   Directors: B. Kent ACA, C.D. Clarke HND, R.P. Diller
South Bank House, Borough Road, London SE1 0AA

Reg No: London 3395162   Telephone: 071 928 7716
VAT No: 41 618231 59   Telex: 988153
                                                 Fax: 071 928 7111

Miss Y. Pollard   17 May 19—
International Shippers Ltd.
City House
City Road
London EC2 1PC

Dear Miss Pollard,

We have arranged for the consignment of computers, the subject of our letter of 12 May, to be sent to Tilbury for loading on to the SS Northern Cross which sails for New Zealand on 18 May.

Enclosed you will find the completed shipping form and bill of lading (10 copies), eight copies of which should be signed and returned to us. I have also attached a cheque in payment of your freight account.

Yours sincerely,

J.D. Simpson

J.D. Simpson
Supervisor

Enc. Shipping form
      Bill of lading (10 copies)
      Cheque No. 0823146

Hartley-Mason Inc.

President: J.R. Mason D.F.A.   Directors: P. Hartley Snr., A. Hartley Jnr.
618 West and Vine Street, Chicago, Illinois
Telephone: 216 818532   Telex: 677312   Fax: 216 349076

Mr E. Jones   19 April 19—
Eddis Jones Forwarding Agents
12 Dockside Street
Liverpool L2 1PP
UNITED KINGDOM

Dear Mr Jones,

The following consignment will arrive on the SS America which is due in
Liverpool on 27 April.

    20 'Lightning' 1000cc motorcycles.
    Packed 1 machine per wooden crate
    Weight 1.25 tons gross
    Size 6' × 3' × 2'
    Markings Cases numbered 1–20 HM
    Value £4,800 each
    Insurance Chicago–Nottingham England (A. R.)
    Invoiced value £96,000

Could you please arrange for the consignment to be delivered to your
clients, Glough & Book Ltd., Nottingham? If there are any problems, please
contact us immediately.

Yours truly,

T. N. Hackenbush

T.N. Hackenbush

11.4.8
Advice of shipment to importer's forwarding agent

In this letter Hartley-Mason Inc. is writing
to a British importing agent advising
them that a consignment of motorcycles
is being sent for them to forward to their
customers, Glough & Book. (Refer
back to 10.5.5/6 for previous
correspondence.)

11.4.9
Advice of shipment to importer

Hartley-Mason now inform Glough & Book that their consignment has been shipped. Glough & Book will accept the bill that the American company has drawn on them, and send the documents to the bank, which hands them to their forwarding agents in Liverpool, who will then be able to collect the consignment on their behalf.

Questions

1 Who are the clearing agents?
2 Who is the agent bank?
3 What must Mr Glough do to receive the shipping documents?
4 Which words in the letter correspond to the following: *should arrive*; *goods*; *made up of*; *signed*; *soon*?

Hartley-Mason Inc.

President: J.R. Mason D.F.A.   Directors: P. Hartley Snr., A. Hartley Jnr.
618 West and Vine Street, Chicago, Illinois
Telephone: 216 818532   Telex: 677312   Fax: 216 349076

Mr B. Glough   19 April 19—
Glough & Book Motorcycles Ltd.
31–37 Traders Street
Nottingham NG1 3AA
UNITED KINGDOM

Dear Mr Glough,

Order No. 8901/6

The above order was shipped on 17 April 19— on the SS America which is due in Liverpool on 27 April.

We have informed your agents, Eddis Jones, who will make arrangements for the consignment to be sent on to you, as you requested.

Our bank's agents, Westmorland Bank Ltd., High Street, Nottingham, will hand over the documents which consist of a shipped clean bill of lading (No. 517302), invoice (No. EH 3314), and insurance certificate (AR 118 4531), once you have accepted our bill.

We are sure you will be delighted when you see the machines, and that they will find a ready market in your country. Meanwhile we are enclosing a catalogue of our new models and believe you will be very interested in the machines illustrated on pp. 103–110. We look forward to hearing from you again in due course.

Yours truly,

T. N. Hackenbush

T.N. Hackenbush

Encl.

Kent, Clarke & Co. Ltd.

Chairman: Lord Matherson   Directors: B. Kent ACA, C.D. Clarke HND, R.P. Diller
South Bank House, Borough Road, London SE1 0AA

Reg No: London 3395162
VAT No: 41 618231 59

Telephone: 071 928 7716
Telex: 988153
Fax: 071 928 7111

Miss Y. Pollard
International Shippers Ltd.
City House
City Road
London EC2 1PC

28 June 19—

Dear Miss Pollard,

Our clients, Delta Computers, Wellingborough, inform us that they
have received a cable from their customers, N.Z. Business Machines,
Wellington, that the SS Northern Cross which was due in Wellington on
June 25 has not yet arrived.

The vessel was carrying a consignment of computers for our clients,
shipped B/L 6715, and they want to know why the ship has been
delayed. A prompt reply would be appreciated.

Yours sincerely,

J.D. Simpson

J.D. Simpson
Supervisor

11.4.10
Delay in arrival of shipment

Goods can be delayed, damaged, or carried-over to another port. In such cases the seller or his forwarding agent will contact the shipping company. (Refer to 11.4.4/5/6/7 for previous correspondence.) Note that the correspondence with the shipping company is through Kent, Clarke, the forwarding agents who sent the goods in this case.

11.4.11
Shipping company's reply to 11.4.10

11.5
Container services

Containers are large steel boxes, 20 to 40 feet in length, can hold most cargoes including liquids, and are transported by lorries or trains to ports where they are loaded on to container vessels and shipped. Because of their sealing to prevent pilfering they are safe, and goods are also protected against constant handling. They are versatile, loading top, front, or side, and can cut a ship's laytime (waiting time) down by 60–70 per cent. Small parcels from different shippers can be grouped together (consolidation) at a depot if they are for the same destination, and special groupage rates are offered to consignees.

Most ports in the world have facilities for loading and unloading containers, and if they do not have them, the container can be delivered to a port with facilities, then loaded on to trucks and taken to the customer.

11.5.1
Documentation for exporting goods by container

A *bill of lading* can be used as it is in ordinary shipments, with the usual conditions applying, i.e. a clean shipped on board bill, naming the port of acceptance (where the goods have been loaded) and port of delivery (where the goods will be unloaded). In this case

---

International Shippers Ltd.

Chairman: Sir Donald Low   Directors: P.R. Castle, D.S.M. Bracking, R.T. Kitson
City House, City Road, London EC2 1PC

Reg No: England 4513869   Telephone: 071 312 5038
VAT No: 12 631541 23   Telex: 951363 INTHIP G
                                                  Fax: 071 312 6117

Mr J.D. Simpson   30 June 19—
Kent, Clarke & Co. Ltd.
South Bank House
Borough Road
London SE1 0AA

Dear Mr Simpson,

In answer to your letter of 28 June, we are pleased to inform you that the SS Northern Cross has now docked in Wellington, but was delayed by engine trouble. I am sure that your customers will now have been able to collect their consignment and apologize for the delay. As you know from previous experience of shipping with us, our line keeps to schedules and this incident was an unfortunate exception. Please contact us if there is any further information you require.

Yours sincerely,

Y. Pollard

Y. Pollard (Miss)

the shipping company only accepts responsibility for the goods while on board ship. But if a *combined transport bill of lading* is used, the place of acceptance and place of delivery may be covered, which means the company accepts door-to-door responsibility, which offers more extensive cover than the bill of lading.

Non-negotiable waybills (see 11.7.3) are also used, but unless instructed, banks will not accept them as evidence of shipment, and they are not documents of title which can be transferred. Although waybills do not have clauses relating to responsibility printed on the back of them, as bills of lading do, container companies will accept the usual liabilities as applying to the waybill.

11.5.2
Documentation for importing goods by container

A *freight invoice* is needed if the sea freight is to be paid in the UK and this is accompanied by an *arrival notification form*, which advises the importer that his goods are coming. On claiming his goods, the customer has to show a *customs clearance form*, which allows the goods to be taxed, copies of the *certificate of origin* (see 11.7.4), if necessary, *commercial invoices*, *import licence*, and *health certificate* for food or animal imports. The *bill of lading* or *waybill* also has to be produced to prove ownership of the goods, and the customs issues an *out of charge note* once the goods have been cleared by them.

This procedure is not unique to container importation, but common to any form of imports. This is one of the reasons why Clearing Agents are employed by either exporters, to get their goods accepted quickly in a foreign country, or importers, to clear their goods in their own country.

11.6
Chartering ships

We saw earlier that the Baltic Exchange was the market for chartering ships and that the vessels were hired through shipbrokers. Once a broker is contacted he will find a ship owner who is prepared to hire his vessel on either a 'voyage charter' or 'time charter' basis.

Voyage charter charges, i.e. taking freight from port A to B, are calculated on the tonnage value of the cargo. For example, if an exporter ships 500 tons of coal at £1.20 per ton, he will pay £600.00 for the charter.

Time charter charges are calculated on the tonnage of the ship (i.e. the weight of the ship) plus running costs of the vessel, excluding wages. So the larger the ship, the more the charterer pays, regardless of whether he ships 500 tons or 5,000 tons.

There are also *mixed charters* combining both time and voyage charters. The contract signed by both parties is known as a *charter party*.

Ships listed on the Baltic Exchange do not run on scheduled routes, and freight rates vary from company to company depending on supply and demand. Correspondence between hirers and brokers, and brokers and owners is done by phone, telex, fax, or cable, with letters confirming the transaction.

11.7
Specimen letters

11.7.1
Enquiry to a container company

Universal Steel Ltd. wants to ship a consignment of steel by container to Hamburg.

UNIVERSAL STEEL Ltd.

Chairman: B. Eltham   Directors: D.E.R. Machin, O.M. Crewit
Furnace House, Granville Road, Sheffield S2 2RL

Reg No: 6217970
VAT No: 31 428716

Telephone: 0742 760271
Telex: 813297 UNEST G
Fax: 0742 610318

International Containers Ltd.   15 March 19—
Buxton House
Mableton Place
London WC1H 9BH

Dear Sirs,

We are a large steel company and wish to export a consignment of steel tubing, approximate weight 16 tonnes, and lengths varying from 2 to 5 metres.

The consignment is destined for Dörtner Industries, Hamburg. Could you pick up the load, transport it to London from Sheffield, and then deliver it to its destination in Germany by the end of April?

Please let us have details of your sailings and freight charges, and we can promise you regular shipments if you quote a competitive rate.

Yours faithfully,

Thomas Pike

Thomas Pike
Export Department

International Containers Ltd.

Chairman: R.L. Nathan ACWA   Directors: T.N. Frost, L.S. Newcombe
Buxton House, Mableton Place, London WC1H 9BH

Reg. No: London 3661515   Telephone: 071 387 6815
VAT No: 62 1431792   071 388 2713
                                                    Telex: 443179 INCONT G
                                                    Fax: 071 387 665516

Mr T. Pike   17 March 19—
Export Department
Universal Steel Ltd.
Furnace House
Granville Road
Sheffield S2 2RL

Dear Mr Pike,

Thank you for your enquiry of March 15 which we received today.
Enclosed you will find details of our rates, shipping schedules, and
documents required for transportation.

The most suitable container for your consignment would be a half-
height container which is 20′ × 8′ × 4′ or, in metres, 6.1 × 2.4 × 1.2. This
can carry a payload of 18,300 kg. It has a solid removable top, and will
protect the metal against all elements.

I would suggest that as the consignment is going to be loaded from
lorry to ship, then transferred again, you should use our Combined
Transport Bill which will cover the goods from point of acceptance to
point of delivery. And if the transaction is on a letter of credit basis, you
should advise your bank that this document will be acceptable instead
of the B/L.

Would you fill out the enclosed Export Cargo Shipping Instructions,
and the Export Cargo Packing Instructions and hand them to our driver
when he calls? Although we accept door-to-door responsibility, we
would advise you to take an all risk insurance policy, and send a copy
of this and three copies of the commercial invoice to us.

contd.

11.7.2
Container company's reply

Questions

1 Which container does Mr Muner recommend?
2 Why is a combined transport bill suggested rather than a bill of lading?
3 Does the exporter need to insure the cargo?
4 When does the SS Europe close for cargo?
5 How are the freight charges estimated?
6 Is there any advantage in the exporter making regular shipments?
7 What sort of liability will the shipping company accept?
8 Which words used in the letter correspond to the following: *charges*; *weather*; *deal*; *complete*; *give*; *timetable*; *worked out*?

– 2 –

Your packing should be adequate, and the cargo marked on at least two sides with a shipping mark which includes the destination port, and these marks should correspond with those on your shipping documents.

The <u>SS Europe</u> sails from Tilbury on March 26 and will arrive in Hamburg March 28, which appears to suit your schedule for delivery. Please note, however, that the vessel closes for cargo on March 24.

You will see from our list of tariffs that charges are calculated by cubic metre or cubic kilogram and that we offer substantial rebates for regular shipments.

If you want us to reserve a space on the <u>SS Europe</u>, please complete the enclosed forms and return them to us as soon as possible.

Yours sincerely,

D. Muner
International Containers Ltd.

Enc. (3)

Shipper	Overseas Containers Limited

OCL

Waybill no
Shipper's ref
OCL booking ref no

Consignee	

Non-Negotiable Waybill

CARRIER

Received in apparent good order and condition except as otherwise noted the total number of containers or other packages or units enumerated below ● for transportation from the place of acceptance to the place of delivery subject to the terms hereof

Delivery will be made to the Consignee named, or his authorised agent, on production of proof of identity at the place of delivery. Should the Consignee require delivery elsewhere than at the place of delivery as shown below then written instructions must be given by the Consignee to the Carrier or his agent. Should delivery be required to be made to a party other than that named as Consignee, authorisation must be given in writing by the Shipper to the Carrier or his agent

Notify Party	

Freight and Charges

Origin zone transport charge

Origin port/LCL service charge

Ocean Freight

Destination port/LCL service charge

Destination zone transport charge

Intended Vessel and voyage number

Intended port of loading

Intended port of discharge

Details of cargo as declared by shipper			Gross Weight	Measurement
Marks and numbers	Quantity and type of package	Description of goods and container number		

SPECIMEN

● Total number of

This Waybill is deemed to be a contract of carriage as defined in Article 1(b) of the Hague Rules and Hague Visby Rules but it is not a document of title to the Goods. The Contract evidenced by this Waybill is subject to the Carrier's standard Bill of Lading terms and conditions and tariff for the relevant trade copies of which may be obtained from the offices of the Carrier and those of his authorised Agents. Except for live animals and Goods which are stated herein to be carried on deck, these terms and conditions are warranted in respect of the sea portion of the transit to apply the Hague Rules or the Hague Visby Rules whichever would have been applicable if the Carrier had issued a Bill of Lading instead of this Waybill

Unless instructed to the contrary by the Shipper the Carrier will subject to the aforesaid terms and conditions process cargo claims with the consignee named in this Waybill. Such settlement if any shall be a complete discharge of the Carrier's liability to the Shipper. Shipper accepts the said standard conditions on his own behalf and on behalf of the consignee and the owner of the Goods and warrants that he has authority to do so.

In witness whereof this Waybill is signed

For the Carrier   (   ) Document

Place of acceptance	

As agent(s) only

Place of delivery	

Place and Date of Issue

11.7.4
Certificate of origin

This document states the origin of the materials used in the production of the goods or certifies that the goods are of a particular origin i.e. that they came from a particular place. The importer needs the certificate to claim preferential duty or special allowances as there has usually been a tariff agreement with the country exporting the goods. Chambers of Commerce issue them, after completion, in sets of three one copy for the Chamber, one for the exporter, and the original for the customer.

See 9.9.2 as a correspondence reference.

Consignor: (Expéditeur:)		SPECIMEN	B 629546

Speirs and Wadley Limited,
Adderley Road,
Hackney London.

EUROPEAN COMMUNITIES
(Communautes Europeennes)

Consignee: (Destinataire:)

Compania de Dowal
Av. Grande 1124
Madrid, Spain

CERTIFICATE OF ORIGIN
(Certificat d'origine)

Consignment by: (Expédition prévue par:)

Ship – IONIAN

THE LONDON CHAMBER OF COMMERCE AND INDUSTRY

THE UNDERSIGNED AUTHORITY certifies that the goods shown below
(L'AUTORITE SOUSSIGNEE certifie que les marchandises désignées ci-dessous)

Serial No.	Packages Number and kind	Marks and numbers	Description of goods	Weight (1) gross	net
	5 cases	SW CIA DOW MADRID 1 TO 5	Electric Drills	254 Ks.	240 Ks.

originated in:
(sont originaires de:)

European Communities – United Kingdom

L. Griffiths.

London, 3rd August, 19 ..
(Place and date of issue)

The London Chamber of Commerce and Industry
(Name, signature and stamp of competent authority)

(1) This entry may, where appropriate, be replaced by others allowing identification of the goods.

DT1/XP/1302

London Grain Merchants Ltd.

Chairman: L. Spencer M.Sc. (Econ)   Directors: B. Meredrew, L. Oban, C.M. Chirmill
Central House, Rowley Street, London EC1
Telephone: 071 742 8315   Telex: 331497 LONGRA G   Fax: 071 742 3319

Keyser Shipbrokers Ltd.   10 January 19—
123–5 Lowland Street
London EC1 2RH

Dear Sirs,

This letter is to confirm our telex to you this morning in which we
asked if you could find a ship of six to seven thousand tons which we
could charter for six months to take shipments of grain from Baltimore,
in North America, to various ports along the South American coast.

We will need a ship that is capable of making a fast turn round and will
be able to manage at least ten trips within the period.

Yours faithfully,

B. Meredrew
Director

11.7.5
Enquiry for a time charter
A London firm wants to charter a ship to transport grain. They contact a shipbroker.

11.7.6
Shipbroker's reply

Keyser Shipbrokers Ltd.

Chairman: P.S. Keyser   Directors: L.M. Nosome, R.N. Landon
123–5 Lowland Street, London EC1 2RH

Reg No: London 818171   Telephone: 071 671 3829/01 670 4211
VAT No: 31 4281563   Telex: 441359 KEYSHIP G
                                               Fax: 071 671 9873

Mr B. Meredrew   12 January 19—
London Grain Merchants Ltd.
Central House
Rowley Street
London EC1

Dear Mr Meredrew,

With reference to your telex and letter, we are pleased to inform
you that we have been able to secure the vessel you asked for.

She is the SS Manhattan and is docked at present in Boston. She has a
cargo capacity of seven thousand tons, is a bulk carrier, and has a
speed of 24 knots which will certainly be able to make the number of
trips you mentioned.

Please cable us to confirm the charter and we will send you the charter
party.

Yours sincerely,

B. Marston
Charter Department

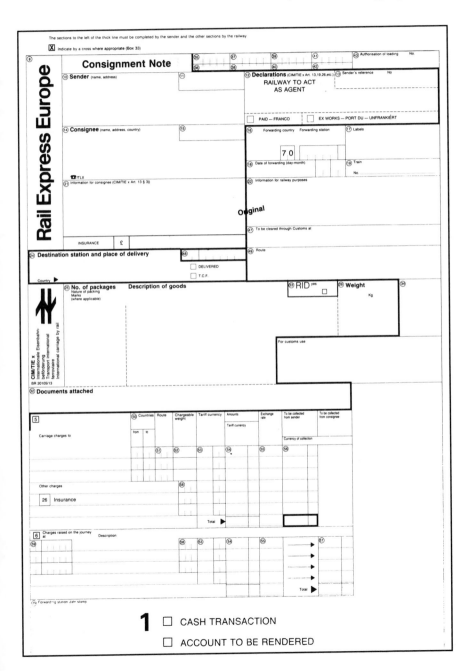

11.7.7
Rail consignment note

11.7.8
Enquiry for a voyage charter

Putney & Raven Merchants Ltd. need a ship to transport a consignment of bauxite.

Putney & Raven Merchants Ltd.

Dealers House, Cantley Street, London WC1 1AR
Directors: M.L. Putney, D. Raven

Telephone: 071 467 3149 (10 lines)
Telex: 886125 PUTRAY G
Fax: 071 467 5959

Reg No: England 615113
VAT No: 21 371942

Keyser Shipbrokers Ltd.
123–5 Lowland Street
London EC1 2RH

7 July 19—

Dear Sirs,

We would like to charter a vessel for one voyage from Newcastle, New South Wales, Australia, to St Malo, Brittany, France, to take a consignment of 4,000 tons of bauxite.

Our contract states that we have to take delivery between 1st and 5th August, so we will need a ship that will be able to load during those dates. Please advise us if you can get a vessel and let us know the terms.

Yours faithfully,

D. Raven

Keyser Shipbrokers Ltd.

Chairman: P.S. Keyser   Directors: L.M. Nosome, R.N. Landon
123–5 Lowland Street, London EC1 2RH

Reg No: London 818171   Telephone: 071 671 3829/01 670 4211
VAT No: 31 4281563   Telex: 441359 KEYSHIP G
                                          Fax: 071 671 9873

Mr D. Raven   10 July 19—
Putney & Raven Merchants Ltd.
Dealers House
Cantley Street
London WC1 1AR

Dear Mr Raven,

You should have already received our fax in which we said that
we had an option on a vessel, the MS Sheraton, which is docked in
Melbourne at present. She has a cargo capacity of 7,000 tons and
although she is larger than you wanted, her owners are willing to offer a
part charter of her.

They have quoted £2.30 per ton which is a very competitive rate
considering you will be sharing the cost. Please will you fax your decision
as soon as possible? Thank you.

Yours sincerely,

B. Marston
Charter Department

11.7.9
Shipbroker's reply

Questions

1 What does an 'option' on a vessel mean?
2 Is the MS Sheraton exactly what Putney and Raven wanted?
3 Why is the chartering cost lower for this shipment?
4 Where is the ship at the moment?
5 Is the whole ship being chartered?

11.7.10
General charter

Adopted by the
Documentary Committee of the
Chamber of Shipping of the
United Kingdom.

RECOMMENDED.

Issued to come into force for fixtures on and after 15th September, 1922.

Code Name :

GENCON.

The Documentary Council of The Baltic & White Sea Conference.

UNIFORM GENERAL CHARTER.
AS REVISED 1922.

(Only to be used for trades for which no approved form is in force).

....19

Owners.	1. IT IS THIS DAY MUTUALLY AGREED between 1
	 2
	Owners of the steamer or motor-vessel.. 3
	of................tons $\frac{gross}{nett}$ Register and carrying about................tons of deadweight cargo, 4
Position.	now 5
	and expected ready to load under this Charter about............................. 6
Charterers.	and Messrs... 7
	of... as Charterers. 8
Where to load.	That the said vessel shall proceed to.. 9
	....or so near thereto as she may safely get and lie 10
Cargo.	always afloat, and there load a full and complete cargo (if shipment of deck cargo 11
	agreed same to be at Charterers' risk) of... 12
	 13
	 14
	 15
	(Charterers to provide all mats and/or wood for dunnage and any separations required, 16
	the Owners allowing the use of any dunnage wood on board if required) which the 17
	Charterers bind themselves to ship, and being so loaded the vessel shall proceed to 18
	 19
Destination.	 20
	 21
	 22
	as ordered on signing Bills of Lading or so near thereto as she may safely get and 23
	lie always afloat and there deliver the cargo on being paid freight—on $\frac{delivered}{intaken}$ quantity—as 24
Rate of Freight.	follows... 25
	 26
	 27
	 28

11.8
Points to remember

1 The method a consignor chooses to deliver his goods depends on whether his main consideration is speed, direct delivery, limiting handling, or economy, and this obviously relates to the type of consignment being sent.
2 Road haulage can be comparatively cheap when transporting relatively small consignments, and offers a door-to-door service. Rail freight services are competitive when shipping bulk goods, and are faster than road transport between terminals. Air transport offers the fastest service, but is restrictive on weight and volume, and can be the most expensive method of sending goods.
3 The 'consignment note' or 'waybill' is the main document used in road, rail, or air transport. It is a *receipt*, not a *document of title*, and therefore not negotiable. An 'advice note' is usually sent to the consignee to inform him that goods are being forwarded, but airlines, as a rule, inform the consignee themselves when the goods arrive.
4 There are various types of vessels available to carry different goods. Their owners may belong to the Shipping Conference and will charge fixed rates for transporting goods.
5 Other vessels can be chartered, on a time or voyage basis or on a mixed charter, through shipbrokers on the Baltic Exchange who will negotiate rates for their clients.
6 The bill of lading is the main document used in shipping and may be 'clean' or 'dirty' ('claused') which explains whether the goods were taken on board in perfect condition,

or if something was wrong with them. Once the bill has been signed by the captain, it is known as a *shipped bill* and the shipping company will now accept responsibility in accordance with the clauses on the back of the document. If the bill is made 'to order' it becomes a negotiable document of title.
7 Containerization is a rapidly growing method of shipment, where goods are loaded into steel boxes which are taken to the docks and then loaded on to special vessels. Container companies use either *combined transport bills of lading*, or *waybills*, but also the usual documents in shipping including the bill of lading.

11.9
Words to remember

road/rail/air transport
transhipment
haulage (trucking)
a freight company
an airline
a forwarding agent
a clearing agent
a private carrier
a consignor
a consignee
a checker
a packer

in transit
a lorry
a van
a container
a passenger liner
a passenger/cargo vessel
a tramp
a tanker
a bulk carrier
a container vessel

roll-on roll-off facilities
a ferry
a barge
a lighter
a goods depot
a terminal

a consignment
a shipment
cargo
a bulk commodity
perishable goods
size
volume (cubic m)
weight (cubic kg)

a despatch note
a consignment note
an air waybill
an advice note
instructions for despatch form
freight charges
customs clearance and handling charges
'contents have been examined'
'contents not examined'

to charter a ship
a shipbroker
The Shipping Conference
The Baltic Exchange
voyage charter charges
time charter charges
mixed charter
charter party
tonnage value
'groupage rates'
export cargo shipping instructions
export cargo packing instructions
a shipping mark
a bill of lading
'clean'/'dirty'/'claused' bill of lading
to order
a shipped bill
freight pre-paid
a shipping note
a rail consignment note

a dock receipt
a wharfinger's receipt

insurance
a policy
door-to-door responsibility
'carrier's risk'
all risks
a claim
compensation
damage
negligence
to inspect goods
fragile
Hague Rules
Acts of War
force majeure
negligence
inherent vice

International Air Transport Association

Insurance

12

Insurance procedures; fire and accident insurance and claims; marine insurance: Lloyd's of London; marine insurance policies and claims

12.1
Insurance procedures

Companies and individuals protect themselves against loss, damage, or injury by taking out *insurance policies*, which are contracts against possible future risks. The usual process of insuring a business or oneself is as follows:

A *proposal form* is completed by the firm or person who wants insurance *cover*. This tells the insurance company what is to be insured, how much the policy is worth, how long it is to run, and under what conditions insurance is to be effected, as the policy may not automatically cover the insured against *all risks. Underwriters*, who will pay compensation in the case of a claim, then work out the *premium*, i.e. the price of insurance.

The premium is usually quoted in pence per cent, i.e. pence per hundred pounds. This means that for every £100 of insurance you will have to pay x pence. So if you insure your stereo for £800 at 25p%, you will have to pay £2.00 per annum for the premium.

If the insurers are satisfied with the information given on the proposal form, they will issue a *cover note.* This is not the *policy* itself, but an agreement that the goods are covered until the policy is ready. Once the policy is sent it will tell the client that he is *indemnified* against loss, damage, or injury under the conditions of the policy. *Indemnification* means that the insurance company will *compensate* the client to restore him to his *original position* before the loss or damage. Therefore, if you insured your car for £4,000 and three months later it was damaged, you would not receive £4,000 for the car, but its *market price*, which might have depreciated by 20% to £3,200. The insurance company will also have the right of *subrogation*, which means they can now claim the wrecked vehicle and sell it for any price they can get.

In the case of injury or death to an insured person, or in the case of *Life Assurance*, where a fixed amount is to be paid over the years so that a total sum, or pension, will be paid at the end of a period, the principle of *benefit payment* comes into operation. This means that the injured person will be paid compensation based on loss of earnings or suffering. Life Assurance payments are calculated on annual contributions, plus interest the company received on investing the premiums.

Insurance companies are large institutional investors on the stock market, and by investing premiums they are able to cover claims for compensation or pay on Life Assurances policies which have matured.

12.2
Fire and accident insurance

12.2.1
Fire insurance

Fire insurance companies offer three main types of insurance policy:
1 insurance of home and business premises and their contents;
2 'special perils' policies, which protect the insured person against loss or damage due to special factors, e.g. flooding or earthquakes;
3 consequential loss insurance, which insures against loss of profit in the period after a fire, e.g. while a factory is being rebuilt.

12.2.2
Accident insurance

Accident insurance covers four areas:
1 *Insurance of liability*, which covers employers' liabilities for industrial accidents, accidents to people attending functions on company business, and motor insurance.

2 *Property insurance*, which is part of the service fire offices provide, but also includes a wide range of protection against riots, terrorism, gas explosions, etc. Usually, the client takes out an *all risk* policy offering full protection.
3 *Personal accident insurance*, which offers compensation in the form of benefit payments to people injured or killed in outings, playing games, e.g. ice hockey, or travelling by train, coach or aircraft.
4 *Insurance of interest* protects firms against making costly mistakes. For example, publishers might want to cover themselves against libel, i.e. being sued for publishing something which damages someone's reputation. Accountants and lawyers protect themselves with insurance of interest. We can also include under this head *Fidelity Bonds*, under which firms insure against their employees defrauding them, or stealing from them.

12.2.3
Claims

Companies and individuals make claims for loss, damage, or accident, by filling in a *claims form*, which tells the insurance company what has happened. If the insurers accept the claim, often after an investigation, they will then pay compensation.

The insurance company will not pay compensation if the claimant was negligent; or suffered the injury or loss outside the terms of the policy; or misled the insurers when obtaining insurance, e.g. overvalued the article; or insured the same thing twice; or gave false information on the proposal form.

The insurer may, of course, offer less compensation than the claimant is asking for. If the claimant disagrees with the offer, he can call in an independent assessor, and then, if necessary, take the case to court. But usually insurance companies are quite reasonable in their assessments, and small claims are sometimes paid without question.

United Warehouses Ltd.

Chairman: B.R. MacDonald A.C.A.   Directors: N.S. Souness, A. Gemill M.Sc., B. Daracott
Head Office, Bruce House, Bruce Street, Aberdeen AB9 1FR

Registered in Scotland No. 166051
VAT No. 54 901013

Telephone: 0224 41615
Fax: 0224 62219
Telex: 247182

Your ref: Our ref: N 3162-1   Date: 6 April 19—

Westway Insurance Co. Ltd.
Society House
Ellison Place
Newcastle-upon-Tyne NE1 8ST

Dear Sirs,

We would like to know if you could offer a comprehensive insurance policy covering us against fire, flood, accident, industrial injury, and theft.

We are a large warehouse selling furnishings to the retail trade, and employing a staff of thirty. The building we occupy belongs to us and is valued, along with the fixtures and fittings, at £250,000 and at any one time there might be stock worth £70,000 on the premises.

When calculating the premium, would you please take the following into consideration:

There are no open fires on the premises as central heating is used, and we have a fully operational sprinkler system which is serviced regularly. There are also numerous fire extinguishers strategically placed throughout, and fire exits on every floor.

The only danger from flood would be from burst pipes, as we are some distance from the river.

Since we began trading six years ago we have never had to claim for industrial injury, and damage to stock has been minimal. Finally, pilferage, which is common in warehouses, has only cost us £400 per annum on average.

Our present policy runs out at the end of this month, so we would require cover as from 1 May, and we would point out that we are changing insurance companies because of the increased rates that our former insurers are charging. So a competitive quotation would be appreciated.

Yours faithfully,

B Daracott

B. Daracott
United Warehouses Ltd.

12.3
Specimen letters

12.3.1
Request for comprehensive insurance

United Warehouses want to change their insurance company. In this letter they ask Westway Insurance for a quotation.

Questions

1 What sort of policy is United Warehouses asking for?
2 How many people do they employ?
3 What precautions have they taken against fire?
4 Is *petty theft* a problem for them?
5 Why are they changing their insurers?
6 Which words in the letter correspond to the following: *full cover against all contingencies*; *store*; *place of work*; *looked after*; *checked*; *inundation*; *small*; *stealing a few things*; *insurance protection*?

12.3.2
Quotation for comprehensive insurance

In this reply to United Warehouses' request, notice that there are three policies available offering cover under different conditions, but the writer draws attention to one of them, and offers to send an agent to explain the details. The rate of 65p% is mentioned for *indemnification*, i.e. to cover the client for compensation based on the market values of stock and machinery.

Westway Insurance Co. Ltd.

Chairman: Sir David Wedge   Directors: M. Orwell I.P.A., C.R. Archer F.I.S., D.F. Clements
Regional Office, Society House, Ellison Place, Newcastle-upon-Tyne NE1 8ST

Reg. No: England 544712   Telephone: (0632) 326115   Ext: 417
VAT No. 61 576192   Fax: (0632) 501116
                                             Telex: 890410

Your ref: N 3162-1   Our ref: I/34/91675   Date: 9 April 19—

Mr B. Daracott
United Warehouses Ltd.
Bruce House
Bruce Street
Aberdeen AB9 1FR

Dear Mr Daracott,

Thank you very much for your letter of 6 April in which you enquired about our insurance cover.

I have enclosed leaflets explaining our three fully-comprehensive industrial policies which offer the sort of cover you require, and I think that policy A351 would probably suit you best as it offers the widest protection at 65p% with full indemnification.

If you wish, I could get one of our agents to call on you to discuss any details that might not be clear, or, if you are satisfied with the terms, please complete the enclosed proposal form and return it to us with your cheque for £195.00 and we will effect insurance as from 1 May this year.

I look forward to hearing from you soon.

Yours sincerely,

N. Sagum
District Manager

Enc. Proposal form

Westway Insurance Co. Ltd.

Chairman: Sir David Wedge   Directors: M. Orwell I.P.A., C.R. Archer F.I.S., D.F. Clements
Regional Office, Society House, Ellison Place, Newcastle-upon-Tyne NE1 8ST

Reg. No: England 544712	Telephone: (0632) 326115 Ext: 417
VAT No. 61 576192	Fax: (0632) 501116
	Telex: 890410

Your ref: A 4517   Our ref: I/47/9165   Date: 17 August 19—

Mr E. Brockway
International Credit Cards PLC
117–120 Hardman Road
Sheffield S2 2RL

Dear Mr Brockway,

Thank you for your letter of August 15, in which you asked about
bonding your employee, Mr Alfred Cade.

We have checked the references you gave us and he appears to have
an excellent record. Therefore, we will cover Mr Cade for £30,000
on the understanding that he will only handle credit cards and
customers accounts. If, however, he is going to deal with cash, would
you please inform us at once?

Insurance will be effected as soon as we receive the enclosed proposal
form, completed by you.

Yours sincerely,

N. Sagum
District Manager

Enc. Proposal form

12.3.5
Quotation for bonding an employee

International Credit Cards have asked if
Westway would bond one of their
employees, i.e. insure him against
defrauding the company. Here is the
reply.

12.3.6
Claim for fire damage

Here is a claim for fire damage from United Warehouses (see 12.3.1–2 for initial correspondence).

United Warehouses Ltd.

Chairman: B.R. MacDonald A.C.A.   Directors: N.S. Souness, A. Gemill M.Sc., B. Daracott
Head Office, Bruce House, Bruce Street, Aberdeen AB9 1FR

Registered in Scotland No. 166051   Telephone: 0224 41615
VAT No. 54 901013   Fax: 0224 62219
                                                  Telex: 247182

Your ref: Our ref: N 3215-1   Date: 16 October 19—

Claims Dept.
Westway Insurance Co. Ltd.
Society House
Ellison Place
Newcastle-upon-Tyne NE1 8ST

Dear Sirs,

Policy No. 184 65314C

We would like to inform you that a fire broke out in the basement of our warehouse yesterday. Although the blaze was brought under control, we estimate that about £8,000 worth of stock was badly damaged.

A Fire Brigade officer informed us that the blaze was probably caused by an electrical short, which he thought must have occurred around midnight. Fortunately, though, the brigade's action prevented extensive damage.

I would be grateful if you could send us the necessary claims forms.

Yours faithfully,

B Daracott

B. Daracott
United Warehouses Ltd.

Westway Insurance Co. Ltd.

Chairman: Sir David Wedge   Directors: M. Orwell I.P.A., C.R. Archer F.I.S., D.F. Clements
Regional Office, Society House, Ellison Place, Newcastle-upon-Tyne NE1 8ST

Reg. No: England 544712
VAT No. 61 576192

Telephone: (0632) 326115   Ext: 321
Fax: (0632) 501116
Telex: 890410

Your ref: N 3215-1   Our ref: I/34/91812   Date: 28 October 19—

Mr B. Daracott
United Warehouses Ltd.
Bruce House
Bruce Street
Aberdeen AB9 1FR

Dear Mr Daracott,

Policy No. 184 65314C

I now have the report from our surveyor, Mr Nulty, who visited your
premises on 18 October to inspect the damage caused by the fire on
the 15th.

From the copy of the report enclosed, you will see that although he
agrees that the fire was probably caused by an electrical fault, he feels
that £4,000 is a more likely evaluation for damage to stock at present
market prices. However, he suggests that we also pay a further £800
for structural damage to your premises. Consequently, we are
prepared to offer you a total of £4,800 in full compensation under your
policy.

If you accept this assessment, would you please fill out the enclosed
claims form and return it to us, with a letter confirming acceptance of
the compensation we have offered?

Yours sincerely,

D. Pruet
Claims Manager

Enc. Claims form

12.3.7
Reply to claim for fire damage

When Westway received Mr Daracott's
claim, they sent a surveyor to inspect
the damage, find out the cause of the
fire, and assess whether £8,000
compensation was a fair estimate.

Questions

1 Who investigated the claim?
2 Why is only £4,000 being offered for
   the damaged stock?
3 What happens to the 'claims form'?
4 What is the £800 compensation
   being offered for?
5 What was the cause of the fire?

12.4
Marine insurance

12.4.1
Lloyd's of London

Lloyd's is *not* an insurance company, but an *international insurance market* consisting of over 260 approved *insurance brokers'* firms and more than 20,000 *underwriters* whose activites are controlled by Lloyd's Council which came into being after the Lloyd's Act 1982, and whose appointments are confirmed by the Governor of the Bank of England.

If insurance is to be effected through a Lloyd's underwriter (and remember there are other insurance associations as well as Lloyd's, e.g. The American Insurance Association), the transaction has to go through a Lloyd's broker who, working on a commission basis, will contact one or more underwriters on behalf of his client to get a competitive rate. Underwriters finance the insurance, which means they will pay the claims, and take the premiums as their fees. They usually work in *syndicates*, spreading the risk. There are more than four hundred syndicates with over 160 involved in *marine insurance*, 170 in *non-marine*, 50 in *aviation*, and 46 in UK *motor insurance*. Members of syndicates write the insurance details on a *Lloyd's slip* which is sent to the Lloyd's Policy Signing Office where it is checked and signed on behalf of the syndicate concerned. The underwriter gets a percentage of the premium he guarantees. If, for example, he accepts 15% of a £1,000 policy, he will be responsible for £150 compensation in the event of a claim and will receive 15% of the premium.

Lloyd's members, as we have seen, are not restricted to marine insurance. Until 1971, they did not generally deal in long-term business, i.e. insurance for more than ten years on a single policy, and this meant that their activities in life assurance were limited. However, in 1971 Lloyd's Life Assurance Ltd. was established and now offers a wide range of life schemes.

Insuring with a Lloyd's member guarantees reliability as all members, like those of the Stock Exchange, have unlimited liability, and there is a fund that will compensate claimants in the event of a member's bankruptcy. In addition to members there are External Names, people who put up money to guarantee insurance and are paid a percentage of the premium. These people are *not* underwriters, but are recommended to syndicates by agents. The largest collective claim ever paid was probably the San Francisco earthquake of 1906, and the largest marine claim probably the *Olympic Bravery*, a new tanker that was written off in 1976, with underwriters paying $50 million in compensation. This explains why underwriters need to spread the risk by working in syndicates.

Lloyd's List, a daily newspaper read throughout the world, gives details of shipping movements, marine and aviation casualties, fires, strikes, etc., and essential information concerning shipping and dry cargo markets. In addition *Lloyd's Shipping Index* offers daily details of the movements of more than 21,000 merchant vessels. *Lloyd's Loading List* provides UK and European exporters with information on cargo carriers to all parts of the world. *Lloyd's Register of Shipping*, though independent of Lloyd's, works closely with the organization, combining to produce vessel classification giving details of age, owners, and tonnage. The highest classification as to seaworthiness and condition is 100–A1.

12.4.2
Marine insurance policies

Insurers will cover consignments under *all risk* policies which will allow compensation in the event of war, strikes, civil disturbances, etc. These policies are in the form of *valued policies* and are based on the stated value of the invoice, plus insurance, freight, and an extra percentage of 10%, 20%, or 30%, etc. profit margin for the consignment.

There are, however, *unvalued policies*, when the value of the goods have not been agreed in advance and are assessed at the time of loss. This means the consignor will, if his goods are damaged or destroyed, get the market price as compensation. The owner of the bill of lading has the right to claims of compensation.

All consignments can be covered against all risks in the form of a valued or unvalued policy. These policies will fall under five main headings:

1 *Time policy*, which insures goods or the vessel for twelve months, e.g. 1 May 1993 to 30 April 1994.
2 *Voyage policy*, which covers the cargo on a voyage from, say, London to Kobe.
3 *Mixed policy*, which covers a voyage from A to B and then for a further period of time. This may be used when a ship is going from, say, Southampton to Bermuda, then doing a series of trips from Bermuda to ports along the North American coast.
4 *Floating policy*, which gives cover for a particular amount, say, £500,000 so that it will not be necessary to continually write a new policy for each cargo that the ship carries. As the cover nears its end, the insurance company advises their client, and the premium is paid to renew the policy.
5 *Open cover agreements*, which are made between the underwriter and shipper, with the latter informing the underwriter, on a declaration form, whenever the shipment is made, and receiving the policy or certificate after shipment. Forwarding agents often have this kind of agreement with insurance companies, allowing them to make shipments, then inform the insurance company *in arrears*, i.e. *after* the shipment has been made. But the arrangement might only cover certain areas, e.g. North African ports, and consequently they would have to make special arrangements if a shipment was outside the agreed area.

12.4.3
Claims

As we have seen, *all risk* policies generally cover against every eventuality. However, clauses should be studied carefully. If a policy is *free from particular average*, in the case of deliberate damage, i.e. damage caused to save the rest of the cargo, as in, say, the case of a fire in a ship, only total loss will be paid by the insurance company, and part loss in the case of major disasters, e.g. fire or collision. If the policy has a *with particular average* clause, then partial loss will be compensated. Therefore, a policy with a WPA clause will cost more.

As in the case of large claims in non-marine insurance average adjusters, i.e. assessors, are called in to examine damage and estimate compensation. In a c.i.f. transaction, the exporters transfer their right to compensation, as the importer holds the bill of lading. In f.o.b. and c. & f. transactions importers hold the insurance policy as they arrange their own insurance.

12.5
Specimen letters

12.5.1
Request for marine insurance quotation

Kent, Clarke & Co. are forwarding agents for Delta Computers (see 9.8.1–8 and 11.4.4–7 for previous correspondence). They ask Worldwide Insurance to quote a rate for their client's shipment to New Zealand, which is outside the terms of their open cover agreement (see 12.4.2).

Kent, Clarke & Co. Ltd.

Chairman: Lord Matherson   Directors: B. Kent ACA, C.D. Clarke HND, R.P. Diller
South Bank House, Borough Road, London SE1 0AA

Reg No: London 3395162
VAT No: 41 61823159

Telephone: 071 928 7716
Telex: 988153
Fax: 071 928 7111

Worldwide Insurance Ltd.
Worldwide House
Vorley Road
London N19 5HD

15 May 19—

Dear Sirs,

We will be sending on behalf of our clients, Delta Computers Ltd., a consignment of 20 computers to N.Z. Business Machines Pty., Wellington, New Zealand. The consignment is to be loaded on to the SS Northern Cross which sails from Tilbury on 18 May and is due in Wellington on 25 June.

Details with regard to packing and values are attached, and we would be grateful if you could quote a rate covering all risks from port to port.

As the matter is urgent, we would appreciate a prompt reply. Thank you.

Yours faithfully,

J.D. Simpson

J.D. Simpson
Supervisor

Enc.

WORLDWIDE INSURANCE Ltd.

Worldwide House, Vorley Road, London N19 5HD
Telephone: 071 263 6216   Fax: 071 263 6925   Telex: 211121

Chairman: A.L. Galvin ACA FIS   Registered in England No. 6 915614
Managing Director: P.R. Erwin CIS   VAT No. 56 341 27
Directors: L. Swanne, T.R. Crowe MC, H.B. Sidey MA

Your Ref: Our Ref: M1-C167932   Date: 16 May 19—

Mr J.D. Simpson
Kent, Clarke & Co. Ltd.
South Bank House
Borough Road
London SE1 0AA

Dear Mr Simpson,

Thank you for your letter of 15 May, in which you asked about cover for
a shipment of computers from Tilbury to Wellington.

I note from the details attached to your letter that the net amount of the
invoice is £22,000, and payment is by letter of credit. I would therefore
suggest a valued policy against all risks for which we can quote £4.35p%.

We will issue a cover note as soon as you complete and return the
enclosed declaration form.

Yours sincerely,

D. Adair

D. Adair
Manager

Enc. Declaration form

12.5.2
Quotation for marine insurance

In this reply to Kent, Clarke, Worldwide
suggest a valued policy, thus covering
the consignment for £22,000 plus
10%, against all risks including war,
strike, and normal and exceptional
damage. Insurance will be effected from
the date the ship leaves port to its
arrival. A *declaration form* gives the
insurance company information about
the shipment so they can prepare an
insurance certificate.

12.5.3
Certificate of insurance

Questions

1 Who will claim compensation if there is damage or loss?
2 Who are the brokers on this certificate?
3 To what destination is the consignment covered?
4 What is the total cover for the consignment?
5 What do the letters *pp* stand for?
6 When must the consignment be shipped?
7 What type of policy is this?
8 What is the name of the ship carrying the consignment?

ORIGINAL   **LLOYD'S**   THIS CERTIFICATE
       REQUIRES ENDORSEMENT

Lloyd's Agent at **Hong Kong** is authorised to adjust and settle on behalf of the Underwriters and to purchase on behalf of the Corporation of Lloyd's in accordance with Lloyd's Standing Regulations for the Settlement of Claims Abroad, any claim which may arise on this Certificate

Exporters Reference

Certificate of Insurance No. C 8700/

This is to Certify that there has been deposited with the Committee of Lloyd's an Open Cover effected by *Barclays Insurance Brokers International Limited* of Lloyd's, acting on behalf of *Speirs and Wadley Limited* with Underwriters at Lloyd's, dated the   1st   day of **January, 19** . and that the said Underwriters have undertaken to issue to *Barclays Insurance Brokers International Limited* **Policy/Policies of Marine Insurance at Lloyd's to cover, up to £100,000 in all by any one steamer** *or sending by air and/or post and/or road and/or rail and/or conveyance and/or location,* machine tools, other interests held covered

to be shipped on or before the   31st   day of December, 19 . from any port or ports, place or places in the *United Kingdom* to any port or ports, place or places in *the World or vice versa, other voyages held covered* and that are entitled to declare against the said Open Cover the shipments attaching thereto.

Dated at Lloyds, London, 2nd October 1979

for the Committee of Lloyd's

Conveyance	From
Cardigan Bay	**London**
Via To	**To**
Hong Kong	**Warehouse, Hong Kong** INSURED VALUE Currency **£4520 Sterling**

Marks and Numbers	Interest
WI	5 Wooden Cases
124	Said to contain
HONG KONG	400 ELECTRIC POWER DRILLS
1/5	Model LM 425
	2 Speed (900 rpm and 2400 rpm)
	425 watt high-torque motor
	2 chucks – 12·5mm and 8mm
	supplied with each drill

We hereby declare for Insurance under the said Cover interest as specified above so valued subject to the terms of the Standard Form of Lloyd's Marine Policy providing for the settlement of claims abroad and to the special conditions stated below and on the back hereof

Institute Cargo Clauses (A) (1 1 82) or Institute Cargo Clauses (Air) (excluding sendings by Post) (1 1 82) as applicable
Institute War Clauses (Cargo) (1 1 82) or Institute War Clauses (Air Cargo) (excluding sendings by Post) (1 1 82) or Institute War Clauses (sendings by Post) (1 1 82) as applicable
Institute Strikes Clauses (Cargo) (1 1 82) or Institute Strikes Clauses (Air Cargo) (1 1 82) as applicable
General Average and Salvage Contribution payable in full irrespective of insured or contributing values

Underwriters agree losses, if any, shall be payable to the order of Speirs and Wadley Limited on surrender of this Certificate.

In the event of loss or damage which may result in a claim under this Insurance, immediate notice should be given to the Lloyd's Agent at the port or place where the loss or damage is discovered in order that he may examine the goods and issue a survey report.
(Survey fee is customarily paid by claimant and included in valid claim against Underwriters.)

This Certificate not valid unless the Declaration be signed by

Speirs and Wadley Limited

     Dated at

     London, 30th July 19 . .

     Signed W. H. Slevin

     pp Speirs and Wadley Limited

Brokers   Barclays Insurance Brokers International Limited
      India House, 81/84 Leadenhall Street, London EC3A 3DJ   144 78 9

GLASTON POTTERIES Ltd.

Clayfield, Burnley BB10 1RQ

Tel: 0315 46125   Registered No. 716481
Telex: 8801773   VAT Registered No. 133 5341 08
Fax: 0315 63182

Mr D. Adair   5 March 19—
Worldwide Insurance Ltd.
Worldwide House
Vorley Road
London N19 5HD

Dear Mr Adair,

We have been insuring individual shipments of our chinaware with you for some time now, and as you have probably noticed we have established a number of customers in North and South America.

As we will be making regular shipments, we wondered if you could arrange open cover for £60,000 against all risks to insure consignments to North and South American Eastern seaboard ports.

We look forward to hearing from you soon.

Yours sincerely,

E. F. Goodman

E.F. Goodman
Export Department

12.5.4
Request for open cover

Glaston Potteries have built up a regular trade with customers across the Atlantic. They now ask for open cover insurance for their shipments.

Questions

1 Why does Glaston want the policy changed?
2 Do Glaston ship general merchandise?
3 What is the destination for Glaston's consignment?
4 Will the policy indemnify against any eventuality, or only in particular cases?
5 Look at letter 12.5.5 and work out Glaston's premium.
6 Which words in the letter correspond to the following: *particular*; *set up*; *general insurance for a number of shipments*; *thought*?

12.5.5
Quotation for open cover

In an open cover agreement, the exporter can be certain that the consignment is insured once he sends the declaration form. Settlement may either be on a monthly or quarterly basis, or per shipment. When insurance cover is nearly used up, the insurance company will inform the client and ask if he wants to renew the policy.

WORLDWIDE INSURANCE Ltd.

Worldwide House, Vorley Road, London N19 5HD
Telephone: 071 263 6216   Fax: 071 263 6925   Telex: 211121

Chairman: A.L. Galvin ACA FIS   Registered in England No. 6 915614
Managing Director: P.R. Erwin CIS   VAT No. 56 341 27
Directors: L. Swanne, T.R. Crowe MC, H.B. Sidey MA

Your Ref: 5/3/19..   Our Ref: M1-C16893   Date: 7 March 19—

Mr E.F. Goodman
Export Department
Glaston Potteries Ltd.
Clayfield
Burnley BB10 1RQ

Dear Mr Goodman,

In reply to your letter of 5 March, I am pleased to say that we can arrange an <u>all risk open cover</u> policy for chinaware shipments to North and South American seaboard ports.

As you propose to ship regularly, we can offer you a rate of £2.48p% for a total cover of £60,000. I am enclosing a block of declaration forms, and you would be required to submit one for each shipment giving full details.

I look forward to receiving your confirmation that these terms are acceptable.

Yours sincerely,

D. Adair

D. Adair
Manager

Enc. Declaration forms

GLASTON POTTERIES Ltd.

Clayfield, Burnley BB10 1RQ

Tel: 0315 46125
Telex: 8801773
Fax: 0315 63182

Registered No. 716481
VAT Registered No. 133 5341 08

Mr D. Adair
Worldwide Insurance Ltd.
Worldwide House
Vorley Road
London N19 5HD

14 July 19—

Dear Mr Adair,

Open Cover Policy OC 515561

Please note a shipment we are making to our customers MacKenzie Bros., Canada, the details of which are on the enclosed declaration form, No. 117 65913.

Yours sincerely,

E. F. Goodman

E.F. Goodman
Export Department

Enc.

12.5.6
Notification of shipment under open cover

Glaston Potteries have made a shipment to Canada.

12.5.7
Claim under open cover agreement

One of Glaston Potteries' shipments to Canada has been damaged.

GLASTON POTTERIES Ltd.

Clayfield, Burnley BB10 1RQ

Tel: 0315 46125
Telex: 8801773
Fax: 0315 63182

Registered No. 716481
VAT Registered No. 133 5341 08

Mr D. Adair   19 October 19—
Worldwide Insurance Ltd.
Worldwide House
Vorley Road
London N19 5HD

Dear Mr Adair,
Policy No. OC 515561

We would like to inform you that a number of pieces of crockery were damaged on our shipment to MacKenzie Bros. of Dawson, Canada. The consignment was shipped clean on the SS Manitoba which left for Canada on 16 September, and you have our declaration form No. 117 65916.

We have already sent our customers replacements but would like a claims form to complete. Thank you.

Yours sincerely,

E. F. Goodman

E.F. Goodman
Export Department

WORLDWIDE INSURANCE Ltd.

Worldwide House, Vorley Road, London N19 5HD
Telephone: 071 263 6216   Fax: 071 263 6925   Telex: 211121

Chairman: A.L. Galvin ACA FIS   Registered in England No. 6 915614
Managing Director: P.R. Erwin CIS   VAT No. 56 341 27
Directors: L. Swanne, T.R. Crowe MC, H.B. Sidey MA

Your Ref: Our Ref: M1-C16910   Date: 23 October 19—

Mr E.F. Goodman
Export Department
Glaston Potteries Ltd
Clayfield
Burnley BB10 1RQ

Dear Mr Goodman,

Policy No. OC 515561

I am sending you the claims form you requested in your letter dated
19 August 19—. We will consider the matter once we have full
details.

I think I ought to point out that this is the fourth time you have claimed
on a shipment, and though I appreciate your products are fragile, and
that in each case the goods have been shipped clean, it would be in
your interest to consider new methods of packing. I agree that the
claims have been comparatively small, but in future you will have to ask
your customers to hold consignments for our inspection to assess the
cause of damage. I should also mention that further claims may affect
your premium when the policy is renewed.

Yours sincerely,

D. Adair

D. Adair
Manager

Enc. Claims form

12.5.8
Reply to claim under open cover agreement

Worldwide are willing to accept Glaston
Potteries' claim, but they are not too
pleased about it.

Questions

1 What sort of policy have Glaston
   Potteries got?
2 Why does the insurance company
   think that their premium may be
   increased when the policy is
   renewed?
3 Why do they think Glaston have
   made so many claims in the past?
4 When will the insurance company
   consider the claim?
5 What does Mr Adair mean by
   'shipped clean'?
6 Which words in the letter correspond
   to the following: *subject*; *information*;
   understand; *goods taken aboard
   without damage to them*; *keep*; *work
   out*; *the cost of insurance*?

12.5.9
Rejection of claim

In this letter Worldwide reject a claim on the grounds that the bill of lading was not clean. Note the transaction could not have been by confirmed letter of credit, as only a clean bill of lading would be accepted. Also that the exporter is entitled to call in his own assessor to inspect the damage, and that if there is a dispute, the case would be settled by arbitration.

WORLDWIDE INSURANCE Ltd.

Worldwide House, Vorley Road, London N19 5HD
Telephone: 071 263 6216   Fax: 071 263 6925   Telex: 211121

Chairman: A.L. Galvin ACA FIS	Registered in England No. 6 915614
Managing Director: P.R. Erwin CIS	VAT No. 56 341 27
Directors: L. Swanne, T.R. Crowe MC, H.B. Sidey MA	

Your Ref: Our Ref: M2-D23140   Date: 28 October 19—

Mr T. Shane
Excelsior Engineering PLC
Valley Estate
Birkenhead
Merseyside L41 7ED

Dear Mr Shane,

Policy No. AR 661 72241

I have now received our assessor's report with reference to your claim CF 37568 in which you asked for compensation for damage to two turbine engines which were shipped ex-Liverpool on the SS Freemont on October 11, for delivery to your customer, D.V. Industries, Hamburg.

The report states that the B/L, No. 553719, was claused by the captain of the vessel, with a comment on cracks in the casing of the machinery.

Our assessor believes that these cracks were responsible for the casing weakening during the voyage and splitting, which eventually caused damage to the turbines themselves.

I am sorry that we cannot help you further, but the company cannot accept liability for goods unless they are shipped clean. See Clause 26B of the Policy.

Yours sincerely,

D. Adair

D. Adair
Manager

12.6
Points to remember

1 *Insurance* is designed to cover a business or individual against risks such as loss, damage, or injury. Numerous types of policies are available to offer cover against eventualities, but the client has to decide which hazards apply to him.

2 *Assurance* is concerned with offering benefit payment either to dependants, in the case of death or incapacity, or in the case of endowment schemes, a lump sum or pension after a number of years' contributions.

3 *Indemnification* is the cover which allows compensation in the event of loss or damage, and is calculated on the market value or depreciation value of goods, not their original value. To be insured, a client completes a *Proposal Form*; the *premium* is then assessed and quoted, in the UK, in pence per cent. On acceptance, the client is issued with a *cover note* which gives him cover until the policy is ready. As insurance is based on the principle of good faith, and supported by laws against fraud, insurance companies accept that the items being insured belong to the client, are not being insured more than once, are of the value stated, and that the client will follow the conditions of the *policy*.

4 *Marine insurance* offers shippers a variety of policies to cover shipments. However, most exporters ship under an *all-risk, valued policy* which covers them against most eventualities and allows them compensation for loss or damage, plus ten per cent.

5 *Open cover* and *floating policies* are used when the exporter makes regular shipments. These give him a total amount of cover which decreases as each shipment's value is declared, but can be renewed.

12.7
Words to remember

an insurance company
a broker
a proposal form
a quotation
a policy
cover
all risk
underwriter
a syndicate
a cover note
indemnification
original position
subrogation

to cover against
to take effect from
to bond someone
to renew a policy

a claimant
to make/reject a claim
compensation
to inspect damage
negligent
to overvalue
an independent assessor
an assessment
valuation
arbitration

life assurance
benefit payment
endowment
fire insurance
'special perils' policy
consequential loss insurance
accident insurance

insurance liability
property insurance
personal accident insurance
insurance of interest
fidelity bonds

marine insurance
all risk policy
valued policy
time policy
voyage policy
mixed policy
floating policy
open cover policy
in arrears
a clause
free from particular average
with particular average
declaration form
an insurance certificate
to ship clean
a clean bill of lading

The American Insurance Association
Lloyd's of London
Lloyd's List
Lloyd's Shipping Index
Lloyd's Loading List
Lloyd's Register of Shipping

Electronic correspondence 13

Fax; electronic mail (email); telegrams; cables; telex

13.1
Fax

The word 'fax' can be used as a noun or a verb, e.g. *a fax*, *to fax someone*. It comes from the word *facsimile*, meaning an exact copy or reproduction. As its name suggests, a fax machine will send a duplicate of the message, document, design, or photo that is fed into it.

Faxing is a means of telecommunication that has developed very quickly over the past few years. There are various models of fax machine which connect to a telephone socket and which work on a system similar to the telephone system. Charges are measured in telephone units and therefore vary according to the time of day and where the fax is being sent.

The different models of fax machine offer a wide range of facilities, including automatic paper feeders, deferred transmission (faxes are sent during cheap-rate periods), automatic redialling if the receiver's machine is engaged, and pre-programmed keys for instant dialling.

The advantages of fax include instant reception of documents, and documentary evidence of what has been transferred. A document can be relayed from one source to hundreds of other receivers, for example, if the head office of a chain store wants to circulate a memo or report to its branches.

13.2
Specimen faxes

13.2.1
Advice of damaged consignment

This fax is from Lynch & Co., who received a damaged consignment and were told by their supplier, Mr Causio of Satex, to return it (see 7.4.3/4).

F. Lynch & Co. Ltd.
(Head Office), Nesson House, Newell Street, Birmingham B3 3EL
Telephone: 021–236 6571   Cables: MENFINCH Birmingham   Telex: 341641

Fax transmission

Message for: D Causio

Address: Satex S.p.A., Via di Pietra Papa, 00146 Roma

Fax number: (06) 481 5473

From: L. Crane

Date: 19 September 19—

Dear Mr. Causio,

This is an urgent request for a consignment to replace the damaged delivery which we received, and about which you have already been informed.

Please airfreight the following items:

Cat.no.	Quantity
RN30	50
AG20	70
L26	100

The damaged consignment will be returned to you on receipt of the replacement.

Yours sincerely,

L Crane

L. Crane
Chief Buyer

Perfect Office Suppliers Limited

Canal Street, Manchester M14 2KQ

Fax transmission

From: Mike Wilson
To: Sue Franks

Sue –

I've been in Bournemouth now since yesterday, and our clients seem to be most enthusiastic about our new range of notepaper. Can you send some more samples and about twenty more catalogues? Please send them Datapost, then I'll definitely get them tomorrow.

Also, just to let you know I'll be in Norwich on Thursday 24th and Friday 25th, and back at the office on the Monday.

Thanks, and see you next week.

13.2.2

This fax is an example of an informal message from a sales representative, who needs something to be done urgently by his Head Office. Notice that the fax is kept brief and clear.

13.3

Electronic mail (email)

Electronic mail is a means of sending and receiving messages – internally, nationally, or internationally. In the UK, Telecom Gold is a leading commercial email service. Subscribers to email need a terminal, such as a personal computer, a telephone line, and a *modem*, which is a device for converting signals to text. Messages appear on the receiver's computer screen.

Email users can also have access to a *mailbox*, which they can call from anywhere in the world and retrieve messages. They receive a mailbox number and a password for confidentiality. Messages can be printed out and kept for reference or filing.

In comparison with telex, email is relatively low in cost, and does not require a trained operator. It is also fast, relatively reliable, and messages can be sent or picked up anywhere in the world, and stored in the mailbox until they are retrieved. This can be particularly advantageous for users who are communicating across international time zones.

Users of the Telecom Gold system can request a personal telex number, and receive messages through email, or send faxes to users on the same system.

13.4

Specimen email message

Here is an example of one type of message, with the capitals representing data on the Visual Display Unit (VDU) and the italics, the messages.

Notice the codes which are the personal numbers of the subscribers, e.g. ABC 123, and the prefixes, e.g. 70: which is the number of that computer system. Also the dot(.) before the word SEND(.SEND), which is a command to the computer.

> mail

SEND, READ OR SCAN: *read*
TO: *German Shipping Lines 70: (ABC123)*
FROM: *Kyser Shipbrokers Ltd. 80: (DEF456)*
POSTED: *15-May-93 12.41*
SUBJECT: *Charter of the MV Orion*

MORE: *yes*

Our clients, Masserey Grain, are willing to accept the charter of the MV Orion at $32.21 per ton. Please confirm that the vessel wil be in Rotterdam ready for loading on 15 June '92.

ACTION REQUIRED: *reply*

TEXT:

Confirmation, the MC Orion will be in Rotterdam loading on 15 June '92, and the charter rate is $32.21 per ton.

.SEND

CDE456 -- SENT

ACTION REQUIRED: *delete*

END OF MAIL

13.5
Telegrams and cables

The words *telegram* and *telegraph* are usually associated with internal communication, while *cable* generally refers to overseas messages. *Telegram* is a noun and *telegraph* can be used as a verb or adjective:

We received your telegram.
Please telegraph your reply.
A telegraph line.

Cable can be used as a verb, noun, or adjective:

I cabled him yesterday.
Please send a cable.
We received a cable message.

There are a number of points to remember when telegraphing or cabling a message. Below is a guide.

```
BUMAN                                                              ──────── Receiver's telegraphic address

CARGO SPACE SS FORTUNA AVAILABLE STOP CONFIRM SHIP
SAILS 10 FEB STOP DELIVER CONSIGNMENT WITH                        ──────── Message
DOCUMENTS SOONEST

TRANSHIP LONDON                                                    ──────── Sender's telegraphic address
```

13.5.1
Layout of telegrams and cables

Although small letters can be used, cables are usually written out in capitals with the telegraphic address of the receiver at the top, the message following, and the sender's address at the end.

Telegraphic addresses are usually made up from the name of the firm, e.g. Denis Robert can be formed into DENRO, or from the name and trade of the company. Figures are also sometimes added.

13.5.2
The word STOP

Although there can be full stops in telegrams and cables, sentences are often broken up with the word STOP.

NEGOTIATIONS SUCCESSFULLY CONCLUDED STOP HOME TOMORROW STOP

YOUR LAST SHIPMENT DAMAGED STOP LETTER FOLLOWS STOP

Occasionally, however, the word STOP can create confusion if the cable is carelessly worded. If, in the second cable above, the sender had used the word WRITING instead of LETTER FOLLOWS to indicate that he was going to write a letter later, the message would have read STOP WRITING, with possibly unfortunate results.

13.5.3
The word REPEAT

This word is often used in cables to emphasize a negative:

DO NOT REPEAT NOT SEND ORDER 18551

Or to emphasize an important detail:

FLIGHT DELAYED BY SIX REPEAT SIX HOURS

13.5.4
Abbreviations

You can use abbreviations in cables, e.g. L/C (letter of credit), B/L (bill of lading) etc., but you must make sure that they are internationally recognized.

Only irrevocable letters of credit which have been confirmed by a bank will be acceptable.

ONLY IRREVOCABLE CONFIRMED L/C ACCEPTABLE

We are prepared to accept your offer on a Cost Insurance Freight basis with payment by bill of exchange at 30 days after sight.

CIF ACCEPTABLE STOP PAYMENT B/E 30 D/S

Notice the special abbreviations *lowest* (as low as possible) and *earliest* or

soonest (as soon as possible), which are acceptable abbreviations in cables.

Could you please give us your most competitive quotation for your MD20 cameras?

PLEASE QUOTE LOWEST FOR MD20 CAMERAS

We would be grateful if you would reply as quickly as possible.

PLEASE REPLY SOONEST

13.5.5
Brief but clear

Economy of words saves money, but if too few words are used, the message becomes confused and will cost more money in the long run. For example, if you received this message from Melbourne, Australia, would you know what to do about it?

JOHN REED ARRIVING STOP MEET AT AIRPORT

The message does not tell us which airport John Reed is arriving at, or which flight he is on. A few more words would have made a difference.

JOHN REED ARRIVING 12 MAY A.M. STOP FLIGHT 441 QANTAS HEATHROW TERMINAL 3 PLEASE MEET

It is possible to omit certain words in cables, provided the meaning remains clear. Articles, pronouns, and prepositions can be left out:

I will send you a copy of the contract on March 1st.

WILL SEND COPY CONTRACT MARCH FIRST

Participles or nouns can be used to replace clauses:
We have received the consignment you sent us last week to replace the damaged goods.

HAVE RECEIVED REPLACEMENT CONSIGNMENT DESPATCHED LAST WEEK

Will you please inform us of the date when the SS Marina arrives in Liverpool?

PLEASE INFORM ARRIVAL SS MARINA LIVERPOOL

13.5.6
Words not figures

It is better to use words rather than figures where money, weight, and size is concerned. The following message from a commodity broker to his client, regarding the purchase of cocoa, is not very clear:

HAVE BEEN QUOTED 27,000 POUNDS STOP SHOULD WE BUY

The figure 7 in the UK can often be confused with the figure 1 in continental Europe. The comma may be confusing (see 2.5.2). The word 'pounds' could refer to weight or, like the words 'dollars' and 'francs' which are also ambiguous, to any of several currencies. So it would have been better to cable:

HAVE BEEN QUOTED TWENTY SEVEN THOUSAND POUNDS STERLING STOP SHOULD WE BUY

13.6
Specimen telegram

13.6.1
Quotation of shipping rates

Here is a reply to an exporter from a shipping company telling him that a vessel is available, and quoting rates. See 11.4.1/2.

LEBATS HONG KONG
SS ORIENT ACCEPTING CARGO 3 MAY TO 7 MAY WHEN SAILING
STOP DUE TILBURY 3 JUNE STOP RATES THIRTY
ONE POUNDS STERLING PER TONNE
FREAST HONG KONG

13.7
Telex

Telegrams and cables can, of course, be sent from the Post Office or telephoned, which means that this form of communication is available for twenty-four hours a day, seven days a week. But there can be short delays between sending the message and its arrival. Telex, on the other hand, is as direct as using the telephone.

The telex has all the advantages of sending a cable and in addition it is available in the office and offers a direct line, with immediate reply. It is available twenty-four hours a day, and can send cables as well as telex messages; moreover, the message can be corrected immediately if there is an error.

As with the telephone, there is a subscribers' directory listing telex users' numbers. There are more than 70,000 UK and 900,000 worldwide lines.

The word *telex* can be used as a verb, noun or adjective:

Please telex us as soon as you have the information.
I will send you a telex.
We have received a telexed reply.

13.7.2
Operating the telex

The telex is a machine like a typewriter, but with a dial on its casing. You can send messages by dialling the receiver's number, or by dialling and using the keyboard for some countries, or by asking the operator at the exchange to connect you.

Once the telex operator has dialled the code, an *answerback* code will appear on the *teleprinter* indicating that the sender is through. If the wrong code appears, the sender merely dials again. The message is typed, as with a normal typewriter, and will appear on the receiver's machine.

Corrections are made by typing five Xs: WE ARE SEDXXXXX SNEDIXXXXX SENDING THE ORDER. (Sometimes E space E space is used: WE ARE SEDE E E SENDING THE ORDER.)

Each telex message is *finished* with a + sign, if the end is not clear, and a + + sign is used after the last message. The sign + ? at the end of a message means either *reply*, *confirm*, or *a further message will be sent*, so that a new call does not have to be made.

Figures or unusual words are sometimes repeated at the end of the message. This is known as *collation*.

13.7.1
Layout of telexes

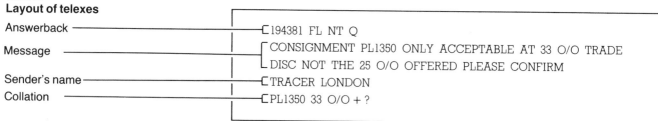

Answerback ———————————— 194381 FL NT Q

Message ———————————— CONSIGNMENT PL1350 ONLY ACCEPTABLE AT 33 O/O TRADE
                        DISC NOT THE 25 O/O OFFERED PLEASE CONFIRM

Sender's name———————————— TRACER LONDON

Collation ———————————— PL1350 33 O/O + ?

13.7.3
Abbreviations

In addition to the abbreviations mentioned at 13.5.4, telex operators also use the following abbreviations which are recognized internationally.

ABS	*Absent subscriber, office closed*
BK	*I cut off*
CFM	*Please confirm/I confirm*
COIL	*Collation please/I collate*
CRV	*Do you receive well?/I receive well*
DER	*Out of order*
DF	*You are in communication with the called subscriber*
E E E	*Error*
FIN	*I have finished my message(s)*
GA	*You may transmit/may I transmit?*
INF	*Subscriber temporarily unobtainable, call the Information (Enquiry) Service*
MNS	*Minutes*
MOM	*Wait/waiting*
MUT	*Mutilated*
NA	*Correspondence to this subscriber is not admitted*
NC	*No circuits*
NCH	*Subscriber's number has been changed*
NP	*The called party is not, or is no longer, a subscriber*
NR	*Indicate your call number/ my call number is . . .*
OCC	*Subscriber is engaged*
OK	*Agreed/do you agree?*
P* (or Figure 0)	*Stop your transmission*
PPR	*Paper*
R	*Received*
RAP	*I shall call you back*
RPT	*Repeat/repeat*
SVP	*Please*

TAX	*What is the charge?/the charge is . . .*
TEST MSG	*Please send a test message*
THRU	*You are in communication with a Telex position*
TPR	*Teleprinter*
W	*Words*
WRU	*Who is there?*
XXXXX	*Error*

*Repeat until transmission is stopped

13.7.4
Telex details

All the points about brevity and clarity in sending cabled messages are relevant to telexing. But there are a number of other points:

Fractions should be typed with a 'shilling stroke': 1/2 for ½; 1/4 for ¼; 15/16 for ¹⁵⁄₁₆; 21–1/3 for 21⅓.

Figures, especially large sums, should be repeated in words: 60,000 SIXTY THOUSAND.

Symbols should be written in words: FIFTY ONE POUNDS STERLING for £51.00; AT for @; 0 0 or PER CENT FOR %.

13.8
Specimen telexes

13.8.1
Advice of inability to supply order

In this telex, Satex of Rome are telling their customer, F. Lynch & Co., that they cannot supply the sweaters they asked for in their order – DR 5871 – and want to know if they can replace this with sweaters of catalogue number N154. Notice the answerback and the collation.

```
341641 TR JM P
CANNOT SUPPLY ITEM R432 ON ORDER DR5871 BUT N154
AVAILABLE PLEASE CONFIRM ACCEPTANCE
SATEX ROME
R432 DR 5871 N15 + ?
```

13.8.2
Acceptance of alternative supply

In their answer Lynch & Co. accept the alternative but want the terms confirmed.

```
285136 ML JR C
N154 ACCEPTABLE ONLY ON SAME TERMS AS R432 NAMELY
33 0/0 DISC CIF
F LYNCH BIRMINGHAM
N154 R432 0/0 CIF + ?
```

13.8.3
Instruction to stockbroker

Here is a telex from a client to his stockbroker asking him to buy shares on his behalf. Note the term *at best*, i.e. the best price the broker can obtain. Also, that a letter will follow.

```
881534 LM TB D
BUY REPEAT BUY 3000 THREE THOUSAND UNION SHIPPING
AT BEST CONFIRMATION FOLLOWS
DALE PRESTON
3000 UNION SHIPPING + +
```

13.8.4
Advice of bank credit

Here is a bank advising their customer that money has been paid into his account. Note that TT means telegraphic transfer of money.

```
901737 PN LT A
YOUR A/C CREDITED TT NINE HUNDRED AND EIGHTY
POUNDS STERLING
NATIONAL BANK OF JAPAN
980 POUNDS STERLING + +
```

```
611531 DM RM B
YOUR ORDER 90103 SHIPPED CLEAN ON BOARD S S ORIENT
SAILING 6 MAY OUR AGENTS FORWARDING DOCUMENTS TO
NORTHERN CITY BANK LETTER OF CONFIRMATION FOLLOWS
LEE BOATBUILDERS
90103 SS ORIENT + +
```

13.8.5
Advice of shipment

This telex is from Lee Boatbuilders Ltd., Hong Kong, advising their customer, International Crafts, that their order is being shipped to them.

```
901174 HM TP L
S S TANAKA MARU NOW DOCKED IN HOUSTON AVAILABLE
FOR SIX MONTHS VESSEL 5000 FIVE THOUSAND TONS HIRE 4
FOUR POUNDS STERLING PER TON TELEX ACCEPTANCE
ALLIANCE SHIPBROKERS LONDON
6 MONTHS 5000 TONS 4 POUNDS STERLING PER TON + ?
```

13.8.6
Shipbroker's advice

Telex from a shipbroker advising an exporter that a vessel is available for a time charter.

```
857811 TR LN P
CONFIRM ACCEPTANCE OF CHARTER FOR S S TINXXXXX
TANAKA MARU SEND US CHIRXXXXX CHARTER PARTY
HERDIS MANUFACTURING SLOUGH + +
```

13.8.7
Reply to shipbroker

This is a reply to 13.8.6. The 'Charter Party' is the contract for chartering a vessel. Notice the corrections in the telex.

13.9
Points to remember

1 The structure and presentation of a faxed letter should be much the same as that of an ordinary letter, but you must state clearly, at the top of the first page, the name of the person you wish to read it.

2 Many offices supply a fax 'lead sheet' which is fed into the machine as a first page, and which gives the receiver details about who the sender is, which company he/she represents, how many pages he/she is faxing, etc.

3 Both fax and email enable people to receive messages and important information immediately.

4 Companies are increasingly using fax and email in place of telex machines. However, remember that telexes, telegrams, and cables are still commonly used in some countries, especially outside Europe.

13.10
Words to remember

a fax
to fax (someone)
receiver's code
electronic mail
email
a modem
a mailbox
a visual display unit (VDU)

a telegram
to telegraph
a cable
to cable
a cable message
a telegraphic address
telegraphic transfer

telemessages
a telex
to telex
answerback
collation

Miscellaneous correspondence 14

Reservations; appointments; hospitality; letters of condolence and congratulations.

In this unit we look at some miscellaneous correspondence, much of which a secretary might deal with in a medium to large-size firm.

14.1
Reservations

14.1.1
Air travel

Dear Sir,

This letter is to confirm our telephone conversation this morning when I arranged for two tickets to be sent to us in the names of P. R. Dell and B. Newsome, our directors, who will be travelling London Heathrow–Rome on flight BA 164 at 10.05 hours, on Wednesday 12 June.

Please send the tickets to us by return, and find a cheque for £210.00 enclosed.

Yours faithfully,

14.1.2
Train travel

Dear Sir,

With reference to my telephone call to you this morning, would you please book a return ticket including couchette in the name of Mr John Miles for London–Paris–Zagreb, leaving on Monday 18 July, and returning Zagreb–Paris–London, on 3 August?

Please could you reserve a seat in a non-smoking compartment?

I would appreciate your sending the tickets as soon as possible and have enclosed a cheque for £188.00.

Yours faithfully,

14.1.3
Hotel

Dear Mr Ruggerio,

This letter is to confirm my telex and your answer of today in which you agreed to reserve two separate rooms with shower and bath, from 12 June to 21 June inclusive for Mr P.R. Dell and Mr B. Newsome, who will be attending the Textile Trade Fair in Rome.

Could you make sure that the rooms are situated at the back of the hotel, as the rooms they were given last year, overlooking the main road, were rather noisy?

I am enclosing a banker's draft for £40.00 as a deposit. Could you please acknowledge receipt?

Yours sincerely,

14.1.4
Conference facilities

Dear Sir,

We are holding our annual conference this year in Nantes and are looking for a hotel which can offer us accommodation and conference facilities from 15 to 18 November inclusive.

There will be 60 delegates, 15 of whom will be bringing their wives. Therefore, we will need 45 single rooms and 15 double with full board for the three days. Provision should also be made for serving morning coffee and afternoon tea in the conference room.

For the meetings we will need a room that can accommodate 60 to 70 people, with sound equipment, and if possible a stage from where lectures and demonstrations can be given.

We will be bringing our own visual aids with us, so it will not be necessary to provide projectors, boards, or screens.

Please would you send us a list of your tariffs and let us know if you are prepared to allow discounts for a block booking. If you can offer a competitive quotation, and satisfactory accommodation and facilities, you can rely on regular bookings from us in the future.

Yours faithfully,

14.2
Appointments

Dear Mr Grane,

Our Chief Buyer, Mr Norman Luman, would like you to contact us with a view to discussing the possibility of setting up a contract with your company to supply us with steel over the next year.

He will be in his office all next week, and if you could write or phone him on 081–573 6621 he would be glad to arrange a meeting with you.

Yours sincerely,

14.2.1
Making an appointment

Dear Mr Grane,

Mr Norman Luman has asked me to confirm the appointment you made to see him. He looks forward to meeting you at 11.30 in his office, at the above address, on Tuesday 2 August.

Yours sincerely,

14.2.2
Confirming an appointment

Dear Ms Hopper,

I am sorry to tell you that Mr Grane will not be able to keep the appointment he made to see Mr Luman on Tuesday 2nd August. Unfortunately an urgent matter has come up in our Lisbon office and needs his immediate attention. He offers his sincere apologies for the inconvenience and will contact you as soon as he returns to London.

Yours sincerely,

14.2.3
Cancelling an appointment

Dear Mr Luman,

Just a line to say that I was pleased we were finally able to meet one another yesterday after having to postpone our meeting two weeks ago when I was called to Lisbon.

I am also pleased we were able to work out the main points of our contract so quickly and were able to come to a mutually acceptable agreement.

It would be useful for us to keep in contact so I will call you in a few weeks or so and perhaps we can discuss how things are going with our supplies or anything else you would like to talk about. I look forward to seeing you soon.

Yours sincerely,

14.2.4
Follow-up after an appointment

14.3
Hospitality

14.3.1
Request for hospitality

A British firm which wants to expand its sales to Scandinavian countries asks a Norwegian business associate to provide help and hospitality on the occasion of a visit to Norway by the company's sales manager. Notice that the letter does not open with the request, but a gentle reminder of the companies' association. The request is also framed in general terms rather than making specific demands.

Dear Mr Deksen,

Thank you for your last consignment. You will be pleased to hear that we are processing another order to be sent to you within the next few weeks.

The purpose of this letter, however, is to ask if you could offer any assistance to our overseas sales manager, Mr Michael Hobbs, who will be visiting Oslo from 11 to 17 May.

You may remember that when you were here a few months ago I mentioned that we intended to expand our sales. We are now looking at the potential of the Scandinavian market, and Michael Hobbs' trip is part of our investigations into the possibilities of our exporting to Scandinavia.

I wondered if, while he was in your city, you would be able to introduce him to wholesalers and retailers in our trade who may be able to give him information with regard to the type of products that we would need to offer to the Norwegian market. He will also be interested in marketing, demand, importing procedures and any other information that would be useful to us.

I understand of course that you are very busy, but if it is not too inconvenient, may I tell him that he may contact you at some time during his stay? The help would certainly be appreciated, and reciprocated if the opportunity arises.

Yours sincerely,

14.3.2
Letter of introduction

This letter would be presented to Mr Deksen in person.

Dear Mr Deksen,

The bearer of this letter is Mr Michael Hobbs, our overseas sales manager, who is visiting Oslo on our behalf to investigate our export possibilities to Norway.

Thank you for your letter of 10 April in which you offered to help him. I will appreciate any assistance you can give, or suggestions you make.

Yours sincerely,

Dear Mr Deksen,

Thank you very much for assisting Michael Hobbs while he was in Oslo.

I know he has already written to you expressing his gratitude, but I would like to add my own appreciation. The introductions you made for him and the contacts and information he gained will be extremely useful in our Scandinavian export programme.

If I can offer you any similar service in the future, please contact me.

Yours sincerely,

14.3.3
Letter of thanks

Dear Mr Grant,

We would like to invite you to attend our award ceremony at Claremont College which is being held on 14 December this year. The proceedings will begin about 2.00 and end around 5.00 in the afternoon, after which a dinner will be given at 7.00 for our prominent visitors.

As one of our distinguished ex-students we would like you to address the parents and students with a short speech of your choice before handing out the awards.

Although we realize you are busy we hope you can find time to accept the invitation and look forward to seeing you.

Yours sincerely,

14.3.4
An invitation

Dear Mr Edwards,

Mr Grant, our director, has asked me to write to thank you and accept your kind invitation to attend the award ceremony and speak at Claremont College on December 14.

He has fond memories of the college where he trained as an engineer, and welcomes the chance to visit it again.

The topic he has chosen to speak on is 'Changing Technology in the next Decade', and he would appreciate it if you would let him know whether this will be an acceptable subject.

Yours sincerely,

14.3.5
Accepting an invitation

14.3.6
Refusing an invitation

Dear Mr Odensa,

Our Chairman thanks you very much for the kind invitation you sent to attend the reception being held next month at your embassy.

Although he would have liked to have come, he will be in America at that time. However, he sends you his best wishes and apologies for not being able to attend, and hopes that you will send another invitation at some future date, when he does not have any commitments.

Yours sincerely,

14.4
Special occasions

14.4.1
Letter of condolence

Letters of condolence should never be written in the third person, i.e. by someone else on your behalf.

Dear Mr Stanton,

I was shocked to hear about the death of your partner, Mr John Brendon, and offer my condolences. He was a fine person and a well-liked man who will be sadly missed by all who knew him.

Please pass my sincerest sympathies on to his family, and assure them that all his associates will have only the fondest memories of him.

Yours sincerely,

14.4.2
Letter of congratulations

Congratulations are also best given directly, not by someone on your behalf.

Dear Mr Carrington,

I would like to offer my congratulations on your being elected chairman of our Trade Association.

No one has done more to deserve the honour, or has worked harder to promote our interests. You can count on me and my company to give you any assistance you require in your term of office, and I wish you every success for the future.

Yours sincerely,

14.5
Points to remember

1 The conventions governing formality should be observed just as rigorously with social correspondence as with business correspondence. The writer, e.g. a secretary, should be aware of the relationship of the sender and the receiver and use appropriate language.
2 Letters of invitation, e.g. to a product launch, should state clearly where and when the event will take place, and some indication of how formal it is.
3 When cancelling an appointment, you should say why you are unable to keep it.
4 Letters of condolence or cogratulation should never be written on someone else's behalf.

14.6
Words to remember

to make a reservation
to accept/refuse an invitation
to make/confirm/cancel an appointment

a letter of introduction
a letter of thanks
a letter of confirmation
an invitation
a letter of condolence
a letter of congratulations
a request for hospitality

In-company communications

15

Memorandums; reports.

15.1
Memorandums

Memorandums are written internal communications which advise or inform employees of policies and procedures that their company has decided to adopt.

The memo may be put on a notice board for everyone to see, or circulated in internal mail to the departments it concerns. In the latter case, the employee usually signs the memorandum to acknowledge that he/she has read it.

There are numerous subjects that memos deal with, from informing staff of a retirement, to announcing important administrative or structural changes in the company.

15.1.1
Layout

Companies often use a special letter-heading for memorandums which gives less information about the company but indicates which department has issued the memo. Compare the letter-heading on the memo at 15.2.1 with the one Westway use for letters (see 12.3.9).

Note that the memo states who it is to, who it is from, the subject, and the date.

Paragraphs in memos are often numbered, as here, particularly when the subject concerns a procedure to be followed.

15.1.2
Guide to contents

Memos may have a *title*, e.g.

Subject: Introduction of shift-work
Subject: Annual Audit
Subject: Pension Scheme

If there is no title, introduce the *subject* in the opening paragraph:

A Shift-Work system is to be introduced next month.

The annual Audit will begin on 1 March 19—.

A Contributory Pension Scheme is to be introduced as from 1 July 19—.

Explain to staff *how* they will be affected:

The shift-work system will affect all employees in this branch of Halliwell & Fischer and will be introduced on a two-shift basis – 06.00 to 14.00 hours, and 14.00 to 20.00 hours. You will be told by department heads . . .

The Auditors will be allotted offices which will mean that some members of staff will be temporarily transferred to other offices in the building . . .

Members of staff will have to join the pension scheme and contribute 6% of their gross monthly salary. The contributions will go towards a retirement benefit plan which at 60 will offer a pension of 70% of gross salary, in addition to the Government scheme.

Unless already stated, the employees must be told *when* the policy becomes effective:

The scheme will begin from 1 February 19—.

The audit will begin on 1 March and should take about three weeks . . .

Contributions to the scheme will be deducted from the pay month ending 1 July 19—.

State *who* will be affected and *where:*

The audit will affect all branches of the company, and warehousemen are reminded that they will have to account for any missing items. Staff will be expected to explain the loss of any equipment, or damage to . . .

The pension scheme will only affect those members of staff who were employed on or before 1 January 19—. Employees who joined after that date will be included in the scheme as soon as they have completed six months' full-time employment with the firm.

Once you have mentioned *how* staff will be affected, *when* the scheme becomes effective, *where* it will operate, and *who* will be involved, you must explain *what* should be done:

Will all employees please see either their supervisors or department

managers, who will let them know which shift they will be working on for the first month? Another memo will be circulated next week, explaining a bonus scheme which will be introduced as part of the new arrangement.

Everyone included in the scheme will receive a booklet giving them details of how the pension plan will work and what benefits they will receive on retirement or in the event of their deaths. A contract with a copy will also be enclosed and you should sign it, then hand it to your departmental manager before 21 June 19—.

Finally, if the memo appears to be complicated, or you think it might not be completely understood by everyone, you should advise them to contact a manager, supervisor, or departmental head, who will explain it to them and consider their comments and complaints, if they have any.

If you have any problems whatsoever with the shift you have been allotted, or cannot work on a shift basis, please tell your supervisor or manager when you see him.

If there are any problems you feel your manager should be made aware of before the auditors arrive, please let him know at once.

The booklet should explain the scheme clearly to you. But if there is anything you do not understand, or if you are already in a scheme that might be affected by the firm's pension plan, please inform your departmental manager as soon as possible.

MEMORANDUM

F. Lynch & Co. Ltd.
(Head Office), Nesson House, Newell Street, Birmingham B3 3EL

To: Department Managers   Date: 10 November 19—
From: The Chief Accountant
Subject: Cheque Identification

Will all Department Managers remind their sales staff that all cheques must be accompanied by proper identification, i.e. cheque, store, or credit cards.

The store has experienced a number of bad debts over the past few months due to customers paying with bad cheques, and as the Christmas rush will soon be with us, this problem could increase unless sales staff are more careful.

Notices are placed round the store to explain the position to customers, but if staff experience any difficulty with a customer they should call over a manager or supervisor to deal with the matter.

T. Braithwaite

T. Braithwaite
Chief Accountant

15.2.1
Memo to Department Managers

Lynch & Co. want to tighten up security in their department stores.

Questions

1 Who sent the memo, and what does it deal with?
2 What should the staff ask customers to do?
3 How are the staff supported, and what should they do if there are any difficulties?
4 What will make the problem worse?
5 Which words used in the memo correspond to the following: *balances that cannot be recovered*; *because of*?

15.2.2
Visit of a customer

Coventry Components are expecting an important visitor to their factory so they circulate this message on their electronic mail computer monitors, see email at 13.2.

Different systems may have a different layout or coding; this message is based on the Telecom Gold System.

Questions

1 What is the memo about?
2 How can employees help?
3 Why is their help so important?
4 Who will escort the visitors?
5 Is any answer expected to this memo?
6 When was the memo sent?
7 Which words in the memo correspond to the following: *parts of an engine*; *a favourable view*; *the way things work*; *giving information*; *very important*?

> mail

SEND, READ or SCAN: *read*

TO: *All managers 90: (COV681)*
FROM: *The Company Secretary - Head Office 90: (COV681)*
POSTED: *3-6-92 15.41*
SUBJECT: *Zorbra Visit*

TEXT:
From 8 to 11 July, Mr George Zorbra of Zorbra Industries, Athens, and two of his colleagues will be looking around the factory, as his firm intends to place a large contract with us to supply them with components over the next three years.

Zorbra Industries is part of the export drive that we have been preparing, to enable us to enter the Greek market. It is therefore essential for us to make a good impression on these visitors.

Although they will be escorted by Micahel Hobbs, our Overseas Sales Manager, it may be necessary for individual employees to answer questions or explain production procedures in their section. Would you therefore ask your staff to be as helpful and informative as possible? It will also be necessary for lunch hours and breaks to be arranged so that there will always be someone available in every section.

Your co-operation in this matter is essential and will be appreciated.

ACTION REQUIRED: *implement*

.SEND

COV681 -- SENT

END OF MAIL

Keyser Shipbrokers Ltd.

123–5 Lowland Street, London EC1 2RH

MEMO

To: All staff   Date: 2 November 19—

From: Head Office

Retirement of D.G. Crayford
Managing Director, and appointment
of Mrs Felicity Fawks.

Mr D.G. Crayford will retire on 20 December 19— and be replaced as Managing Director by Mrs Felicity Fawks whose appointment begins as from 2 January 19—.

Mr Crayford has been with the company for 30 years, and has been Managing Director since 1985. The Board, his colleagues, business associates, and staff, I am sure would like to take this opportunity to thank him for his excellent work in organizing and running the company to make it the successful concern it is today. His good-humoured presence will be missed by all those who worked with him, and we offer our best wishes to his successor.

Mr Crayford's leaving will not affect the present policy of the company.

Would all Department Managers please attend a meeting in room 358 on Monday 3 December at 15.30 hours, where they will be introduced to Mrs Fawks?

P.S. Keyser

P.S. Keyser
Chairman

15.2.3
Retirement of Managing Director

Notice how this memo takes the opportunity to announce the retirement; advise everyone of the new appointment; thank the ex-Managing Director, and welcome his successor; inform the staff there will be no changes in policy; and announce a meeting. Therefore, you can see that it is not necessary to confine a memo to a specific topic, as long as there is a link between the subjects. However, a memo that dealt all at once with, say, canteen facilities, punctuality, and a new accounting system, would not be read properly, or would confuse those who read it.

15.2.4
Automation

This memo is issued to employees to
explain that automated machinery is
being introduced into the factory, but
that job security will not be affected.

Questions

1 Why are the machines being
  introduced?
2 Will they mean redundancies?
3 How will they help employees?
4 Who have the management
  negotiated with for the introduction of
  the machines?
5 Which words in the memo
  correspond to the following: *enlarge*;
  expand; *output*; *learning new skills*;
  putting in (equipment); *servicing*?

Panton Manufacturing Ltd.   **MEMO**
Panton Works, Hounslow, Middlesex, TW6 2BQ

To: All employees   Date: 6 February 19—
From: The Managing Director

As part of the company's expansion programme over the next year, we are
introducing RS 100 and DS 100 machines which will increase productivity
and lower costs of production to make us more competitive in overseas
markets.

The new machinery will not in any way affect employees' job security, but
will ensure it, as it will make us more efficient. It will also release men from
boring, dirty jobs, and allow retraining for more technical and interesting
work here.

Union representatives have already been consulted and have promised
their co-operation in installing and maintaining the machinery. If any
employee feels apprehensive about the changes, they should see their
Union representative who will explain the situation to them.

D. Panton

D. Panton
Managing Director

MEMORANDUM

L. Franksen PLC
Prince of Wales Road, Sheffield S9 4EX

To: All employees   Date: 15 July 19—
From: The Managing Director

Cutting output and redundancies

The company has been running at a loss for the past three years, due to rising costs of production and a fall in demand for our products because of the economic situation.

It is therefore with regret that we have to announce that one third of the work force will be made redundant over the next month as production will be cut by forty per cent.

Those employees affected will be advised within the next fortnight and will receive full severance pay, plus holiday pay, which, we hope, will help them until they find new jobs.

We express our sympathies to those affected and would like to thank them for their help in the past and their co-operation in these unfortunate circumstances.

L. Franksen

L. Franksen
Managing Director

15.2.5
Redundancies

Questions

1 Why is the company making redundancies?
2 How many people will be affected?
3 What is going to happen to production?
4 What compensation is offered to those affected?
5 When will those being made redundant be advised?

15.2.6
Take-over of the company

This faxed memorandum is to the staff of a company that is about to be taken over. In this case, it is essential to explain exactly what is hapening and what is going to happen, as employees will naturally want to know about their job security. Notice how the main points are carefully laid out, and that the memo is written almost immediately after the take-over to prevent rumours spreading. Employees are also encouraged to ask supervisors and union representatives questions. It is bad industrial relations not to advise employees immediately in this situation, as secrecy only creates suspicion, and even those with secure jobs might leave for fear they might be dismissed.

MEMO FAX
Fax: 071 940 6668

Bedix Calculators Ltd.
Bedix House, Richmond, Surrey TW9 1DW

To: All employees in all branches
From: J.L. Bedix, Director

Date: 21 October 19—
Subject: Control of Bedix Calculators by Prendall Industries

You are probably aware from reports in the press that Bedix Calculators has been taken over by Prendall Industries and is now part of the Prendall group of companies.

Details of the take-over and how it will affect employees will be sent to everyone before the end of the week. However, this memo is being circulated to reassure you of the following:

1 There will be <u>no redundancies</u> as a result of the take-over, although there will be some reorganization.

2 <u>Reorganization</u> will take place over the next year as Prendall intend to <u>expand</u> Bedix Calculators' production so that it will become a major electronic component supplier to their own industries.

3 <u>Salaries and wages</u> will <u>not</u> be affected.

4 <u>Management positions</u> will <u>not</u> be affected, although Organization and Management Consultants will be looking at our methods of production with a view to improving efficiency.

5 Bedix Calculators will retain its own name and identity and fulfil all contracts and obligations it was committed to prior to the take-over.

The Board of Directors, management, and Union representatives of Bedix Calculators have already met with Mr Prendall, who has given us the above undertakings both verbally and in writing. However, if you wish to ask your supervisors or Union representatives about anything regarding the new situation, please do so, and I am sure they will clear up any doubts or misgivings that you might have.

J. L. Bedix.

J.L. Bedix, Director

15.3
Reports

Reports are used in every area of administration, and may announce, explain, or recommend policy. They may initiate and begin a sequence of events to start new schemes, introduce fresh approaches, or develop new methods of operations. They may also be the result of events that need investigation and explanation.

Reports can come from *external agencies* which have been called in by the firm to review problems, e.g. Organization and Management Consultants, or business associates, e.g. surveyors' reports or credit investigation agencies (see 8.8.6).

Reports may also come from *internal sources*, when management are asked to investigate the possibilities of increasing efficiency in the company.

15.3.1
Guide to contents

The length of a report depends on the complexity of the subject it deals with, but all reports follow a similar pattern, as follows:

Title
The title of the report always explains its contents. Here are three examples of titles which immediately tell you what the report is about.

'The development of small industries in Nigeria'

'The limitations of the Consumer Protection Act 1989'

'The problems of English-language teaching in London Colleges of Further Education'

Introduction
The introduction might be a summary of the report and the circumstances or conditions that initiated it. It could also lay out the objectives and limitations of the enquiry.

Background
All reports, regardless of whether they are specialized or not, must give a background to the subject of the study. This allows the reader to see how the situation arose, and how it can be corrected, improved on, or changed.

Facts
This section is essential to all reports as it explains the situation that exists and offers evidence to support the statements that the writer is making. If the reader is to be convinced that changes in a situation are necessary, well-selected and well-presented facts will influence him.

Conclusions
Conclusions are the ideas you have formed from the evidence you have looked at. Whereas facts are objective statements, conclusions draw together all aspects of the situation as you see it.

Recommendations
These follow from conclusions and are the suggestions that you are making to improve, or change, the current situation.

15.4
Specimen reports

15.4.1

This report from the Sales Director suggests that his company should enter the mail order business. Notice that this is a summary of a much larger report containing statistical data which it refers to throughout the report.

Questions

1 How long has the research into the project taken?
2 Why do they believe there is a potential market in mail order?
3 Which is the best market for the company to enter?
4 What would be the problem with other areas of mail order selling?
5 How much would the company have to invest to go into the mail order market?
6 Where will the company get the money from to invest in the project?
7 When should the board meet to discuss the project?
8 Which words in the report correspond to the following: *because of*; *buying*; *breakdown of figures*; *garments*; *yearly account*; *money which cannot be recovered*; *future*; *information*?

_____ MEMORANDUM _____
SP Wholesalers PLC

To: The Board of Directors   Date: 15 October 19—

From: D. Logan, Sales Director

<u>Introduction of Mail Order Service</u>

I have now completed the research we began in July of this year into developing a mail order service. You will find all the statistical and graphic data attached to this report, but in summary, the research team came to the following conclusions.

Market

Over the past six years there has been a steadily expanding market both here and in the other single European market economies towards mail order buying. This has been due to three main reasons – range of selection, convenience, and the credit facilities this form of selling offers. However, the main area of development, which has expanded by 8 per cent over the period, has been in clothes purchasing, especially children's clothes in the age range of 4–15 years, see p.9 of Statistical Analysis, attached.

With regard to other sales items such as electrical appliances, household utensils, carpeting, linens, and general furnishings, we found that although there has been a 2.7 per cent increase in sales over this period, the investment in stocks would be too large to undertake in the initial period, see pp 23–27 of Analysis. We can reconsider these areas in the future.

Finance

If we concentrate on the garment area of the market supplying all age groups, we estimate an increase in investment of our annual budget of 4.8 per cent, and this includes administration, warehousing, expanding stock, producing catalogues, advertising, distribution, agents' commissions, and bad debts. This will increase our present turnover in this area by 7 per cent over a two year trial period, see pp 15–18 of Analysis.

Our finance department suggests that this increase in capital investment should come from share issues rather than loans because increasing rates of interest will cut into profits.

Conclusions

With our main competitiors already considering this market, and its international potential in the European community, we suggest that on the basis of what has been said, and the data we have collected, it would be feasible to enter the mail order business by 19—. Once you have studied the details, I would suggest a meeting before the end of this financial year.

D. Logan
Sales Director   *D. Logan*

Delta Computers

Bradfield Estate, Bradfield Road, Wellingborough, Northamptonshire NN8 4HB

To: ——   Date: 31 August 19—

From: J.M. Norman

Declining Sales in Germany

1   I was sent out to Germany last month to find out why sales have fallen by 40% over the past two years, and while there I interviewed a number of our leading customers who were very helpful in explaining how and why German demand for our products has contracted.

2   Between 1983 and 1990 we were one of the leading exporters to Germany from this country, with an annual turnover of £2.6m from that market, with our share of the market never below 10% of their imports for our product. However, in 1991 it was evident that we were losing ground despite increased advertising and promotion. Although our customers maintained regular orders, the orders themselves were smaller, in some cases half their previous net values.

This fall in demand continued until two years ago when we found our share of the market had fallen to six per cent, and from that time has shrunk to three per cent.

3   Our market researchers have already produced two reports explaining the decrease in demand, and my trip and interviews have confirmed their findings.

Our exports have become more expensive to buyers, despite the European single market economy, and as our customers saw this as a trend, they began to look for new suppliers which they found in the Far East.

These countries, who were keen to earn hard currencies and develop their Information Technology industries, were prepared to cut their prices, in some cases by 60%, while at the same time maintaining the quality and standard of the products. They also offered first rate after-sales service, long-term guarantees, cheap transportation, and short-term delivery dates.

contd.

15.4.2
Sales Manager's report

This internal report suggests far-reaching changes in production and marketing. A report of this sort may be even more detailed and supply figures and forecasts to help Directors make a decision on whether they wish to increase their capital investment to stay in the market.

Questions

1 How did the Sales Manager who wrote the report get his information?

2 Did customers stop ordering?

3 Have there been any previous reports on the German market?

4 Where did the German customers get their new supplies from and why were they buying from their new suppliers?

5 What recommendations does the Sales Manager make with regard to prices, distribution, agents, and advertising?

6 Which words in the report correspond to the following: *discover*; *become smaller*; *obvious*; *fashion*; *maintenance (of products)*; *fall*; *maintaining standards*; *putting money into a business*?

– 2 –

It may be of little consolation, but in the face of this competition most of our rivals in the West have also experienced a decline in sales to this market.

4 The solution to the problem calls for drastic price cuts and a total reorganization of our methods of production and service. But if we are prepared to force our way back into this market, I would suggest the following:

a) Review production methods and introduce improved technology to cut costs, and enlarge production capacity to effect economies of scale, producing in mass units regardless of whether there are orders or not, so that we can supply immediately from stock.

b) Improve distribution and order processing so orders can be met quickly and delivery dates guaranteed.

c) Find new suppliers of raw materials who are prepared to allow generous trade, cash, and quantity discounts, so that we can pass the reduced prices on to the customers.

d) Offer extended guarantees on products and improve quality control to strengthen our reputation in the market.

e) Establish a service base, and agents in Germany.

f) Increase advertising and promotion so that our brand becomes identified with the product, and expand our sales force in Germany, again, possibly through agents.

5 I realize that this will mean increased capital investment, but unless we are prepared to invest in our future in this market, we will find within five years that we have no market to invest in.

J.M. Norman
Sales Manager (Europe)

ACE ADVERTISING ASSOCIATES

B.R.M. House, Kensington Church Street, London W8 4BN

Preliminary Market Research Report for   Date: 1 April 19—
Katz Electric Ltd.

We have completed our market research on testing consumer reaction to your brands and products, and attached you will find a statistical analysis which is the result of that research. This preliminary report is a summary of our findings, conclusions, and suggestions which you might like to discuss with us after you have considered the results.

Our survey was based on discussions moderated by a psychologist who took a number of groups, some who used and some who did not use your products. On the results of the discussions we constructed a questionnaire which was presented to a random sample of 500 people reflecting the population distribution of this country. We asked them about their preferences and awareness of your products compared to others on the market, and from this Usage and Attitude Study we produced a profile of your brands compared to other companies' brands.

The lists attached show the statistical breakdown in answers to our questions, and in summary they suggest the following:

1   Although your products are stocked in leading stores and your name is well known, there is a feeling that in spite of their dependability, they are over-priced and old-fashioned. Younger people, 15–25 age group, associate your brands with appliances used by their parents, and the 25–35 age group associate the brands with the 1970s.

2   Your name featured very low on the list when people were asked to name a brand of electric fire, vacuum cleaner, iron, and refrigerator. You will see from the attached survey that less than 10% of the sample knew that you had recently put the 'Popup' toaster on the market.

contd.

15.4.3
Agency report

The next report comes from an outside agency and is written at the request of the company, Katz Electric, who are manufacturers of domestic appliances. They are losing ground in the market and have employed an advertising agency, with their market research resources, to find out why. The Agency has submitted a preliminary report based on their market research, which they hope will persuade Katz Electric to attend a presentation in which the Agency will propose a campaign to advertise Katz.

Questions

1 How did the market research people get their information about Katz Electric's products, and what reaction did they find to them?
2 What does the list attached to the letter show?
3 Why does the advertising agency think that Katz does not have a good image on the market, and what do they suggest to improve it?
4 Which symbol do they suggest they use?
5 How should the products be packaged?
6 Which media do they suggest they concentrate on?
7 What does the advertising agency say it could do if Katz allows them to handle their account?
8 Which words in the report correspond to the following: *investigation*; *data breakdown*; *brief details*; *controlled*; *out of date*; *poor selling techniques*; *put together*; *associated*; *material and design of product*; *prominent*?

– 2 –

We believe that poor marketing is the main reason for the old-fashioned image people have of your products, and there is a lack of brand identification which we are sure can be overcome with a well-presented advertising campaign. So we have compiled the following suggestions which we think will develop a new image for you.

1 Establish a symbol that will be identified with all your products. The most obvious appears to be a cat, a domestic animal for domestic products, which is also associated with your name.

2 Your present advertisements give the impression of functionalism. We suggest glamourizing the ads, maybe with an exotic cat and girl which will always be recognized when seen.

3 Improving the packaging of the products, perhaps by using bright colours, and maybe even eccentric designs, with your symbol always standing out.

4 We noticed you have not been selective in placing your advertisements. For example, it would be better to concentrate on women's magazines rather than national newspapers, and we would suggest afternoon television commercials rather than just evenings, as more women are at home and that is the market you are aiming for. You will also get a cheaper rate than during prime time.

There are many other points we could make, but we think they could be better illustrated at a presentation. So if, after studying the information enclosed, you are interested in us going ahead with a full presentation, please let us know. I am sure that if we handle your account we could effectively improve your sales.

G. Grover
Marketing Director

15.5
Points to remember

1 A memo should indicate clearly at the top who it is to, who it is from, what it is about, and the date it was written.
2 Memos can be addressed to one individual or a group of people within a company.
3 Reports prepared by market researchers and advertising agencies are often aimed at improving the efficiency and profitability of a company.
4 Reports tend to follow a fixed pattern, thus enabling the readers to locate easily the sections which are of particular interest to them, and to refer to them quickly in meetings.

15.6
Words to remember

a memorandum
a memo
internal mail

a report
to report
agency report
internal report
market research

Personnel appointments

16

Applications; curriculum vitaes; unsolicited applications and replies; covering letter for c.v; invitation for interview; offering a position; conditions of employment; confirming acceptance

16.1
Advertisements

Advertisements (ads) for employment appear in all the media including radio and television. However, newspapers and magazines are usually the main source for vacancies. Most 'ads' use abbreviated forms to announce conditions of employment, especially in the 'small ad' section for appointments, e.g. *Wntd sec. full-time fr smll mnfg co. Gd slry. 5-day week, hrs 9–5 usl bnfts.* (Wanted, secretary for full-time employment for small manufacturing company. Good salary, five days a week, hours of work 09.00 to 17.00, and the usual benefits in terms of conditions and holidays.)

Other abbreviations that might appear include *clk* (clerk), *accnts* (accounts), *mngr* (manager) *asst* (assistant), *vacs* (vacations). Terms like *m.* (male), *f.* (female), are no longer permitted by law.

16.2
Applying for a position

Generally, the terms *vacancy*, *post*, position, or *opening* are used instead of the word *job* in applications.

16.2.1
Opening

If replying to an advertisement, as with most correspondence, it is better to simply state what you are doing, and remember to give a date or reference.

I would like to apply for the position of Programmer advertised in this month's edition of Computer Technics.

I am writing to you concerning your advertisement on 12 May in The Guardian, for a bilingual secretary to work in your export department.

I am answering your advertisement for the post of Bank Trainee which appeared in yesterday's Times.

I am replying to the advertisement of 18 June for a Sales Manager which you placed in The Export Journal.

If applying for a position which has not been advertised, you can open like this:

I am writing to ask if you might have a vacancy in the (your) general office/ sales/export/accounts department for a(n) clerical assistant/salesperson/ export manager/accounts clerk.

If someone associated with the company suggested you write to them, you can open thus:

I was recommended by . . . . . . who is currently working in/who has had a long association with your firm/who is one of your suppliers/customers, to write to you/contact you concerning a possible post in your/the . . . . . . department.

(subject and class, mentioning any special topics that would be relevant to the position).

At present I am employed by (name of firm) where I deal with/am employed as (title)/am employed in (department)/ concerned with (description of work), and I have been there for (number of years), since (date).

There is no need to give any more information at this stage, so the letter can be closed:

Please can you send me an application form and any other relevant details?

Would it be possible for you to send me an application form and further details?

I would be grateful if you could send me an application form, and if in the meantime you need any further details about me, I would be happy to supply them.

16.2.2
Application form requests

If your enquiry is only for an application form, you can give some brief details about yourself, then ask for the form. It is worth remembering, at this point, that your letters, in these cases, are not for the positions themselves, but are for interviews.

These examples can also be used for unsolicited applications, i.e. when applying for a post that has not been advertised.

I am 23 years old, was educated at (secondary school) which I left in (date) having taken (leaving certificate). I graduated from (college/university) in (date) with a (diploma/degree) in

16.2.3
Curriculum vitae

Some companies do not send application forms, but prefer applicants to supply a curriculum vitae (c.v.) which is your personal and working history, see 16.3.5 for an example.

There should be a covering letter with application forms and c.v.s, either explaining points that might not be clear, or giving further information to emphasize your suitability for the post.

Remember to quote any reference numbers or job titles that have to be mentioned, and if an application form has been sent, thank the company.

16.2.4

Opening

Your c.v. should be mentioned in the second paragraph to a letter answering an advertisement.

Thank you for your letter of (date) and the application form for the post of (title). I have now completed the details and am enclosing the form.

I am enclosing my curriculum vitae for the position of . . .

The enclosed c.v. is for the above post.

16.2.5

Summary of details

You will see that I graduated from (college)/left (name of school) in (date) where I got (degree; diploma; certificate). I then began work with (name of firm) as (job title), where I was trained as (title), and was involved with (brief description of duties).

If you have had more than one job, you could explain why you left each position. This is often left for an interview. But you should never use explanations such as leaving for more money, better fringe benefits, advantages besides salary, e.g. better pension, health scheme, social facilities, car, or conditions. Whether it is justified or not, employers do not like to feel staff leave companies for these reasons.

You should also not state you were bored with the work you were doing, after all, you accepted the job; and never criticize the firm you worked for, the products or services they offered, or staff you worked with.

Explanations for leaving a company could include the following:

I left (name of firm) in (date) as (new employer) offered me a chance to use my (skills or specialized knowledge, e.g. languages, knowledge of computers, etc) . . .

In 19— I was offered a chance to join (name of company) where there was an opportunity for me to gain more experience in . . .

I was offered promotion (a chance to advance) by (name of company) in (date) and therefore left (company) as this meant I could (explanation) . . .

I joined (name of company) in (date) as they offered an opportunity for advancement, being a much larger concern.

16.2.6

Explanation of previous experience

Most application forms give limited space to expand on previous duties in a company; what you did, how many people were involved, what your detailed responsibilities were. Without elaborating too much or boasting, you should stress your responsibilities and authority in the company(ies), projects you undertook, changes you effected, or schemes you introduced.

While I was at (name of company) I took responsibility for (title) and this meant I (description); within (period of time) the firm/department was able to (description of improvements) . . .

During my time at (name of firm) I worked on several (description) schemes which were very successful as they meant (description) . . .

At (name of company) my duties included (description). This gave me more experience in (description) which was very valuable when I moved to (name of next company).

(Name of company) encouraged day release at (name of college/institute) where I studied (subject) and took a (degree/diploma/certificate) in (date). After two more years of management experience I joined (name of company).

16.2.7
Reasons you are applying

All companies will want to know why you are applying for a particular position. This not only means explaining why you want the job but why you think your particular skills and experience would be valuable to the firm.

I am particularly interested in the position you offer as I know my previous experience and academic background would be valuable in this area of (engineering; teaching; accountancy, etc.).

I am sure I would be successful in this post as I have now gained the experience and skills that are required.

As (title of post) I know my background in (area of work) would prove valuable to you, especially as I have been dealing with (explanation) . . .

This position would require someone who has had extensive experience of (area of work) which I gained both academically and commercially at (college and companies).

16.2.8
Close

At the end of the letter, look forward to the interview and offer to supply more information if necessary.

I look forward to hearing from you. However, if there is any further information you require in the meantime, please contact me.

Please let me know if there are any other details you need. Meanwhile, I look forward to hearing from you.

I hope to hear from you in due course. Please let me know if you would like further information about me.

I will be able to give you more detailed information at an interview, and I look forward to seeing you.

The Manager
Mitchell Hill PLC
Merchant Bank
11–15 Montague Street
London EC1 5DN

Fürstenweg 110
D—3000 Hannover 71

21 June 19—

Dear Mr Curtis,

I am writing to you on the recommendation of David McLean, Assistant Manager in your securities department.

A year ago Mr McLean was on a banking course here with me in Hannover, and he suggested that I should contact your company and mention his name. He told me that you often employ people from other countries on a one-year basis, if they have had banking experience.

I am a 28 year-old employee of the International Bank in Hannover, working in the Overseas Securities Department, and have been with this organization for the past two years, since graduating from the University of Munich in 19— with a degree in Economics.

As well as speaking fluent English, I also have a very good working knowledge of French.

In my present position as Assistant to the Director of the International Securities Department, I deal with a wide range of investments from companies throughout Europe, buying shares and bonds for them on a worldwide basis.

My bank encourages all its staff to spend a year abroad for the experience of working with different systems, and my Director would be willing to give you a reference.

I would like to spend a year or so in the UK to gain experience in securities investment with a British bank, and in exchange, I think my experience and languages would prove useful to your organization.

If you think it would be possible to offer me a position, please send me an application form where I will be able to give you more specific details about myself.

I look forward to hearing from you in due course.

Yours sincerely,

Marcus Bauer

Marcus Bauer

16.3
Specimen letters

16.3.1
Unsolicited letter

Notice in this letter how the applicant first mentions how he knows of the company, then gives brief details of his age, education, and experience, then refers to his Director who approves of staff spending time abroad. Finally, he tells the bank why he wants to join them for a temporary stay in the UK, and asks for an application form. Of course, he could also include a c.v. with the letter, but knows the practice of this firm is to send application forms.

Questions

1 How did Mr Bauer hear about the bank he is applying to?
2 What does he do in the bank where he now works?
3 What are his qualifications?
4 Why does his bank encourage people to go on overseas courses?
5 What does he want the UK bank to send him?
6 Which words in the letter correspond to the following: *suggestion*; *getting a qualification*; *various methods of doing things*; *particular*?

16.3.2
Reply to unsolicited letter

Mitchell Hill Plc
Merchant Bank

11–15 Montague Street   London EC1 5DN

Telephone: 071 625 3311/2/3
Telex: 971135 Fax: 071 625 4019
Cable: MITHIL (London)

Fürstenweg 110   29 June 19—
D–3000 Hannover 71

Dear Mr Bauer,

Thank you for your letter of 21 June 19—, in which you enquired about a
one-year traineeship in our Securities Department in the UK.

I have spoken to Mr McLean, who recommended you to contact us, and he
remembers you from the course you did together.

We do employ staff from overseas banks, with experience, and could
probably find an opening for you in the Securities Department around the
end of this year as one of our current overseas trainees is leaving in
September.

I am enclosing an application form and booklet giving you details of
Mitchell Hill, salary structure, and conditions of employment. Would you
please complete the application form and sent it to Mrs Helen Griffiths,
Personnel Department, at the above address. Meanwhile, could you ask
your Director, Mr Strauss, to send me a reference for you, and we would
appreciate another reference, possibly from one of your Professors at
Munich University.

Once I have received these details we can consider your application.

I look forward to hearing from you.

Yours sincerely,

Sheila Burrows

Sheila Burrows (Miss)
pp David McLean
Securities Manager

Application form Ref:	Mitchell Hill Plc Merchant Bank
Post:	11–15 Montague Street, London EC1 5DN

Surname (Mr Mrs Miss Ms) Bauer	Forename(s) Marcus

Maiden name —	Age 28 Date of birth 12 Nov 19—

Marital status Single	No of children — Ages —

Address Fürstenweg 110, D–3000, Hannover 71

Tel daytime (49) 312–885533	Tel evening (49) 312–251068

Next of kin Mr Kurt Bauer, father (see above address)

Education	School/univ/college	From	To	Address
Secondary	Friedrich-Ebert Gymnasium	19—	19—	Herrenhaüser Str. D–3000 Hannover 21
Higher	Universität München	19—	19—	Hittorfstr. D-8000 München

Examinations Title	Grade	Subject(s)	Date
Diplom	1	Business studies/ Economics	19 —
Abitur	1		19 —
LCCI Higher		Business English	19 —
Cambridge Proficiency	B	English	19 —

Have you any of the following skills?
Tick appropriate box

- ☑ Typing ..35.. wpm
- ☐ Shorthand .... wpm
- ☐ Word processing
- ☑ Keyboard skills
- ☑ Bookkeeping
- ☐ Accounts
- ☑ Telex
- ☑ Customer contact
- ☑ Driving licence
- ☑ Filing

Languages	Fluent	Good	Fair
French		√	
English	√		

Employers Name and address	From	To	Position and duties	Salary
International Bank Georgenplatz 108 D–3000 Hannover 1	19—	19—	Assistant to Director of International Securities Dept. Buying and selling securities	£16,000

Names of two referees besides employers
Herr Prof. K. Weil, Universität München, Hittorfstr., D-8000 München Herr Dr G. Grass, as above

Can we approach your employer for a reference?
☑ Yes   ☐ No

Hobbies/activities
Reading, chess, skiing, swimming, and tennis

When will you not be available for an interview?
Date(s) before 5 Sept

Date 17 July 19—   Signature

16.3.4
Covering letter for c.v.

In this example, notice the applicant immediately explains what the letter is about. She then goes on to expand on her present duties and emphasizes these and any other information that she feels is relevant to the advertised position, ignoring the duties in her previous employment which have no relevance to this particular post. Most importantly, she explains why she is applying for this particular vacancy and the qualities she can offer the company. Note that if she offered her current employers as referees, she could mention that she would prefer the company she is applying to not to approach her employers until after an interview.

Questions

1 What position is Ms Brice applying for?
2 What does the abbreviation P.A. mean?
3 How did she learn about IT?
4 What reason does she give for wanting to join ICS?
5 Which words in the letter correspond to the following: *ask for*; *everyday duties*; *continued with*; *materials used with a computer, e.g. discs*; *managing*; *real*?

Your Ref: KH 305/9

Mrs J. Hastings
Personnel Officer
International Computing Services PLC
City Road
London EC3 4HJ

25 Westbound Road
Borehamwood
Herts
WD6 1DX

18 June 19—

Dear Mrs Hastings,

I would like to apply for the position advertised in *The Guardian* on 16 June for a Personal Assistant to the Sales Director.

As you will see from my c.v., much of the work I do in my present position is that of a PA. I deal not only with the routine work of a secretary, but also represent the Assistant Director at small meetings and functions, and am delegated to take a number of policy decisions in his absence.

Your advertisement asked for a knowledge of languages. I have kept up my French, and learnt Italian for the past two years at evening classes, and have regularly visited Belgium and Italy with the Assistant Director, acting as an interpreter and translator for him.

I am also familar with the latest developments in Information Technology, having just completed a one-month course at The City College, in addition to previous day release courses I attended when I was with Johnson Bros.

I am particularly interested in the situation you are offering, as I would like to become more involved with an IT organization. I am quite familar with many of the software products that ICS manufacture for office technology.

As well as my secretarial skills and experience of running a busy office, I am used to working with technicians and other specialized personnel in the field of computers. I have a genuine interest in computer development and the people involved in the profession.

Please let me know if there is any further information you require. I look forward to hearing from you.

Yours sincerely,

Carol Brice (Ms)

Encl. c.v.

Curriculum vitae

Date of Birth:	25 February 19—
Name:	Carol Brice
Present address:	25, Westbound Road, Borehamwood, Herts, WD6 1DX
Telephone number:	081 953 9914
Marital status:	Single

Education and qualifications:

1980–1985	Mayfield School, Henley Road, Borehamwood, Herts, WD6 1DX GCE in English Language; French; History; Geography; and Art.
1985 – 1987	Hilltop Further Education College, Kenwood Road, London NW7 3TM Diploma in Business Studies.

Work experience:
Oct '87 – Dec '88

Johnson Bros. Plc, 51–55 Baker Street, London W1A 1AA
Type of Company: Retail Chain Stores
Post: Junior Secretary
Responsibilities: Secretarial work including typing; shorthand; correspondence; copying reports and minutes from shorthand notes; tabulating data; filing; answering customers' calls; mail distribution; and general office duties.

Jan '89 – present

National Auto Importers Ltd., Auto House, Sidmouth Street, London WC1H 4GJ
Type of Company: Car importers
Post: Secretary to Assistant Director
Responsibilities: Dealing with all correspondence; taking minutes at meetings and writing up Assistant Director's reports; receiving customers and suppliers; dealing with home and overseas enquiries; making decisions on behalf of A.D. in his absence; and representing the company at various business functions.

Other information: While working I have attended various evening courses for Italian and French, and have also been on a special Information Technology course at The City College. My interests include tennis, badminton, swimming, and reading.

References: Mr B. Norman, Assistant Director, National Auto Importers Ltd., Auto House, Sidmouth Street, London WC1H 4GJ.

Mrs T. R. Bradley, Senior Lecturer, Business Studies Dept., Hilltop Further Education College, Kenwood Road, London NW7 3TM.

Current salary: £14,000 per annum

16.3.5
Curriculum vitae

There are various layouts for a c.v. and this is just one example. Some c.v.s may have a section for supplementary information, where reasons for applying for the position and leaving previous and present employment are included, as well as personal qualities and skills which the candidate feels are relevant to the job. In this example, however, this material is included in the covering letter, see 16.3.4.

Questions

1 What was Ms Brice's position at Johnson Bros?
2 Name three of her duties at National Auto.
3 Which words in the c.v. correspond to the following: *unmarried*; *stenography*; *cataloguing and keeping data*; *acting for*; *wages*?

International Computing Services plc

City Road
London EC3 4HU

Telephone: (071) 625 4443 (10 lines)
Fax: (071) 625 3012/3108
Telex: 295386

Your ref:
Our ref: KH 305/59

Date: 29th June 19—

Ms Carol Brice
25 Westbound Road
Borehamwood
Herts
WD6 1DX

Dear Ms Brice,

Thank you for your application of June 18 for the post of Personal Assistant to Ms Frances Newman, our Sales Director.

Ms Newman has asked me to write to you inviting you for an interview at 15.00, on Thursday 12 July 19—.

Please come to the reception on the ground floor at the above address and ask for me, and I will meet you.

Please bring with you any certificates, diplomas, or references that you have. Meanwhile, would you phone me on Ext. 217 to confirm that you will be able to attend the interview.

I look forward to hearing from you.

Yours sincerely,

Anne Levin

Anne Levin (Mrs)
pp Frances Newman
Sales Director

16.4
Making a decision

16.4.1
Turning down an applicant

There are various reasons why a company may not offer a candidate a job, and these include lack of qualifications, competence, i.e. they do not think the applicant has the ability or experience to handle the post, or there are too many applicants of similar qualifications and ability, so the company makes a choice based on nothing more than the personality of the interviewee at the time of selection. Therefore, how you present yourself at an interview is as important as how you present yourself in your application. It is worth noting that it is rare for a candidate to be told why he or she has been refused.

Thank you for attending our selection board on (date), but we regret to tell you that you were not successful in your application. We hope you will be able to secure a position in the near future.

We regret to tell you that we are not able to offer you the post of (title) which you applied for on (date). We hope you will soon find the position you are looking for.

We are sorry to say that we are unable to offer you the position of (title) for which you were interviewed on (date), and hope you will be more successful in the future.

We have decided not to accept any applicants who were interviewed for the post of (title), and are readvertising the vacancy.

16.4.2
Offering a position

Letters to successful applicants can vary in length and detail depending on the type of post, whether the company has a standard printed contract, or if the position is so specialized that they need to give details of the terms of employment, see example at 16.4.4.

16.4.3
Openings

We are pleased to inform you that you were successful in your interview for (title) which you attended on (date).

Thank you for seeing us on (date). We are prepared to offer you the position of (title) which you applied for.

I am pleased to tell you that we are offering you the post of (title) which we discussed at your interview on (date).

The selection board have approved of your appointment as (title).

The bank has agreed to accept you for the post of trainee subject to the usual references.

16.4.4
Details

As we discussed in your interview, your duties will include . . . Working hours are from 09.00 to 17.00, Monday to Friday, and overtime wil be paid at time-and-a-half rates. You are entitled to all Bank Holidays, plus three weeks' vacation after one year's service. There is a Staff Contributory Pension Scheme, which you will be eligible to join after your first year of employment.

Two weeks' notice of termination of employment is required by both you and the company.

Enclosed with this letter you will find full details of your conditions and terms of employment. Please read these carefully and if you have any questions, contact me as soon as possible.

Would you please check the following which was agreed at your interview:

*Title: Maintenance Engineer.
Commence: 8.30, Monday 9th March 19—.
Duties: Servicing all company products.
Hours: 8.30 a.m. to 6.00 p.m.
Days: Monday to Friday.
Holidays: Three weeks annual leave, time at discretion Supervisor, plus all Public Holidays.
Sick leave: Ten days per annum.
Annual Pay: £12,000.
Overtime: Time-and-a-half. Double time for Public Holidays.
Pension: Non-Contributory Pension Scheme at 7% of annual pay.
Benefits: Subsidized staff canteen. Social Club. Full use of company vehicle.
Notice: One month's notice either side.*

Your traineeship will commence on Monday, 14 November and terminate on Friday, 11 October 19—. Although this is a temporary position, you will be subject to all the terms and conditions of a full-time bank employee in the Securities Department, for details of this, see Mitchell Hill Employee's Guide, where pages 15 to 18 mostly concern you.

16.4.5
Close

Generally, a company will welcome the new employee, possibly inviting questions about the terms and conditions of employment (if anything is not clear), and ask for written confirmation of acceptance. In the UK, the law demands that firms offer contracts of employment, and these are often sent with letters offering a job, asking the applicant to sign one copy and return it with their confirmation.

I look forward to seeing you in my office at 09.00 a.m. on Monday 10 January 19—. If there are any questions concerning the enclosed conditions, please contact me immediately. Otherwise, return the enclosed Contract of Employment, signed, with your letter of acceptance.

Your Contract of Employment is attached to this letter. Please will you sign one copy and return it to the Personnel Officer, Mr T. Wright, with a note confirming you have accepted the position. I will see you at 08.00 on Monday 9th March, when I can welcome you to the organization and give you details of your duties.

Please meet me at my office in the bank at 08.30 on Monday 14 November, so I can introduce you to the other members of staff, and Mr Jenson, who you will be working with. If there is anything in the handbook you do not understand about your conditions of employment, please let me know as soon as possible.

16.5
Accepting a position

Letters confirming that you accept a position can be brief, as long as they mention the relevant points.

Thank you for your letter of 23 December 19—, offering me the position of (title). I look forward to seeing you at 09.00, on Monday 10 January, and enclose one signed copy of the Contract of Employment.

I am returning a signed copy of my Contract of Employment which you sent me with your letter of 15 February. I confirm that I will be able to commence with you on Monday 9 March at 08.00, and look forward to seeing you then.

Thank you for offering me the temporary position of trainee in your bank, starting on Monday 14 November. I have read the handbook and relevant details concerning the position, and accept the conditions. I look forward to meeting you and Mr Jenson at 08.30, when I begin with you.

<table>
<tr><td colspan="2">

International Computing Services plc
</td></tr>
</table>

City Road London EC3 4HJ	Telephone: (071) 625 4443 Fax: (071) 625 3012/3108 Telex: 295386
Your ref: Our ref: KH 305/9	Date: 25 July 19—

Ms Carol Brice
25 Westbound Road
Borehamwood
Herts
WD6 1DX

Dear Ms Brice,

I am writing on behalf of Ms Frances Newman to tell you that you were successful in your interview on 12 July for the post of Personal Assistant.

Your duties will commence at 09.00 on 10 October 19—, but we would appreciate it if you could arrive at 08.30, so that we can introduce you to the staff, and acquaint you with office procedures.

Full details of your terms of employment are on pp 9–14 of our employees' handbook, ICS 661, but, as we discussed at the interview, your hours will be subject to requirement, and no overtime will be paid. This is compensated for by an annual bonus paid to administrative staff, based on annual profits.

Your starting salary will be £16,000, with annual increments of 9 per cent in the first three years, and subject to negotiation thereafter. During this period you will be allowed three weeks' vacation a year, and four weeks after three years, rising to a maximum of six weeks. In addition to the listed fringe benefits, which include a Non-Contributory Pension Scheme at 8% of your gross salary; free medical insurance; staff discounts on our products, etc.,

Please look at the relevant sections of the handbook carefully, and if you have any queries, contact me.

I look forward to welcoming you to the company, meanwhile, would you sign one of the two copies of the Contract of Employment enclosed and return it to Mrs J. Hastings, Personnel Officer, at the above address, with your confirmation accepting the post.

Yours sincerely,

Anne Levin

Anne Levin (Mrs)
pp Frances Newman
Sales Director

16.6
Specimen letters

16.6.1
Letter offering position

Questions

1 Which job has Ms Brice been selected for?
2 Why does she need to come to the office early?
3 Where will she find information about her conditions of employment?
4 When does this firm offer pay rises?
5 What must she do when she confirms she will take the job?
6 Does the firm offer anything else besides a salary?
7 Which words in the letter correspond to the following: *become familiar*; *to work when needed*; *increases*; *benefits besides salary*; *money taken off purchases by employees*; *questions*?

16.6.2
Letters confirming
acceptance

Your Ref: KH 305/9   25 Westbound Road
                                            Borehamwood
                                            Herts
                                            WD6 1DX

                                            27 July 19—

Mrs J. Hastings
Personnel Officer
International Computing Service PLC
City Road
London EC3 4HJ

Dear Mrs Hastings,

Please thank Mrs Levin for her letter of 25 July in which she offered me the
post of PA to Frances Newman, your Sales Director.

Please inform her that I am very pleased to have been offered the position,
and confirm that I will begin at 08.30 on Monday 10 October 19—.

I accept all the terms in Mrs Levin's letter and conditions in the employees'
handbook, ICS 661, and I am enclosing a signed copy of my Contract of
Employment.

I look forward to starting on the above-mentioned date.

Yours sincerely,

Carol Brice

Carol Brice

Enc. Contract of Employment

16.7
Points to remember

1 The word *job* should not be used either in advertisements or applications. The terms *vacancy*, *post*, *position*, or *opening* are more appropriate.
2 If requesting an application form, keep the letter brief, but provide essential details about yourself. When returning the form, you should include a covering letter, expanding on details that might not be clear, or pointing out areas of your responsibility or your achievements. But keep this as brief as possible, as most application forms or your own c.v. should have a section where this information can appear.
3 When writing to a prospective employer, remember to explain why you left your previous post, but do not complain about the salary or conditions. Concentrate rather on the positive aspects of the post you are applying for, such as the greater potential for promotion, or your particular suitability for the type of work offered. Explain what you can offer your new employer in terms of experience or expertise, and why you particularly want the post.

16.8
Words to remember

advertisement (ad)
small ad

personnel
staff
employer
employee
employment

vacancy/post/position/opening/
appointment/job
application/applicant/candidate
recommendation/reference/referee

temporary/permanent post

interview/interviewer/interviewee
duties
minutes
shorthand
filing
office technology/information
technology

salary
annual/per annum/yearly
fringe benefits
Non-Contributory Pension Scheme
time-and-a-half
leave/holiday(s)/vacation
Bank Holiday/Public Holiday(s)
sick leave

(weeks') notice/termination of
employment

junior secretary/trainee
director
personnel officer
personal assistant (PA)
application form
unsolicited letter
confirming letter (for job)
contract of employment
curriculum vitae (c.v.)

Index

The references in bold type are to specimen letters.